IMAGES
of America

ATLANTA'S PUBLIC ART

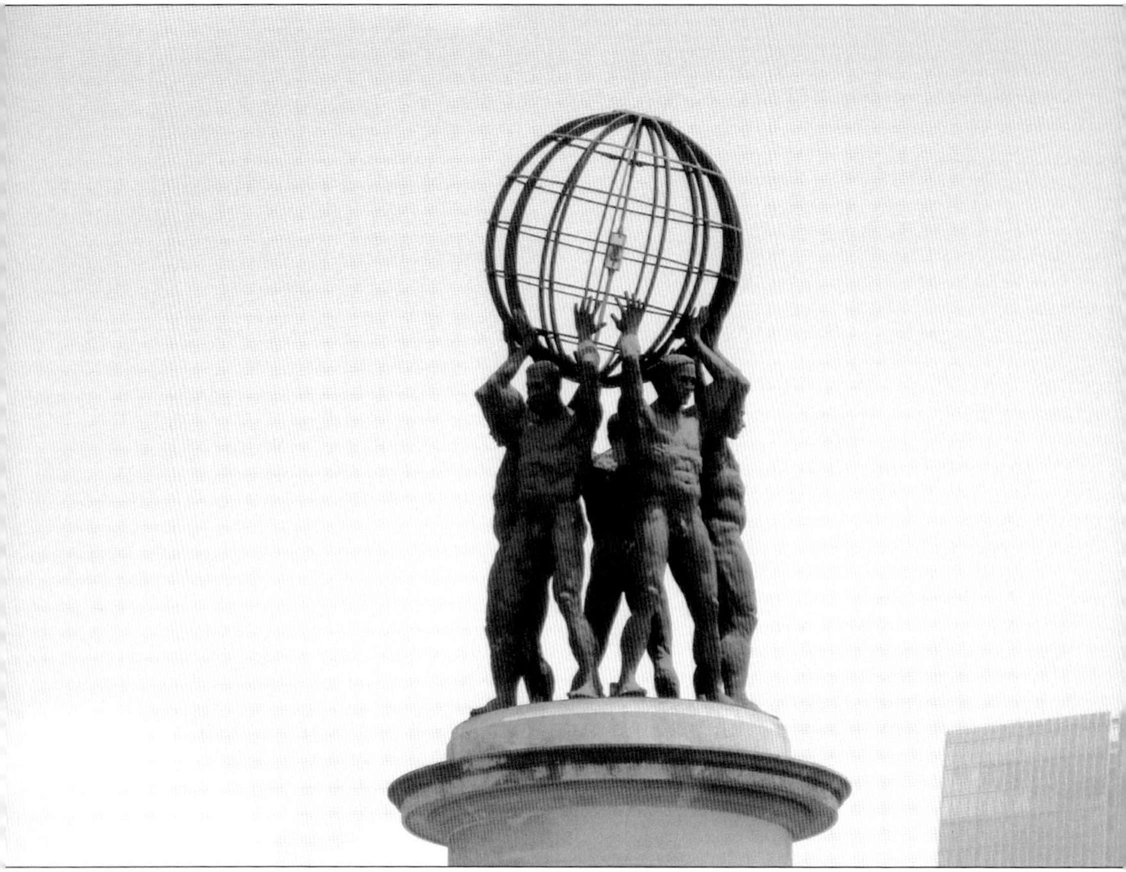

One of Atlanta's most notable landmarks of public art was the product of an international competition for an emerging international city. Known as the Prince of Wale's World Athletes Monument, the design is based on the winning concept of Anton Glikine of St. Petersburg, Russia, calling for a ring of atlases supporting a globe, and subsequently sculpted and cast in bronze composite by Atlanta sculptor Martin Dawe of Cherrylion Studio and installed on a neoclassical base. Celebrating the 1996 Centennial Olympic Games hosted by Atlanta, the monument (supported by the Prince of Wales Institute of Architecture) subsequently became a gathering place for mourners at the time of the death of Princess Diana, and its site was then named Princess Diana Memorial Plaza. (RMC.)

On the Cover: John Portman's monumental sculpture titled *KR*+C (see page 55) combines, in its abstract forms and title, references to Georgia Tech's pursuit of knowledge, advancements in research, and expressions of creativity. Fabricated of three identical forms, connected at different angles and arranged in an interlocking composition, the sculpture, also known as *Koan*, references the dialogues, paradoxes, and riddles of Zen Buddhism. As Georgia Tech president Ángel Cabrera observed, the sculpture stands "tall and unavoidable, ready to shake our rational minds." (RMC.)

IMAGES
of America

ATLANTA'S PUBLIC ART

Robert M. Craig

ARCADIA
PUBLISHING

ISBN 978-1-4671-0739-6

Published by Arcadia Publishing
Charleston, South Carolina

Printed in the United States of America

Library of Congress Control Number: 2021945984

For all general information, please contact Arcadia Publishing:
Telephone 843-853-2070
Fax 843-853-0044
E-mail sales@arcadiapublishing.com
For customer service and orders:
Toll-Free 1-888-313-2665

Visit us on the Internet at www.arcadiapublishing.com

To the memory of Frank Parker, who introduced me to art history

Contents

ACKNOWLEDGMENTS

This book is indebted to the online documentation of Atlanta murals by Art Rudick at streetartmaps.org. Rudick's timely and thorough recording of new street art, while "archiving" erased, painted over, or vandalized older murals, makes his website the "go-to" resource for researchers, Atlanta citizens, and tourists interested in viewing Atlanta's over 1,000 murals on site. With interactive maps, tags for directions, and artist profiles, Rudick's website is a well-conceived, thoroughly executed, and up-to-date resource that was invaluable to this author's fieldwork.

For the sharing of postcards, lending of books, and sharing information and/or researching for this project, I remain grateful to Christopher K. Craig, Richard D. Funderburke, Jennifer Richardson, Janice Simon, Kenneth H. Thomas Jr., and Thomas Turner.

Unless otherwise indicated, all photographs are by Robert M. Craig (RMC.)

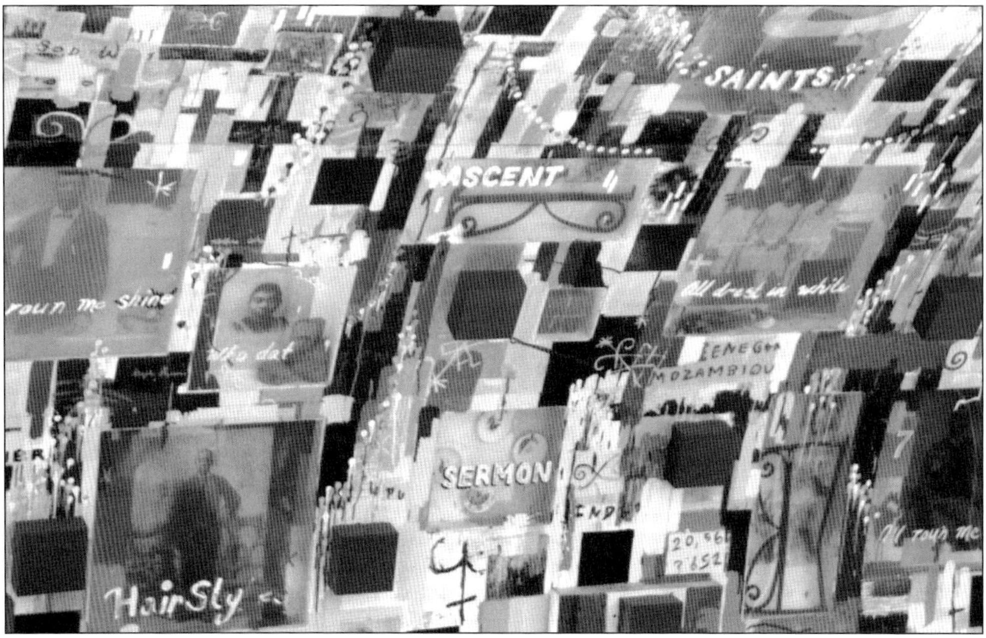

Saints by Radcliffe Bailey is a mixed media collage at the Atlanta airport, mounted on the curved wall above escalators leading from Concourse E to the automatic people movers below. Installed in 1996, it is the largest site-specific installation on the concourse and explores the theme of migration. Bailey incorporates archival photographic images, objects symbolic of power, text, stencil, and bright colors of paint as background, to explore various aspects of African American culture. A rhythm of blue and black squares and crosses punctuates the long mural, whose subtext defines the church and its leaders as major influences on the city's history. (RMC.)

Introduction

Public art featured in this book includes monuments and statuary sited in public parks, in urban plazas, and in street mediums as well as an extensive variety of murals by street artists adorning masonry walls of factory and commercial business, covering retaining walls along sidewalks and roads, surfacing piers, overheads, and walls of bridge underpasses, and painted over multi-floor skyscraper facades. Both sculpture and painting can be representational or abstract, realistic and immediately legible to the observer or fanciful, geometric, or expressionist. The subjects, styles, and meanings are varied and include historic themes, sports, music, cartoons, photorealistic portraiture at super-graphic scale, and social and political activism.

Among the noted sculptors executing statues in Atlanta are nationally known traditionalists Daniel Chester French, Charles Keck, and Solon Borglum; contemporary artists Thornton Dial, Albert Paley, and (in glass) Dale Chihuly; and local Atlanta sculptors, Julian Hoke Harris, George Beasley, Martin Dawe, and John Portman. Atlanta displays a rich collection of public work by nationally significant sculptors. Similarly, street artists have come to Atlanta from Barcelona, Paris, Rome, Buenos Aires, and elsewhere to execute large urban murals and then move on to Los Angeles, New York, Louisville, or Miami to paint anew. Local artists such as Alex Brewer, also known as Hense, grew up in Candler Park, attended Grady (now Midtown) High School, and has developed an international reputation as an abstract artist who has been awarded commissions around the world, including a commissioned abstract work for the High Museum of Art. Hense's work ranges from reupholstering in paint an entire church exterior in Washington, DC, wrapping grain silos in Australia in bright abstract colors, and executing a huge urban mural in Peru and another right here on Fourteenth and Peachtree Streets in Atlanta, his hometown; indeed, there are multiple examples of Hense's murals throughout the city. Atlanta's public art is truly an international art in an international city.

Public art can be ephemeral, however, especially outdoor murals which can easily fade or deteriorate due to exposure to weather and pollution. Some street murals are painted over by other muralists or sometimes updated by a new work by the same artist. In the worst cases, street art is tagged by graffiti artists who one would think would not disrespect another artist's work, but alas, the palimpsest of street art is ever in evidence, layer upon layer, and may be part of the dynamic of street life. The Krog Street tunnel exhibits the most caustic and guttural of the graffiti artists' patois. In contrast, isolated businesses throughout the city adorn sidewalls with a rich tableau of abstract, floral, and figural painting intended to beautify. With over 1,000 murals already documented in Atlanta, it is remarkable that so many remain in original locations, sometimes refreshed, but even when overpainted, one finds new expressions of interest reflecting the dynamism of urban life. The city becomes an outdoor museum of art at super-scale.

One might expect outdoor sculpture to have greater longevity, and excellent work by prominent sculptors does remain in situ throughout the metropolitan region. However, outdoor sculpture also has its cycles and vicissitudes. Local arts councils sponsor temporary exhibits of sculptural art and only purchase some of the work for permanent display. A 2013 campus exhibition of outdoor sculpture titled "Engineered Art: An International Sculpture Exhibit at Georgia Tech" featured 15 works curated by internationally acclaimed, Chattanooga-based sculptor John Henry, of which eight were acquired by the university and are today part of the campus's permanent collection. The Roswell Arts Fund sponsors sculptural art in public spaces rotating temporary and permanent installations in public parks, along the riverside, and at the public library. Of those on display at any given time, only five of the year's ten works are purchased for permanent display. Sandy Springs, a new city with a new interest in establishing itself as a cultured community, has a new performing arts center, an excellent community theater producing professional musicals, and one of the better collections of interesting sculptures scattered around its "City Springs" town plaza.

In Atlanta itself, the City of Atlanta Mayor's Office of Cultural Affairs supports nonprofit arts and community organizations and provides project support to neighborhood associations and individual artists living and producing work in Atlanta. With regard to murals specifically, the nonprofit organization Living Walls "creates intentional, thought-provoking public art to inspire social change and activate public spaces." Art on the Beltline has contributed to the enhancement of the experience of thousands who walk, run, or bicycle throughout the Beltline trails, a renewal of the inner rail line and industrial corridor that represents one of the most notable developments in the city's improved urban life in recent years. Sculptures along the pathways, murals on bridge abutments, piers, and retaining walls, and whole industrial warehouse walls converted to floral murals or abstract canvases make up a remarkable collaboration in public space, landscape, adaptively reused and contemporary architecture, and public art. Even here, however, murals can be transitory, and if our collective attention span is being increasingly reduced by modern fast-paced technology, one can only stay tuned, and a new mural will enrich next month's perambulations along the Beltline.

Art is intentional; its purpose is to communicate, to evoke response, to express ideas, and to educate. It can convey a social or political message, as do civil rights, social justice, and Black Lives Matter murals scattered throughout the city. Art and its represented subjects can contribute to cultural and societal pride: in West End, a mural covering the full depth of a major retail store's sidewall tells "Herstory," a play on the word "history," and depicts female community leaders who made a difference to the lives of neighborhood citizens. Iconic civil rights leaders such as Martin Luther King Jr., Ralph David Abernathy, John Lewis, and many others are subjects of murals large and small, as well as of statuary and monuments across Atlanta. Pop culture heroes, from Hank Aaron to the rappers Outkast, are depicted on large murals. And immigrants from Hispanic to Southeast Asian, and cultures from African to Caribbean, are subjects of exotic, narrative, and commemorative murals celebrating other cultures within the urban mix that is Atlanta.

Like architecture, sculpture is three-dimensional and, therefore, experiential. A painting typically calls for the observer viewing a canvas frontally, and while optical illusionary art might take on a different cast and even reveal different forms and subjects if one moves closer or takes a distant view, or moves laterally to view the canvas obliquely, paintings normally assume a two-dimensionality and frontal view. On the other hand, one moves through the spaces of a building, and observers move around sculptural works to view the art from varying vantage points. This dynamic quality of sculpture encourages, for instance, an observer of Bernini's *David* to circumnavigate the sculpture. Capturing the moment when David actually throws the stone at Goliath, Bernini creates a dynamic, almost kinetic work. Unlike Michelangelo's *David*, contemplative of what is to come and at rest, Bernini's *David* is caught in the act and appears full of the energy and ardor of the action. We walk around the work to note the grimace on David's face, the muscles of his back and shoulders, and the dynamic profiles of a human figure that takes on different aspects from each vantage point. The same is true of Rodin's *L'Ombre* on the grounds of Atlanta's High Museum, a work whose very pose bears the weight of the tragedy at Orly that generated the statue's gift from the French Government to the city of Atlanta. Interestingly, Rodin's figure's hand shows that the sculptor was familiar with Michelangelo's similar treatment of David's overscaled hand. One cannot resist walking fully around such masterworks, seeing the art in its changing dimensions in space and time.

Robert Clements, who taught for a quarter-century at the art school of the University of Georgia, takes full advantage of this multidirectional character of three-dimensional art. For instance, in his sculptural work at Isabel Gates Webster Park in Atlanta titled *Yes, We Can* (see also page 146), Clements displays his frequent use of painted sheet steel cut in action figures (dancing, playing musical instruments) whose orientation differs and thus offers the viewer different profiles as one walks around the sculptural work. A full-profile figure becomes a thin linear edge as one moves from north to east of the work, and an undisclosed figure on the east side gradually comes into full profile as one moves to the south side. The sculpture's pedestal features ceramic tiles incorporating the career goals as envisioned by students of the nearby elementary school, who participated in the fabrication of the work by decorating the base. Clements appreciated the untrained character of this art, the foundation from which the mature work in fire-engine red steel emerges above to a height of 18 feet.

Categorizing the sculpture *Yes, We Can* becomes of little import. It is abstract and figural, folk and explicitly avocational conveying to students that "they can be whatever they set their minds to." Judge Isabel Gates Webster, the namesake for the park that is home to this sculptural work, was studying in Boston when Rev. Martin Luther King Jr. urged her to come to Atlanta to fight for civil rights (which she did). It was Clements, by the way, who coordinated the $800,000 Folk Art Sculpture Park in Atlanta for the 1996 Centennial Olympics.

While a short volume such as this cannot but scratch the surface of the subject of Atlanta's public art, as an introductory sampling of the art on public view, *Atlanta's Public Art* illustrates the breadth of scope, widespread talent, varied expressions, and multifarious subject matter of the city's works of art. Websites exist that map the locations, identify the artists, and illustrate in color the hundreds of works of art in Atlanta and surrounding towns making up the metropolitan region. It is a rich collection, and the readers' excursions into corners of the city new to them will become acts of discovery that are rewarding, aesthetically enriching, and educational.

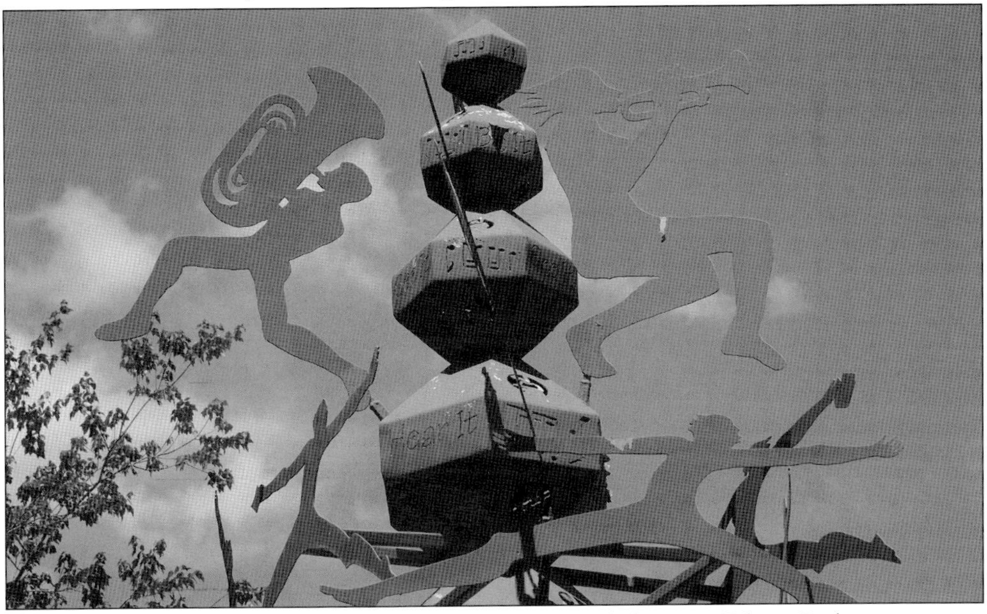

Robert Clements's *Yes We Can* sculpture at the entry to Isabel Gates Webster Park composes an array of figures playing musical instruments and prancing as though in a marching band, each single-figured vignette composed of flat sheet metal painted red, and arranged around tiered knobs stacked atop a terra-cotta enriched pedestal. The panels of the base were designed by local students and added an untrained character to the imagery. In contrast, the composition above is sophisticated and spatially charged with an energy that is intoxicating, inviting observers to circumnavigate the artwork in order to see the changing profiles of the flat action-figural profiles. (RMC.)

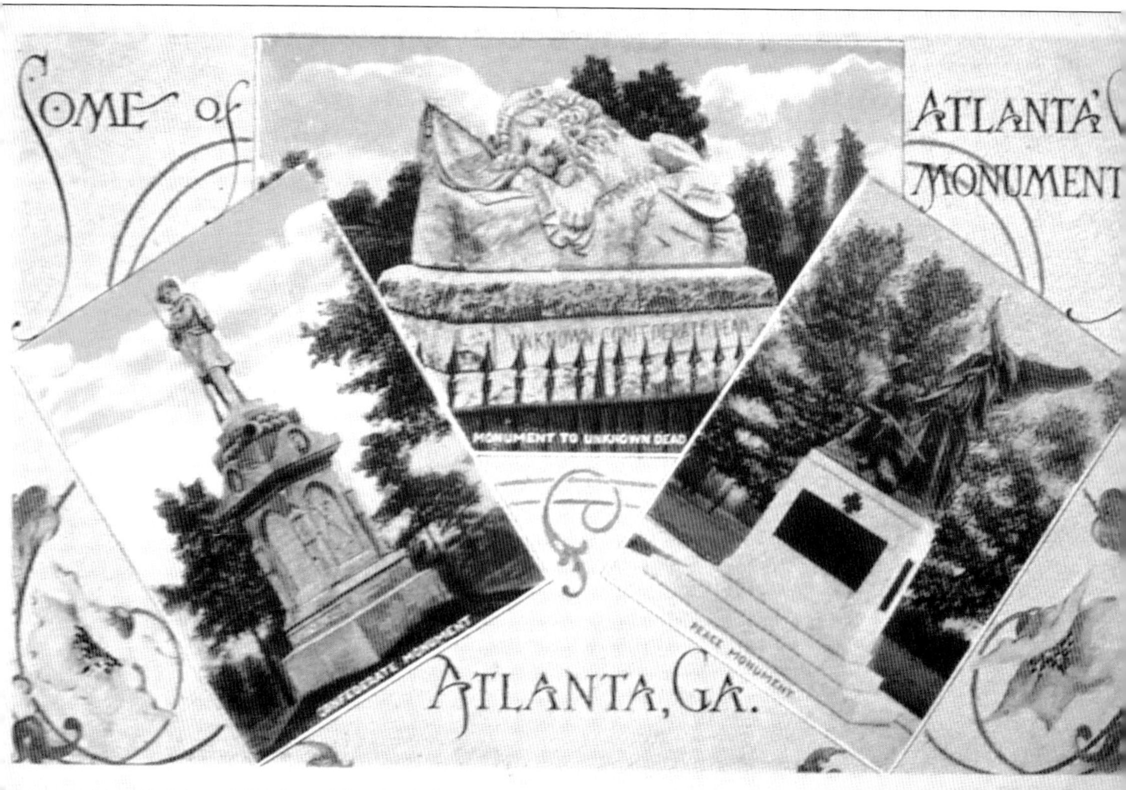

The three images featured in this historic postcard of "Some of Atlanta's Monuments" are associated with the Confederacy and with three of the city's most notable landscapes: Oakland Cemetery (center), Westview Cemetery (left), and Piedmont Park (right). The 1894 *Lion of the Confederacy*, based on the *Lion of Lucerne* (Switzerland), is dedicated to unknown Confederate dead buried at Oakland Cemetery. Five years earlier, the Confederate Veterans Association of Fulton County erected the Confederate Monument at Westview "in memory of our dead comrades," a work regrettably recently vandalized. The third sculpture is the 1911 Peace Monument by Allen Newman of New York commemorating the 1879 march of the Gate City Guard, a "Northern Mission" of peace from Atlanta to New England. The bronze Goddess of Peace holds an olive branch and commands a kneeling Confederate soldier to lower his rifle. (Courtesy Kenneth H. Thomas Jr.)

One

Historic Public Art

Public art in Atlanta featured in this chapter is either early in the date of its design and making or represents a historical event or personality of lasting historical significance. Much of this artistic work is aesthetically traditional rather than abstract. It commemorates notable events, sentiments, or the life and contribution of individuals of the past important to our cultural memory. Monuments and older statuary from the late 19th and early 20th centuries, weathering in public parks and passed by joggers almost unnoticed due to their familiarity, are thought by some to be a community's public "antiques." As artistic expressions of earlier societies, the art may convey sentiments or express values we may now reject. For citizens living in a virtual world, used to pixel art and digital aesthetics, the art of "the establishment" may be dismissed simply as old-fashioned, passé, or irrelevant, and thus expendable. Taken further, some historical art in today's fraught society, no matter its artistic merit or historical worth, runs the risk of being the object of a secular iconoclasm, the target of ideological extremism that dismisses and would destroy the artistic merit, craftsmanship, historical significance, and educational value of an evocative art for the sake of assuaging a narcissistic, ideologically induced reflex of projected personal offense.

Thus, a monument to dead military men in Westview Cemetery, erected in late Victorian times by their comrades (elder surviving veterans of the Civil War), was significant in its time and would remain so today as history remains significant; the military monument withstood the anti-war isolationism of the early-20th-century progressive era and remained intact during the contentious Vietnam Era when returning soldiers were spat upon, but today, the statue and its base are splattered in red paint and disfigured presumably by someone offended because the soldier buried in the ground below or represented by the figural statue above, had fought in civil unrest over 150 years ago, but on the wrong side.

Admittedly, art has meaning, and different observers' intellectual understanding or emotional reactions to the art's content may vary, but as Ruskin noted, art is not made "for present use alone; let it be such work as our descendants thank us for." Let us "[plant] forests that our descendants may live under their shade." I would call upon every "activist" with a cause targeting public art to first read "The Lamp of Memory" in Ruskin's *The Seven Lamps of Architecture*.

Atlanta is a relatively new city, founded in 1837 when Boston was already over 200 years old. On the other hand, Atlanta's railroads, interstate highways, and now airport (the busiest in the world) have made Atlanta the leading city of the South and an international crossroads. The city's rich culture is linked in significant ways to the rise of a New South, to the civil rights movement, and to an immigrant and transcultural society whose influences on public art extends from African, Hispanic, Asian, and Caribbean cultures to American history in its broadest context, expressive of cultural values of home, community, social justice, and human rights. While today's art may be more frequently abstract, historic art is figural, traditional, enhanced by inscriptions, ennobled as equestrian art or monumental statuary in public plazas, and reliant on realism. Historic public sculpture reflects a period of time when a citizenry demanded that art be equated with beauty. Men and women who made contributions to society were memorialized in statuary and portraiture intended to commemorate their deeds and contributions to posterity. The intention was not to look for the failings in an imperfect society but to value the good and to accept Ruskin's promise that "a time is to come when those stones will be held sacred because our hands touched them." Might we, better than finding offense (at a Confederate monument, for instance), accept that the "glory is in the Age, and in that deep sense of voicefulness . . . nay even of approval or condemnation," and that our city's historic art "long washed by the passing waves of humanity" has merit and value enhanced by time and embodied in the very craftsmanship and labor of its making. (Quotations are from John Ruskin's *The Seven Lamps of Architecture.*)

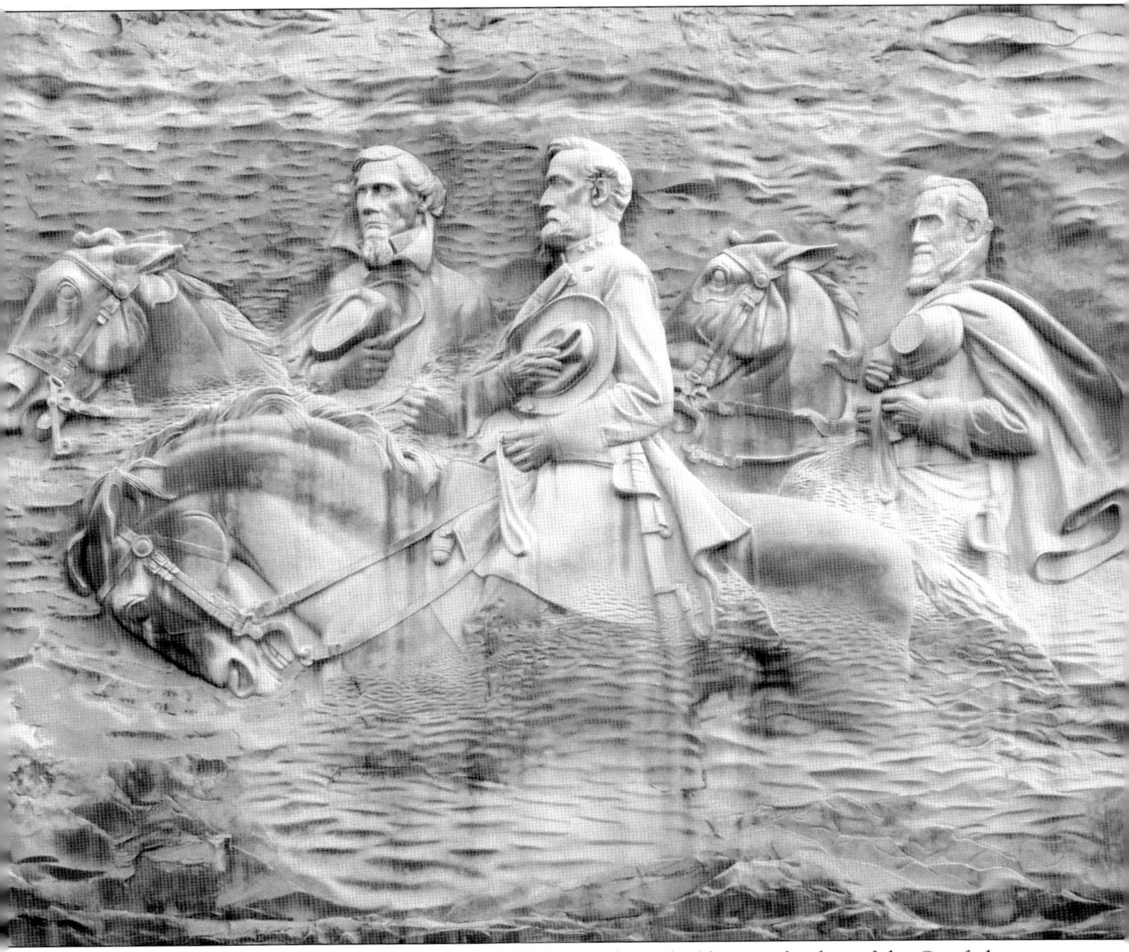

On the north face of Stone Mountain, the world's largest bas relief features leaders of the Confederacy including, from left to right, Jefferson Davis (1808–1889), Robert E. Lee (1807–1870), and Stonewall Jackson (1824–1863). The carving was begun in 1916 by Gutzon Borglum (1867–1941), who later carved the four presidents on Mount Rushmore. Borglum originally envisioned five groups of figures including 65 officers and a cavalry of some 700–1,000 figures, a scheme that was simplified to the 90-foot-high-by-190-foot-wide composition ultimately executed. By January 1925, the head of Lee was completed but subsequently dynamited following financial disagreements and Borglum's dismissal in 1925. Borglum also destroyed his models. Sculptor Henry Augustus Lukeman (1872–1935) resumed the work in 1925 projecting a smaller design, but the work stopped again in 1928. Finally, between 1963 and the carving's dedication in 1970, Walker Hancock (1901–1998) worked to complete the project, which was finally finished in 1972 by Roy Faulkner (1832–2016). By 2015, Stone Mountain Park, which officially opened in 1965, was touted as the most visited destination in the state of Georgia. (Courtesy Ron Fuller, Pixabay.)

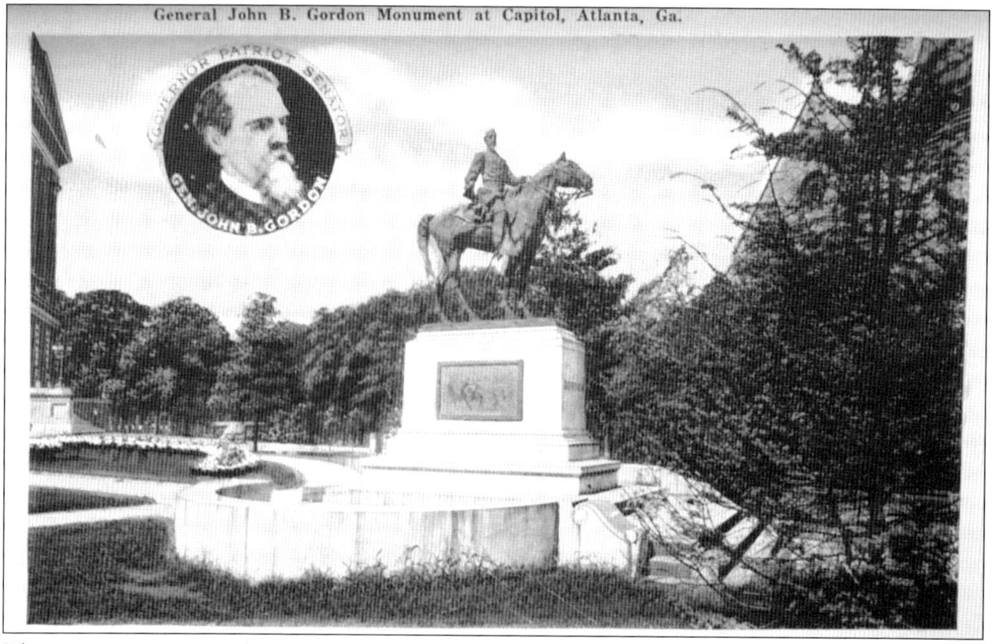

The equestrian statue of Lt. Gen. John Brown Gordon (1832–1904) is the work of Solon Hannibal Borglum (1868–1922), brother of Gutzon Borglum, and dates to 1904–1907. During the Civil War, Gordon served under Robert E. Lee in the Confederate States Army and, after the war, entered politics, serving in the US Senate from 1873 to 1880 and 1891 to 1897 and as governor of Georgia between 1886 and 1890. (Courtesy Kenneth H. Thomas Jr.)

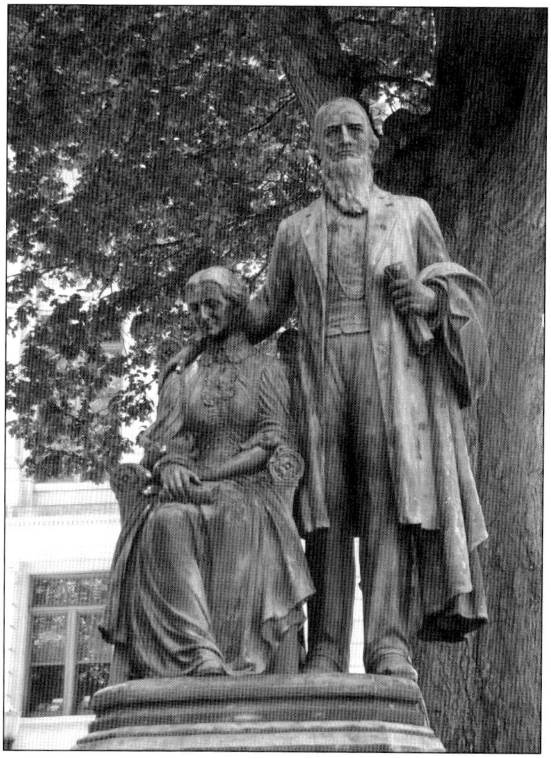

Joseph Emerson Brown (1821–1894), represented here with his wife, Elizabeth Grisham Brown (1826–1896), was Georgia's governor before and during the Civil War, serving from 1857 to 1865. He was elected to the US Senate and served from 1881–1890, the years during which Gordon was not there. The 1928 Brown statue, located in the capitol grounds, is the work of Giuseppe Moretti,(1857–1935), sculptor of the huge *Vulcan* (1903–1904) in Birmingham, Alabama. (RMC.)

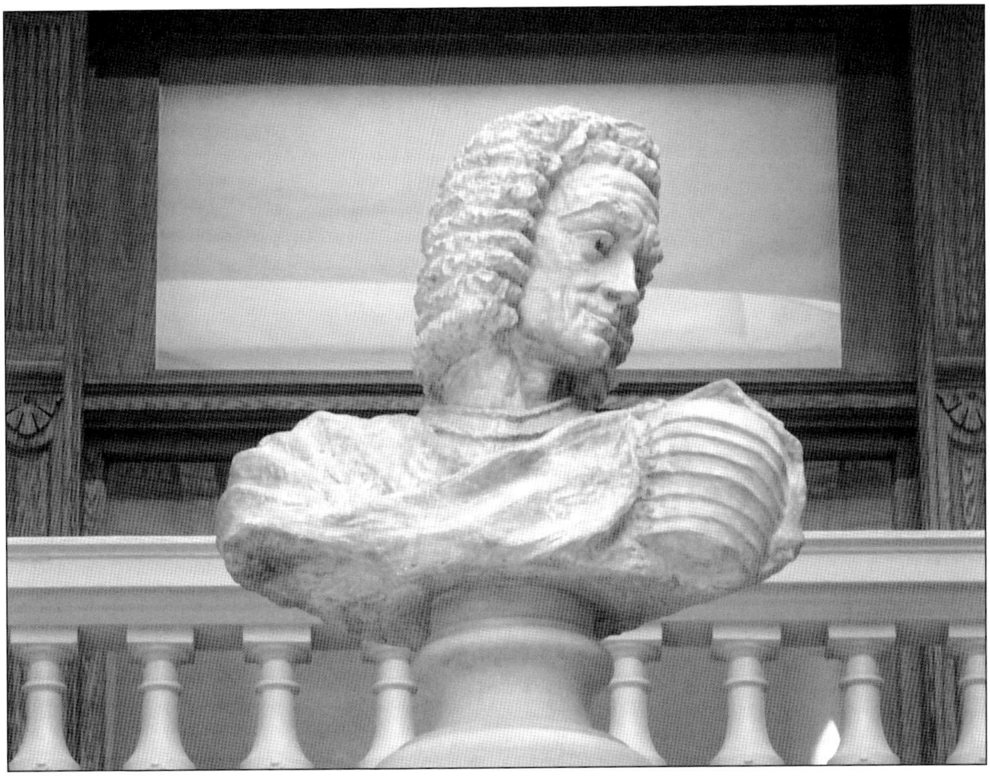

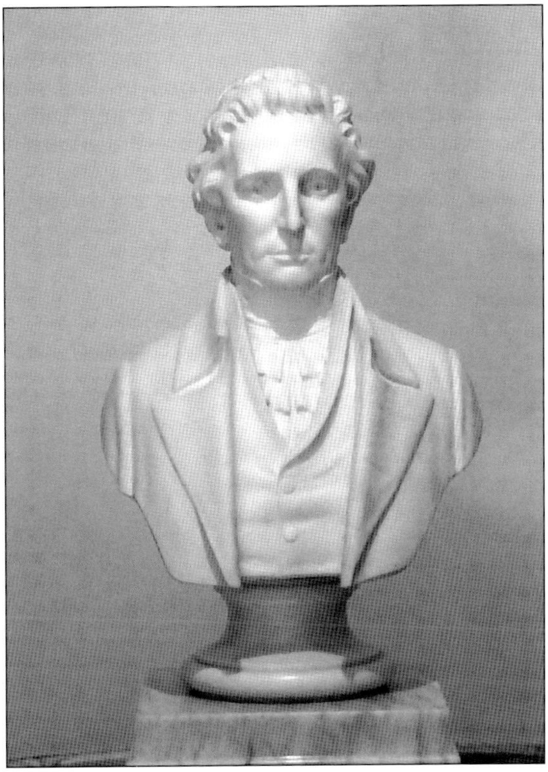

Inside the state capitol rotunda are sculptural busts and statues of prominent historic figures in Georgia history. Overlooking the central space from the upper floor is a Georgia pink marble bust of James Edward Oglethorpe (1696–1785), inscribed, "To the people of Georgia by Eric Underwood, London, England," and dated 1941. Oglethorpe founded the colony of Georgia and, in 1733, led the expedition of colonists that landed at and established Savannah. (RMC.)

Also from the colonial era is John Adam Truetlen (1733–1782), a former indentured servant and, later, political leader during the American Revolution, who helped write Georgia's first constitution and, in 1777, was elected Georgia's first governor. Killed by mob action in 1782, perhaps by Tories who resented his support of the revolution, Truetlen is represented here by a bust of white Georgia marble executed by Bryant Baker around 1959. (RMC.)

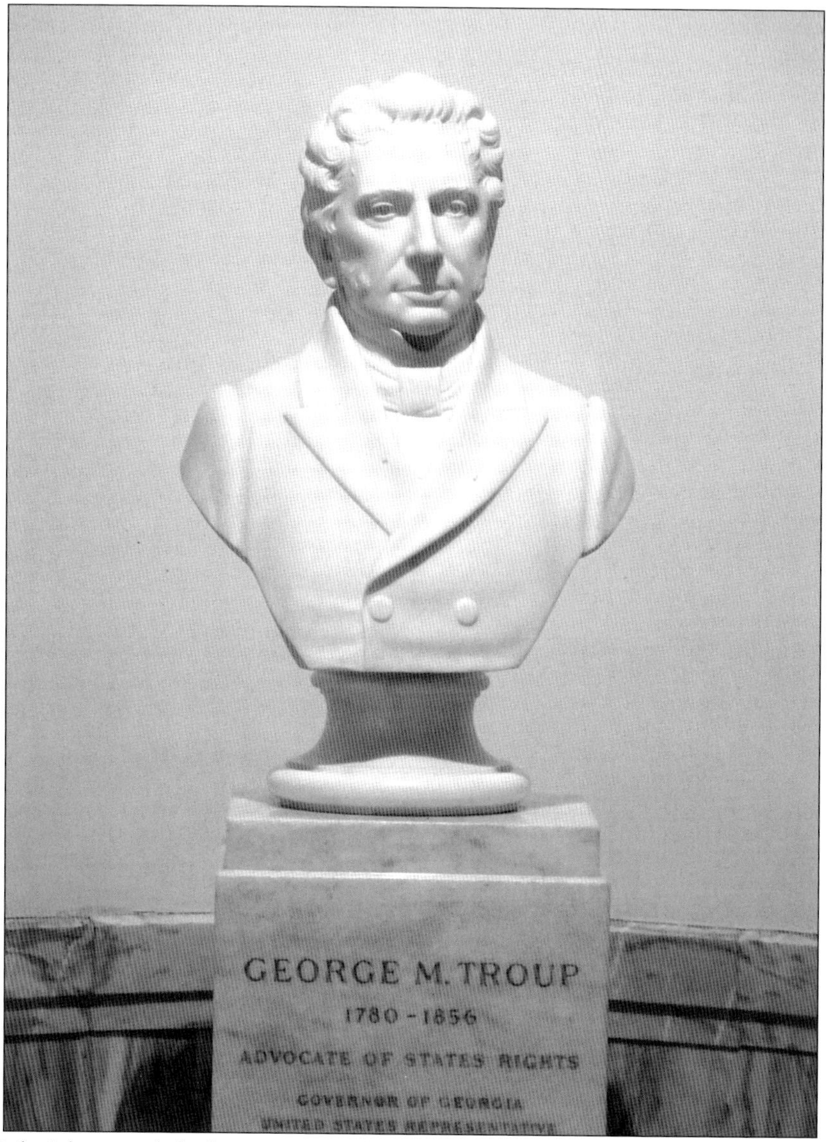

Bryant Baker's busts include three signers of the Declaration of Independence from Georgia [Button Gwinnett (1735–1777), who served in Georgia's colonial legislature and the 2nd Continental Congress; George Walton (c. 1749–1849); and Lyman Hall, (1724–1790)]; Archibald Bulloch (1730–1777), a revolutionary soldier and Georgia's first chief executive; and Abraham Baldwin (1754–1807), founder of the University of Georgia in 1785 and a delegate to the constitutional convention of 1787. Baker's busts of early national figures include William H. Crawford (1772–1834), a member of the US Senate from Georgia (1807–1813), minister to France (1813–1815), and secretary of war (1815–1816), both under President Madison, and secretary of the treasury (1816–1825) under Madison, Monroe, and John Quincy Adams. Finally, the sculptor's bust of Benjamin Hawkins commemorates the man who served 20 years as principal temporary agent for Indian affairs south of the Ohio River (1796–1816). Baker's c. 1958 bust (above) is of George M. Troup, namesake of Troup County in northwest Georgia and a proponent of Monroe's policy of manifest destiny who supported the removal of Creek Indians from western Georgia to the new Louisiana Territory (RMC.)

Alexander H. Stephens (1812–1883) served as vice president of the Confederacy under Jefferson Davis, although he initially opposed secession and frequently opposed the policies of President Davis. Prior to the Civil War, Stephens served in the Georgia Assembly (1836–1841), the Georgia Senate (1842), and the US House of Representatives (1845–1853 and after the war 1873–1882). He was elected governor of Georgia in 1882 but died in office four months later. (RMC.)

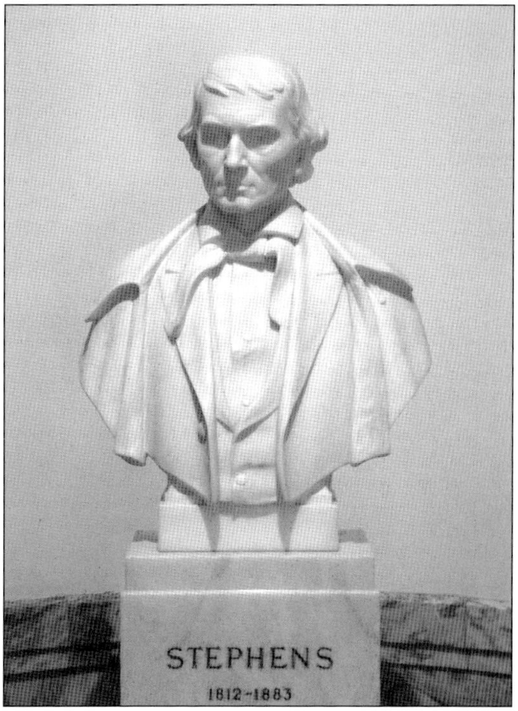

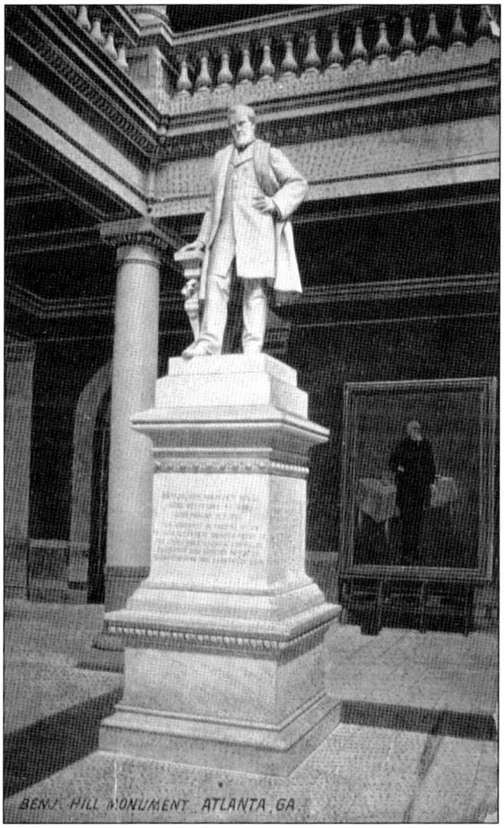

The statue of Benjamin Hill (1823–1882) was originally sited at the intersection of Peachtree and West Peachtree Streets (today's Hardy Ivy Park) but moved to the capitol rotunda in 1890. The Italian marble statue (almost 13.5 feet high) was carved by New York sculptor Alexander Doyle (1857–1922) in 1885. During the Civil War, Hill was a member of the Confederate Senate and a spokesman for Jefferson Davis. (Courtesy Kenneth H. Thomas Jr.)

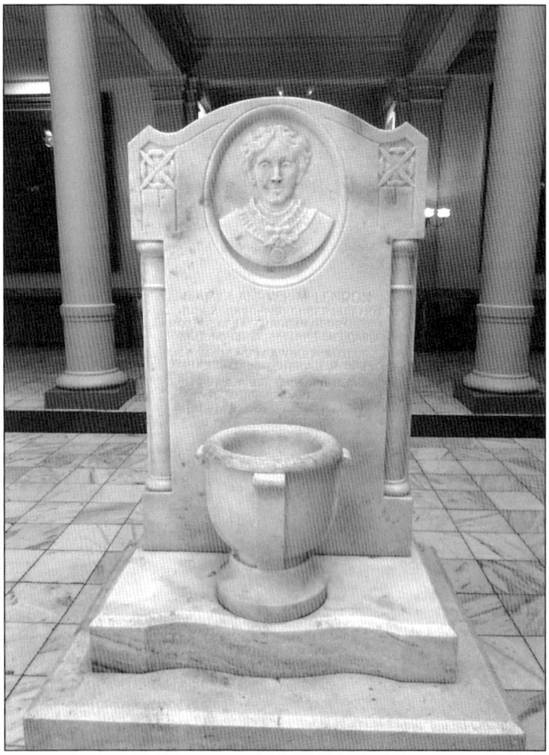

Mary Latimer McLendon (1840–1921), seen left, was known as the mother of suffrage in Georgia and was also active in the prohibition movement. During her lifetime, she witnessed the passage of both the 18th and 19th Amendments to the US Constitution. Her 1923 fountain/monument was the first monument dedicated to a woman to be installed in the capitol. Moina Bell Michael (1869–1944), pictured below, a professor at the University of Georgia, was inspired during World War I by Canadian poet John McCrae's opening lines from "In Flanders Fields," where "poppies blow / Between the crosses row on row," and she originated the idea of wearing a red poppy as a symbol of remembrance of those who served in the war. Known as "the Poppy Lady," she is memorialized in the rotunda by a bust carved in the 1930s by Steffen Thomas (1906–1990). (RMC.)

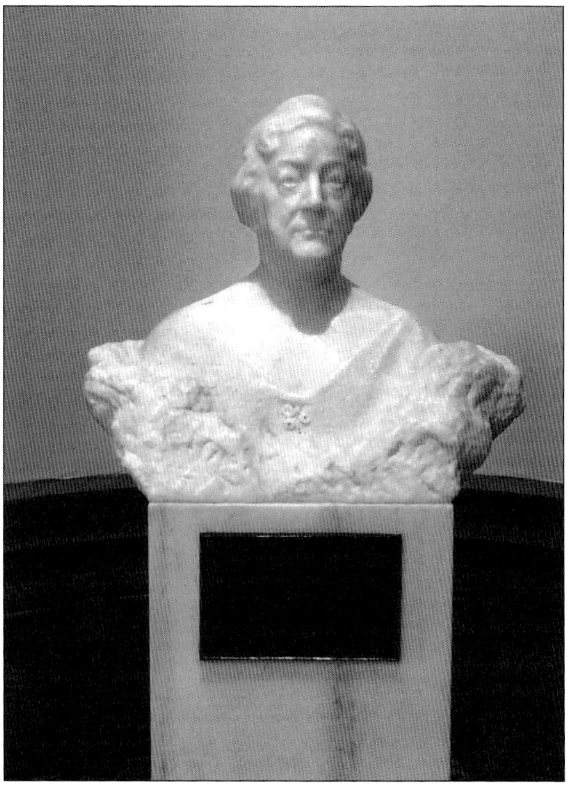

The most commanding work of public art outside the capitol is *The Goddess of Liberty*, also known as *Miss Freedom*, 1888, a hollow copper painted figure rising 26 feet above the capitol's gold dome. Although the sculptor is unknown it is thought the work was ordered by the capitol's architects Edbrooke and Burnham and fabricated at the W.H. Mullins Manufacturing Company in Salem, Ohio. The statue was restored in 2004. (RMC.)

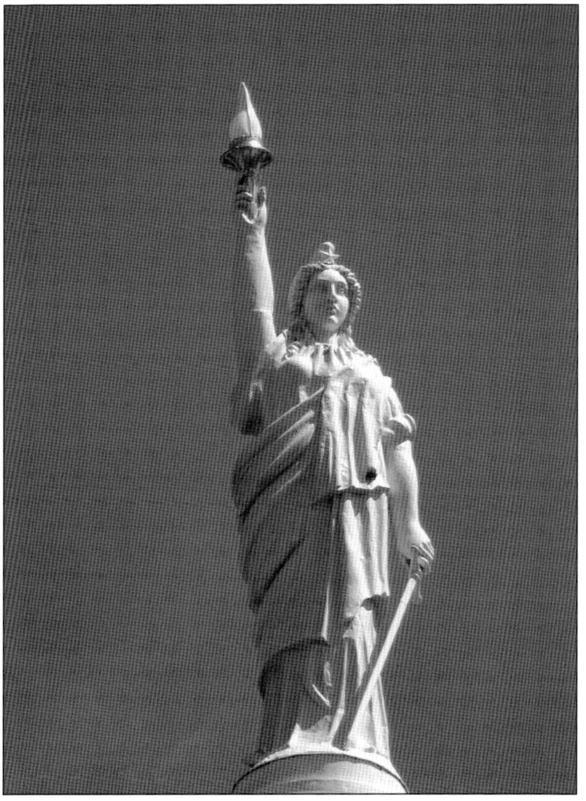

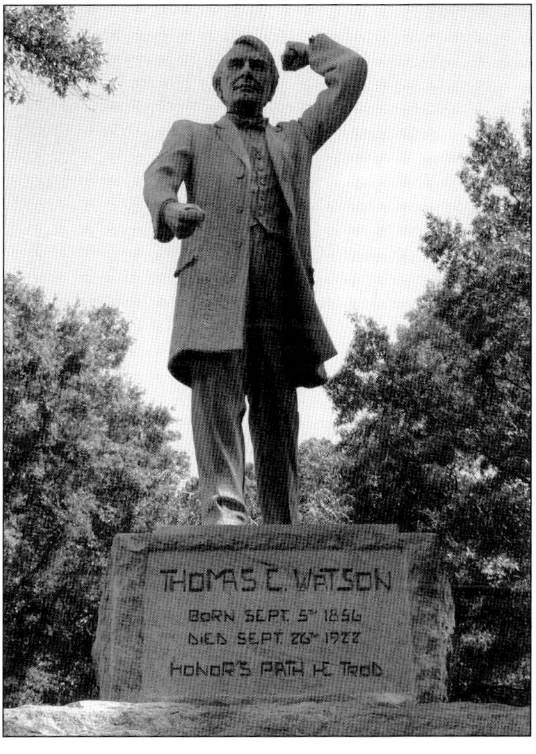

The statue of fiery Thomas E. Watson (1856–1922), dedicated in 1932, used to greet visitors on the steps of the capitol until it was moved across the street in 2013 to Georgia Plaza Park. Watson's prominence in politics reflected his early opposition to lynching and advocation of expanding suffrage to African Americans. By 1908, as a People's Party candidate for president, his white supremacist views were distinctly anti-Semitic and anti-Catholic. (RMC.)

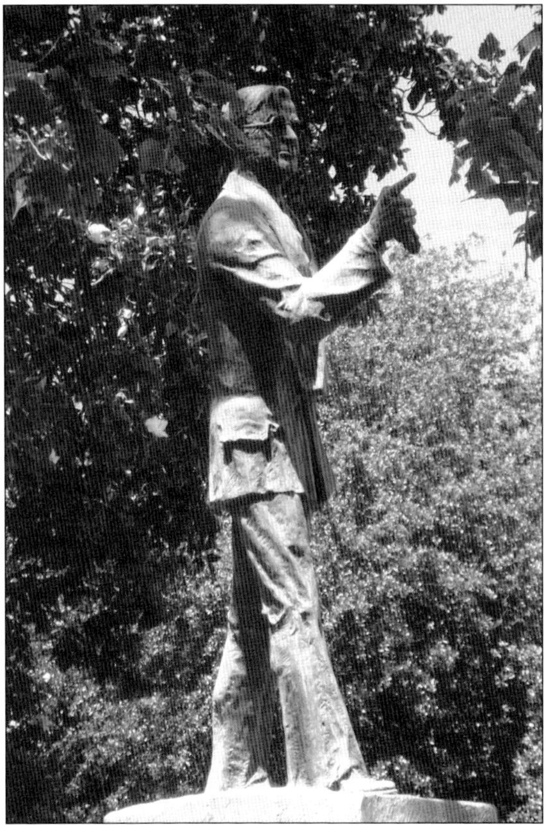

Eugene Talmadge (1884–1946) and his son Herman Talmadge (1913–2002), served as Georgia governor in 1933–1937 and 1941–1943 (Eugene) and 1947–1955 (Herman). Herman Talmadge went on to the US Senate from 1957–1981. Eugene Talmadge was a segregationist and white supremacist notably encouraging the firing of the dean at the University of Georgia for his advocacy of integration of university classrooms, resulting in the removal of accreditation from state universities. Herman Talmadge was only 33 when he became governor, and throughout his terms as governor and US senator, the younger Talmadge continued the family tradition of opposition to integration and civil rights legislation, ordering schools to be closed rather than desegregated. During his US Senate career, Talmadge was a prominent member of the Watergate Commission. The elder Talmadge statue (1949, left) is by Steffen Thomas and the younger one (1990, below) is by James Killian Spratt (1950–). (RMC.)

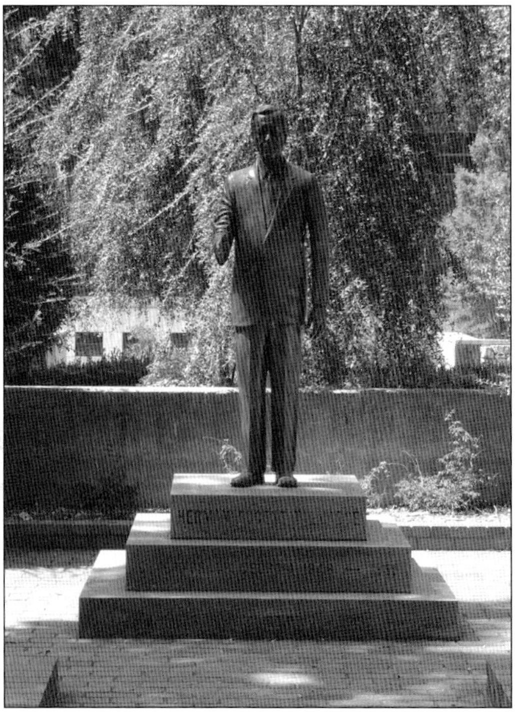

The 1997 statue of Ellis Arnall (1907–1992), Georgia governor from 1943 to 1947, is by Zenos Frudakis (1951–). One of the most effective governors in the state's history, Arnall accomplished much in his single term, achieving accreditation of the university system after Herman Talmadge's interference in academic affairs (see page 20), establishing a teachers' retirement system, and as a wartime governor, helping to make Georgia the first state to lower the voting age to 18. (RMC.)

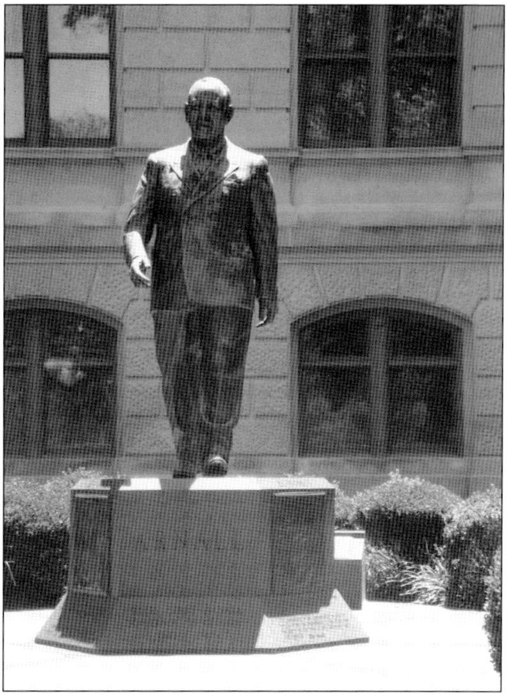

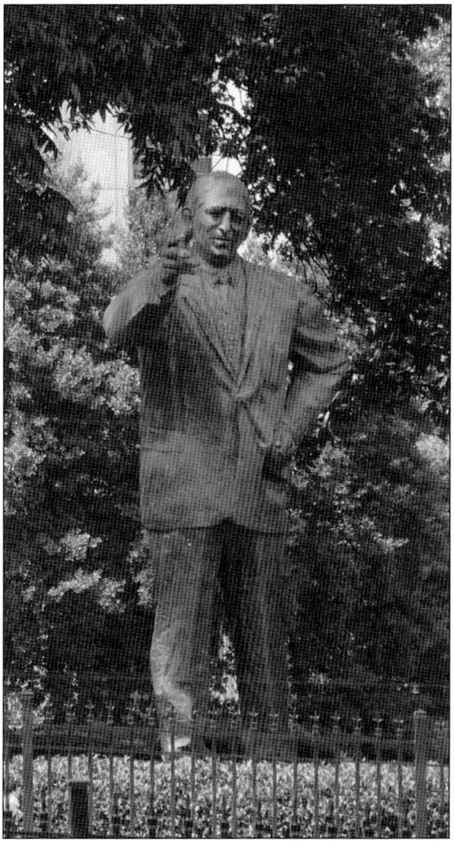

Richard Russell Jr. (1897–1971) was governor of Georgia from 1931–1933, but his most impactful political activity was in the US Senate for almost 40 years (1933–1971), where he and his dominating conservative coalition, led the Southern opposition to the civil rights movement and blocked passage of civil rights legislation. When Lyndon Johnson signed the Civil Rights Act of 1964, Russell led a Southern boycott of the 1964 Democratic National Convention. (RMC.)

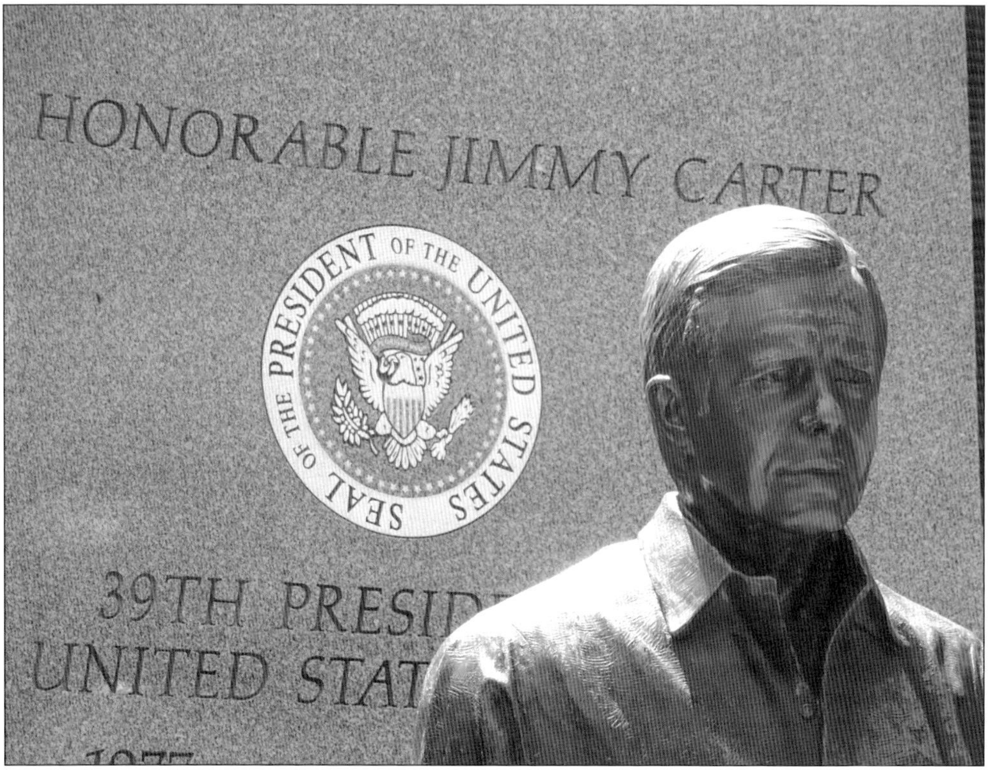

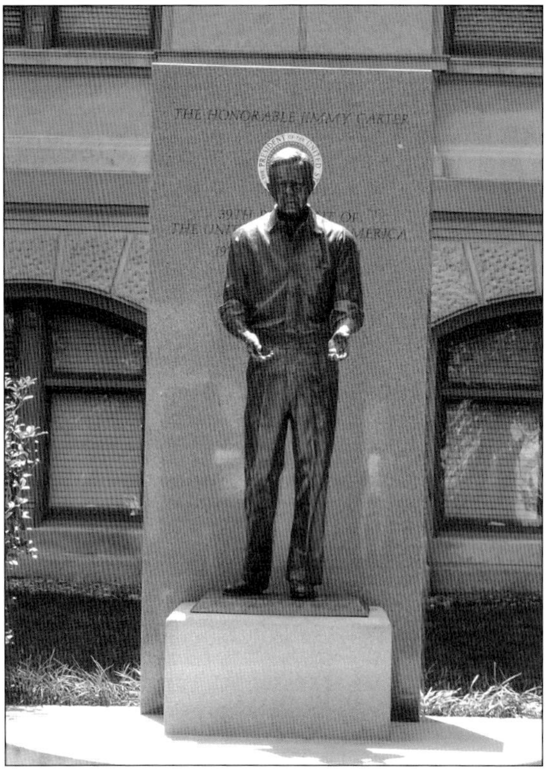

As governor of Georgia from 1971–1975, James Earl "Jimmy" Carter (1924–) drew national attention for his support of African American civil rights and racial desegregation. Carter had been in the Georgia Senate (1963–1967) when Lester Maddox (who preceded Carter as governor) famously refused to serve black customers in his Atlanta Pickrick restaurant. In 1976, Carter was elected US president; his single term in office was highlighted by the Arab-Israeli Camp David Accords and the Iranian hostage crisis. Carter's post-presidency activities garnered universal praise. In 2002, he received the Nobel Peace Prize for "his decades of untiring effort to find peaceful solutions to international conflicts, to advance democracy and human rights, and to promote economic and social development." Carter's statue (unveiled in 1994) is the work of Frederick Hart (1943–1999), the sculptor of *The Three Soldiers* at the Vietnam Memorial in Washington. (RMC.)

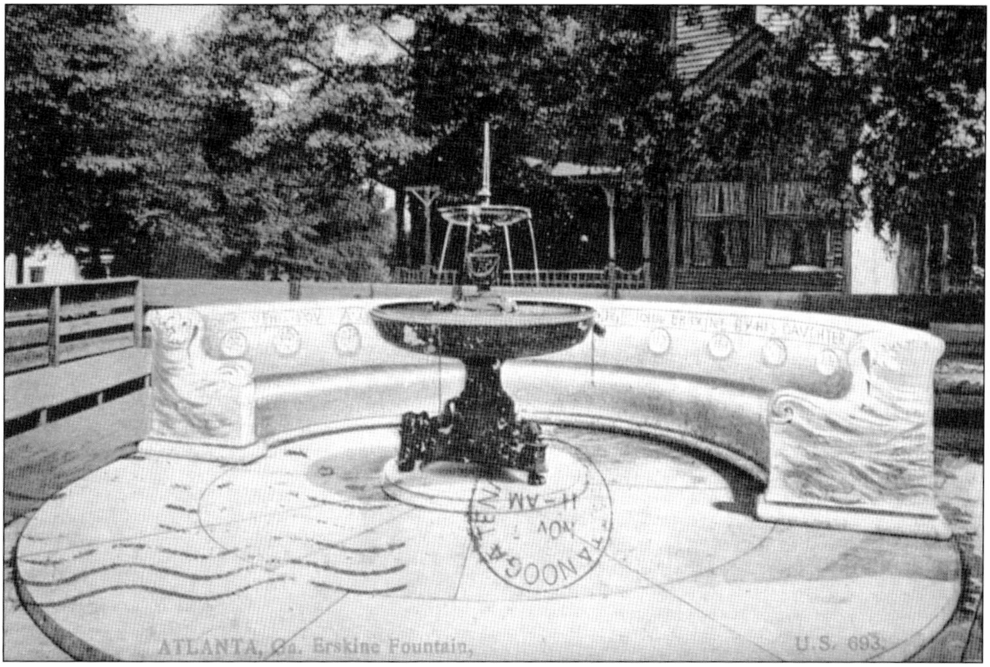

The Erskine Memorial Fountain was originally sited in what is now Hardy Ivy Park (replacing the Benjamin Hill statue; see page 17), but in 1912, it was moved to Grant Park. Designed in 1896 by J. Massey Rhind (1858–1936) with curved bench carvings displaying ocean themes and signs of the zodiac, it was Atlanta's first public fountain. Dedicated to federal judge John Erskine (1813–1895), it was a gift to the city by Erskine's daughter. (Courtesy Kenneth H. Thomas Jr.)

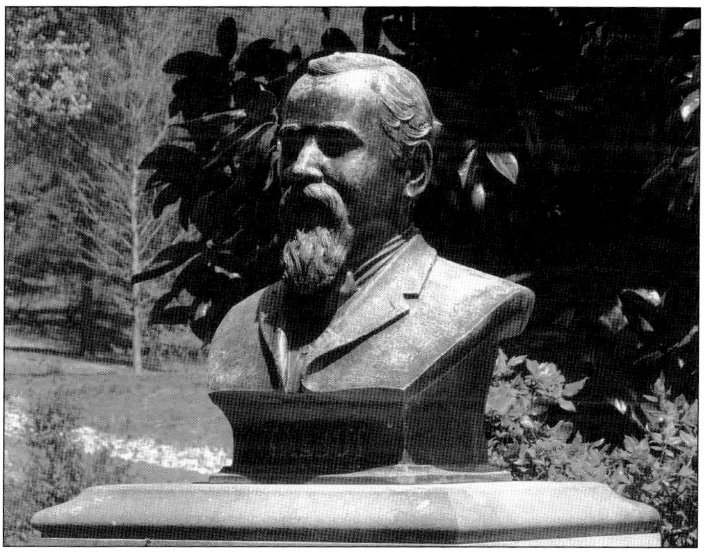

The bronze bust on Tennessee marble base, sited in front of the Cyclorama Building in Grant Park, was erected in 1948 by the membership of the International Association of Machinists in memory of its founder and president, Thomas Wilson Talbot (1849–1892), marking the centennial of his birth and the 60th anniversary of the organization. (RMC.)

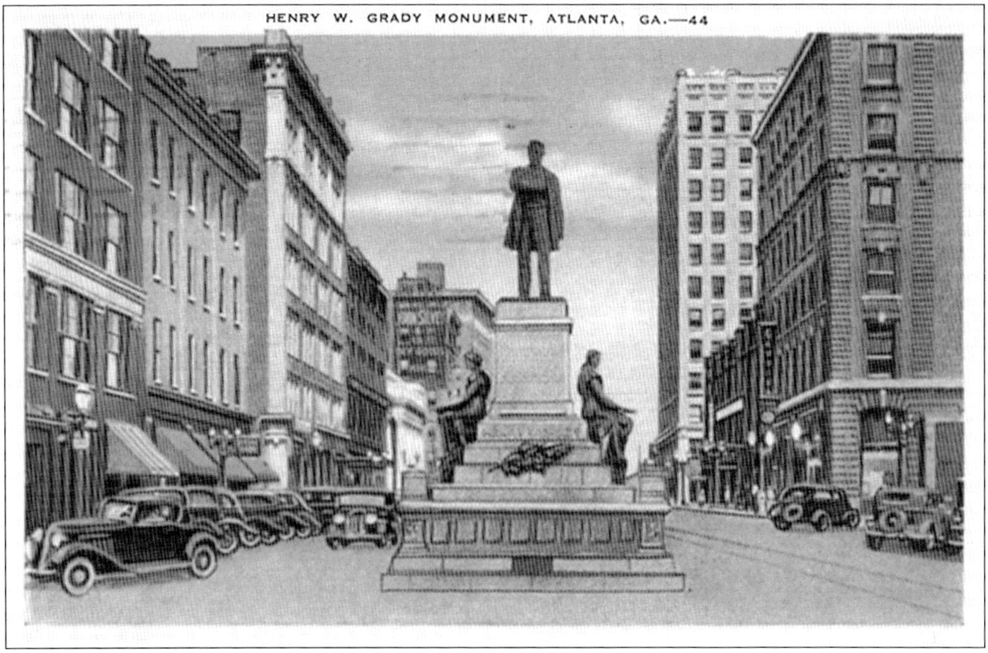

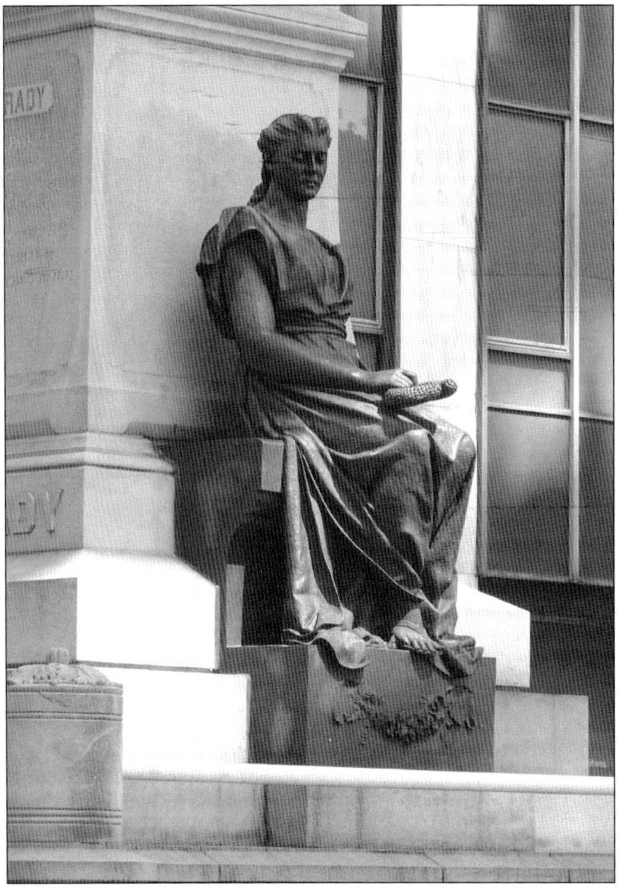

Henry Grady, the namesake of Grady Hospital, Grady High School, and here Grady Square, is best known for his advocacy of a post–Civil War "New South doctrine" which sought to encourage northern industrial and commercial interests to invest in the South, especially Georgia. As editor of the *Atlanta Constitution* (and an effective orator), he was an influential voice, but his support of John Brown Gordon (see page 14) for governor, a former Confederate general with alleged ties to the Ku Klux Klan, has prompted recent calls for the Grady statue's removal. Designed by Alexander Doyle in 1891, cast in bronze in Massachusetts, and mounted here on a Georgia granite base, the monument originally fronted the Victorian Gothic US Post Office and Customs House, which served briefly as Atlanta City Hall. Grady died in 1889 at the age of 39. (Above, courtesy Kenneth H. Thomas Jr.; left, RMC.)

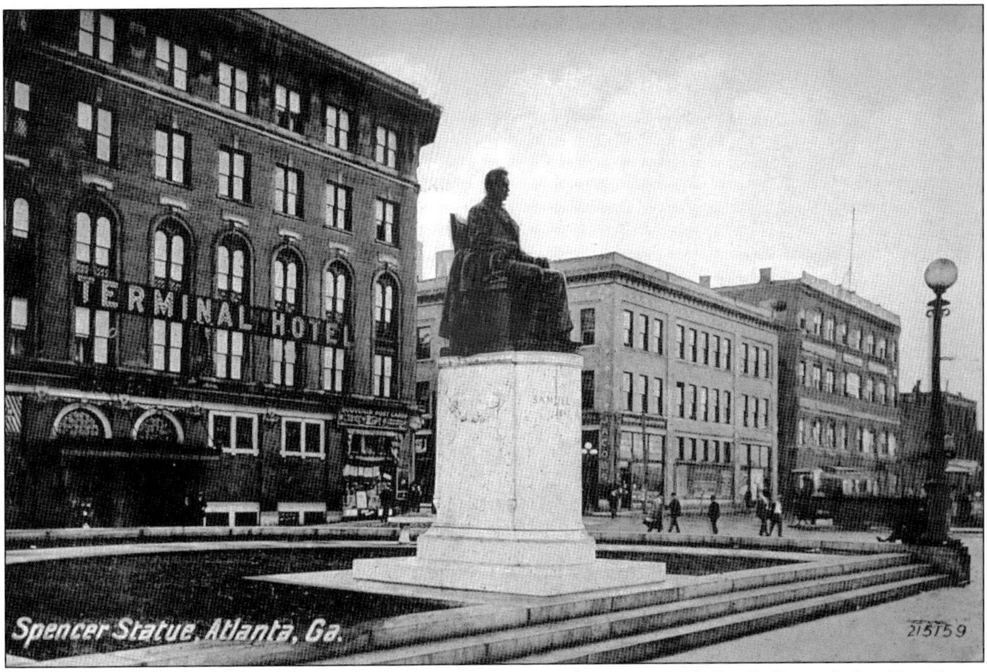

Civil engineer, president of six railroad companies, and considered the father of the Southern Railway system, Samuel Spencer was ironically killed in a train wreck in 1906 at the age of 59. His 1910 statue by Daniel Chester French (1850–1931) sits on a plinth designed by architect Henry Bacon (1866–1924), the same sculptor/architect duo who created the 1914–1922 Lincoln Memorial in Washington, DC. Some 30,000 Southern Railway workers contributed to the cost of the statue. The Spencer monument was originally sited in front of Atlanta's Terminal Station, moved briefly to Brookwood Station, moved again in 1996 to Hardy Ivy Park, and is now located at Norfolk Southern Railroad headquarters at 1200 Peachtree Street NE. (Above, courtesy Kenneth H. Thomas Jr.; below, RMC.)

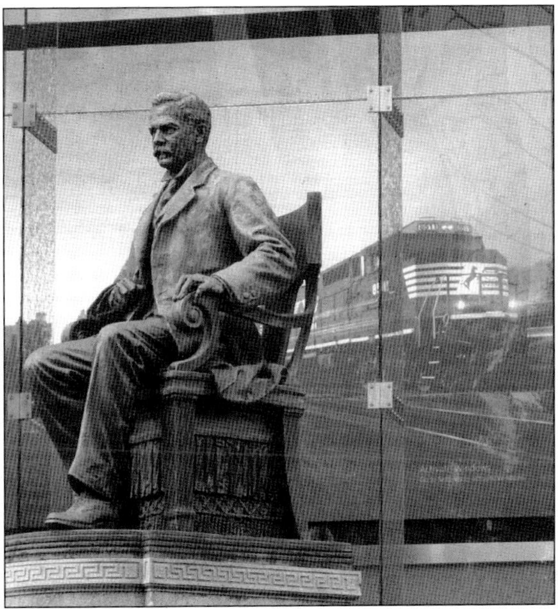

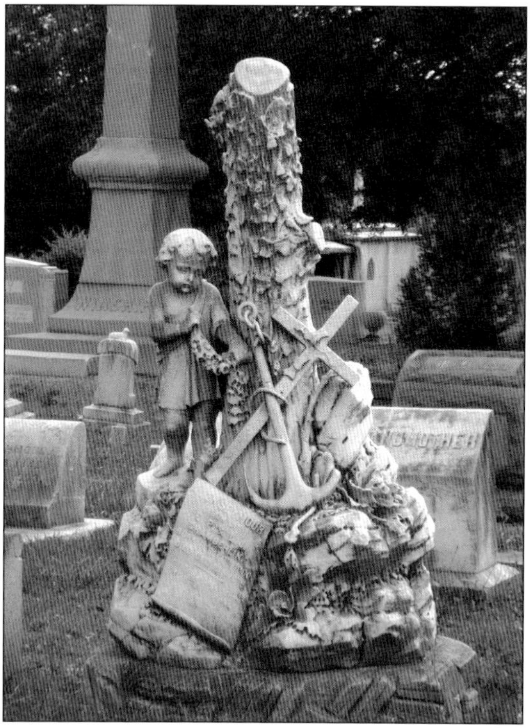

Oakland Cemetery is a microcosm of Victorian taste and societal sensibilities. Established in 1850, it offers a landscape full of architecture and sculpture, including impressive mausoleums, decorative columns, obelisks, and statuary, as well as figural sculptures of angels, mourning females, and innocent children, the latter a commentary on 19th-century infant mortality. The Allen Seymour Chamberlin (1860–1875) monument records the death of a 15-year-old. (RMC.)

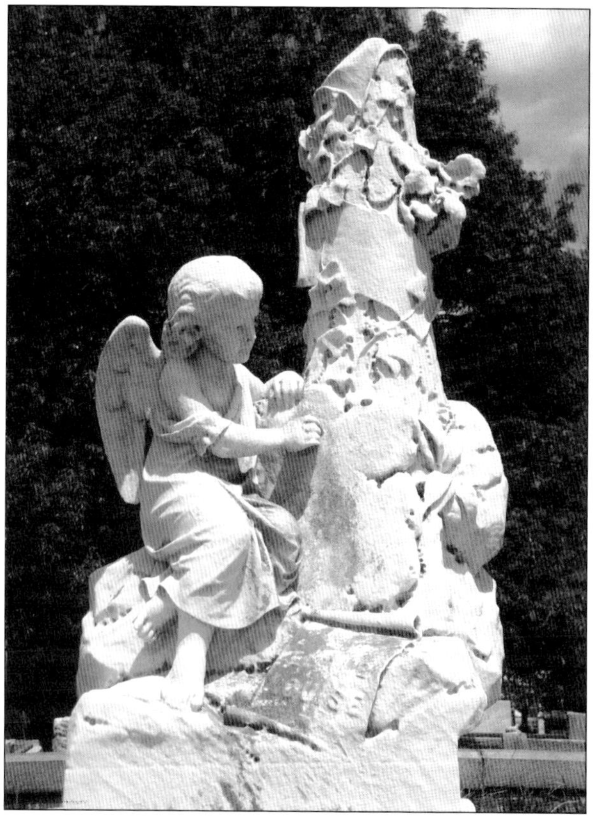

Hugh T. and Josephine Inman were pioneer settlers of Atlanta and became one of the wealthiest families in Georgia. Their children, Hugh (1879–1881) and Louise (1883–1888), died before age two and at age four and a half, respectively. Louise's cherub stands in front of a broken tree stump symbolizing Louise's life cut short, while the cherub inscribes on a stone tablet Louise's brief life story. (RMC.)

One of the most charming artworks at Oakland Cemetery is the "Out in the Rain" fountain fabricated in 1913 by the J.L. Mott Iron Works (New York City), possibly a replica of a c. 1876 sculpture by Galloway & Graff of Philadelphia, itself possibly duplicating a sculpture exhibited in the Italian section of the US International Exhibition of 1876. (RMC.)

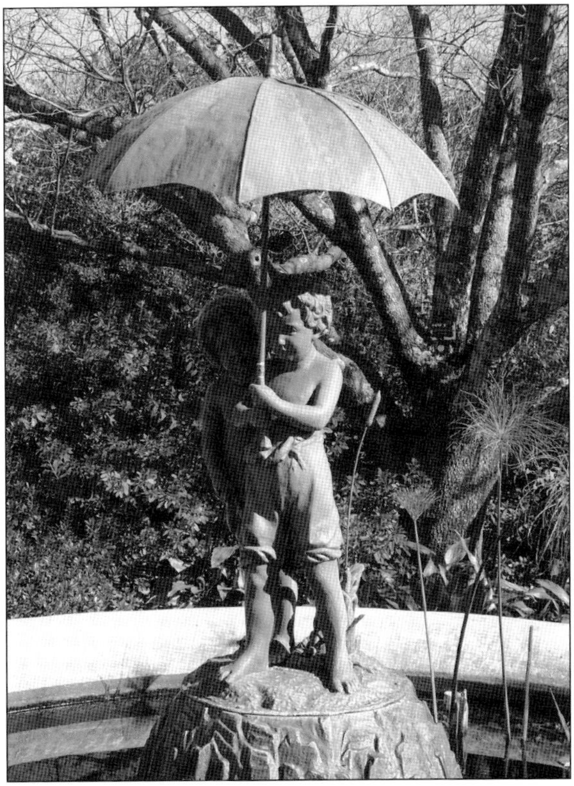

At the Grey family monument at Oakland is a figure of the weeping mythical Greek character Niobe who taunted the goddess Latona boasting of her fourteen children while Latona had but two. Latona's children, Artemis and Apollo, retaliated by killing Niobe's children. Inconsolable, Niobe fled to Mount Sipylus where she was turned to stone, but her grief was so great that the stones continued to weep. (RMC.)

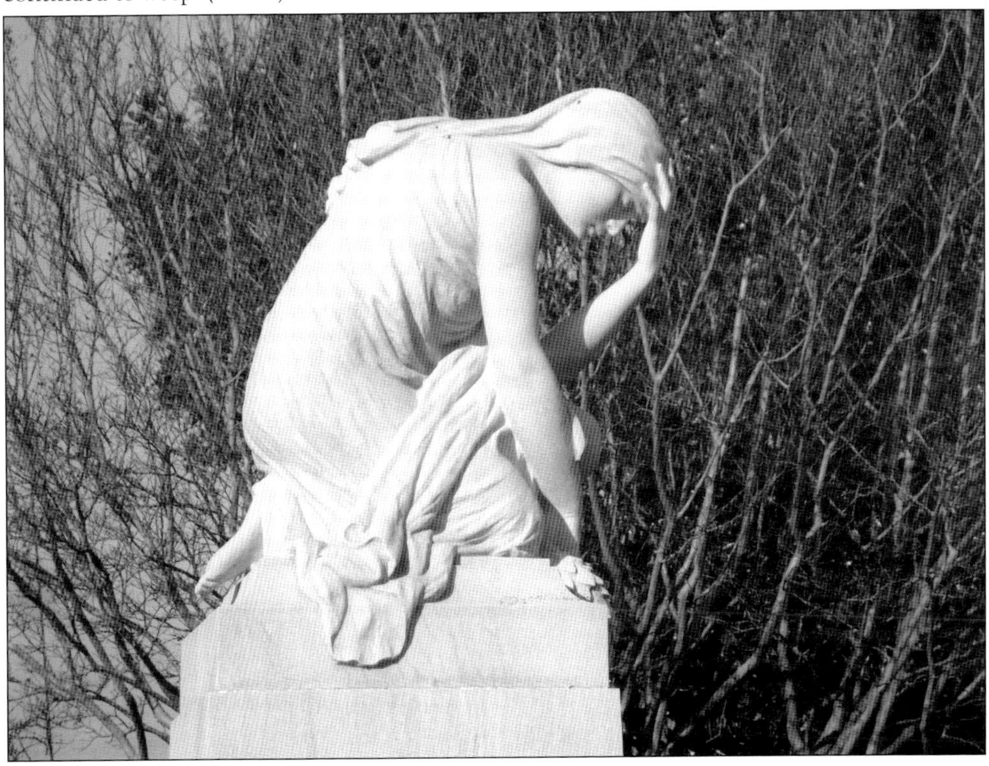

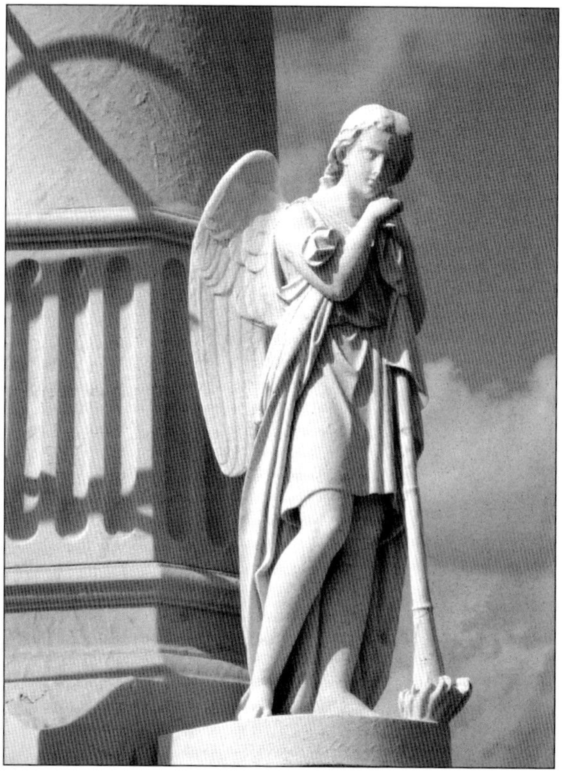

Angels are frequent subjects for sculptural treatment of cemetery monuments, as evidenced at the base of the noble column at the monument of Joseph Emerson Brown (see page 14). Atop the high column symbolizing life is Gabriel holding a trumpet; the two angels look down at people coming up to heaven, their trumpets turned down (sometimes interpreted as torches representing a life snuffed out). (RMC.)

One of the most artistically beautiful sculptures at Oakland Cemetery is the angel on the Mary Glover Thurmond monument, whose face may be an idealized rendering of Mary herself. The angel replicates the design of Daniel Chester French at the Angie Kinsey monument (1911) in Woodlawn Cemetery, the Bronx, New York. Mary Thurmond was known as "the Angel" due to her frequent gifts of flowers to local hospitals. (RMC.)

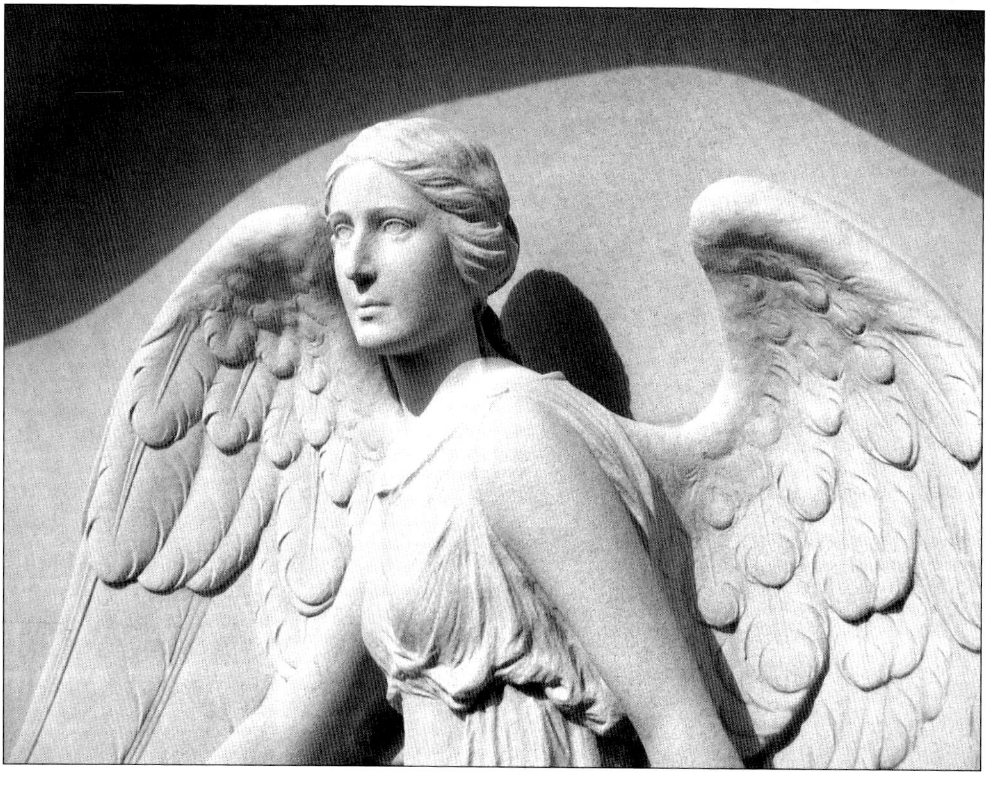

Confederate monuments abound throughout the South, adorning town squares, the grounds of county courthouses, and cemeteries. The Confederate Veterans' Association of Fulton County Monument at Westview Cemetery is as much a peace monument as a memorial to the "lost cause"; its inscription quotes the Bible: "they shall beat their swords into plowshares and their spears into pruning hooks; nation shall not lift up sword against nation, neither shall they learn war anymore." The Peace Monument, also known as *Cease Firing*, in Piedmont Park conveys a similar message (see page 10). A 1911 work of Allen Newman (1875–1940) of New York, the bronze sculpture shows the Goddess of Peace holding an olive branch and commanding a kneeling Confederate soldier to lower his rifle. The monument commemorates the 1879 march of the Gate City Guard, a "Northern Mission" of peace from Atlanta to New England. (RMC.)

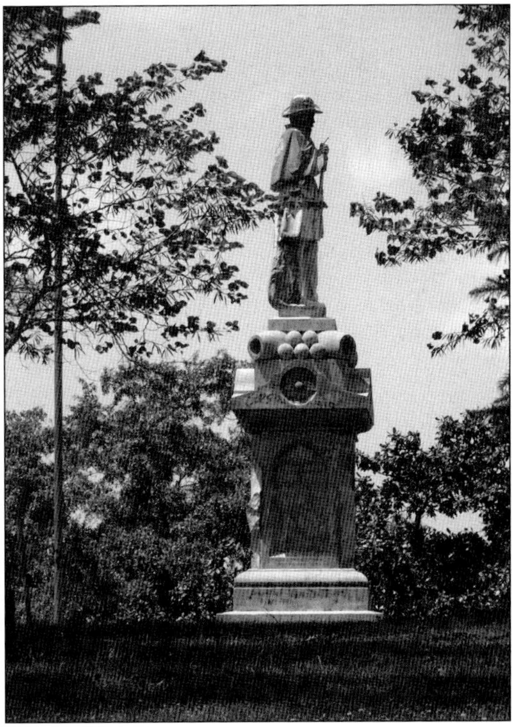

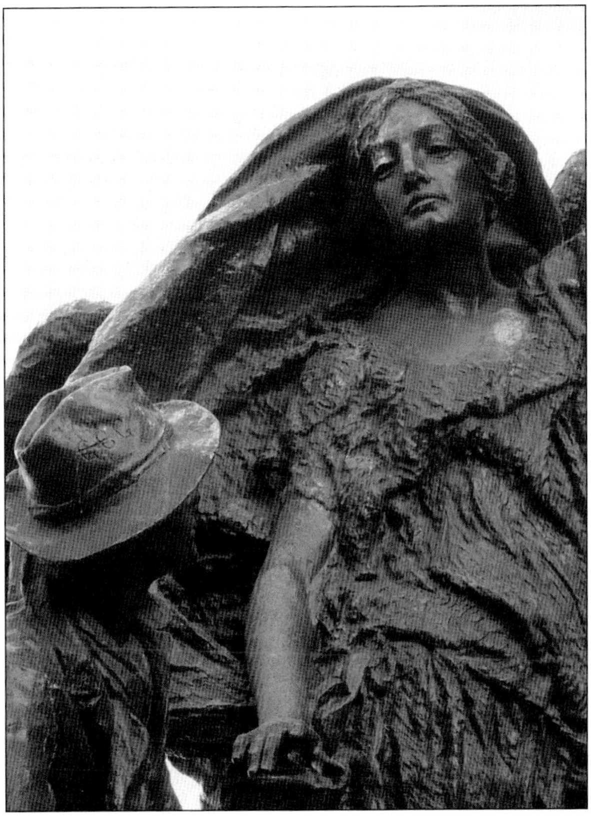

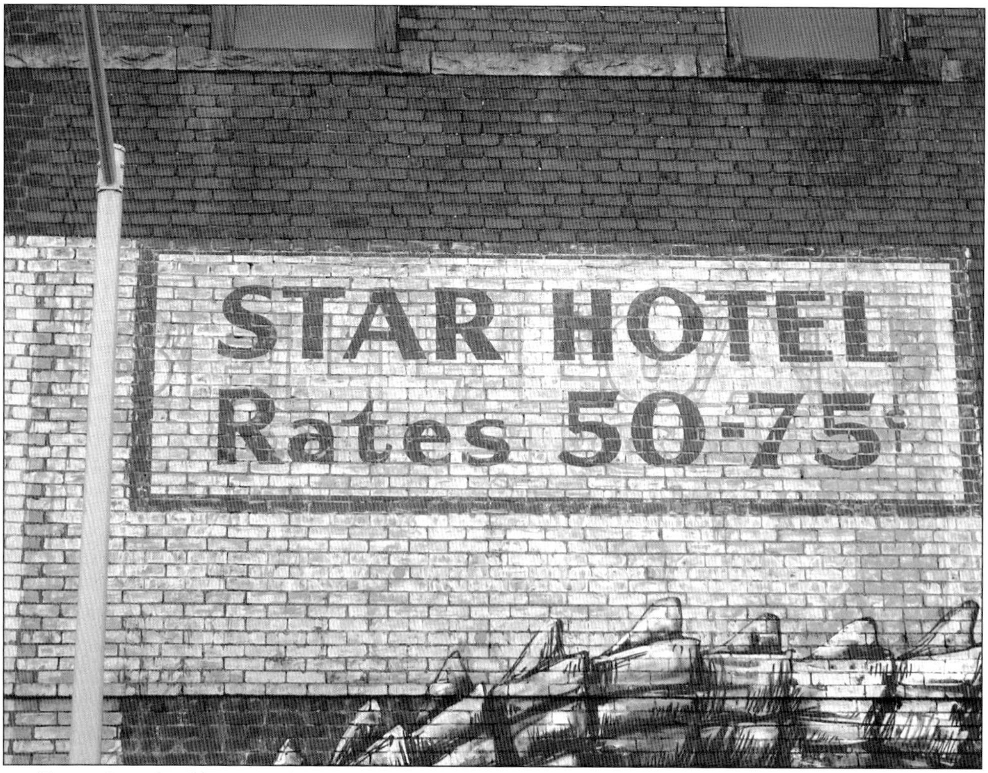

Wall murals on buildings took on an early role as advertisement, the ancestors of today's freestanding highway billboards. Often historic urban buildings retain "ghosts" of such signage, and a particularly intact example is the Star Hotel's advertisement of room rates on Atlanta's historic "Hotel Row" on Mitchell Street SW. Contemporary artists frequently duplicate familiar historical signage, most notably images of Coca-Cola, an early advertiser on building flanks (see page 151). (RMC.)

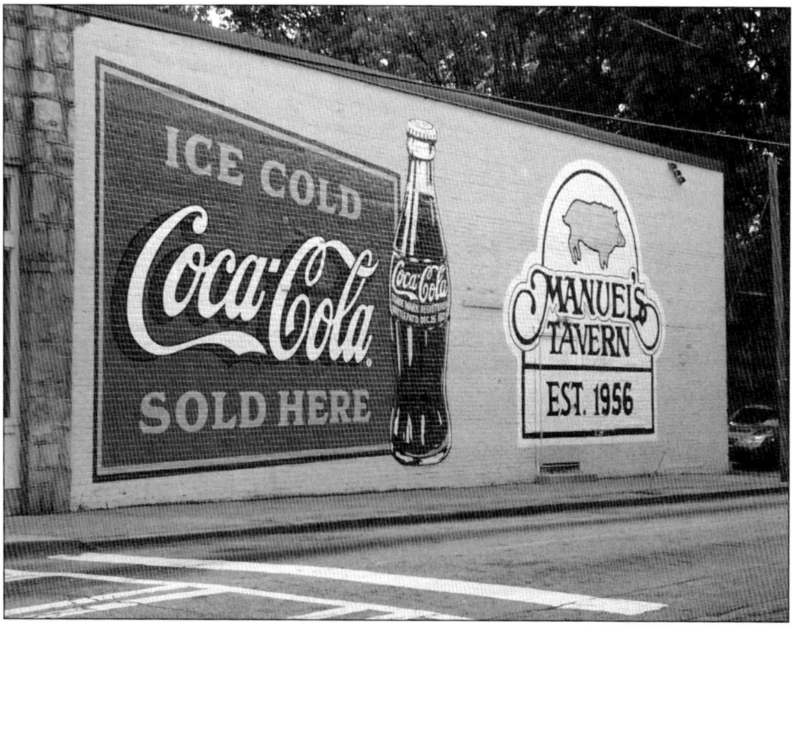

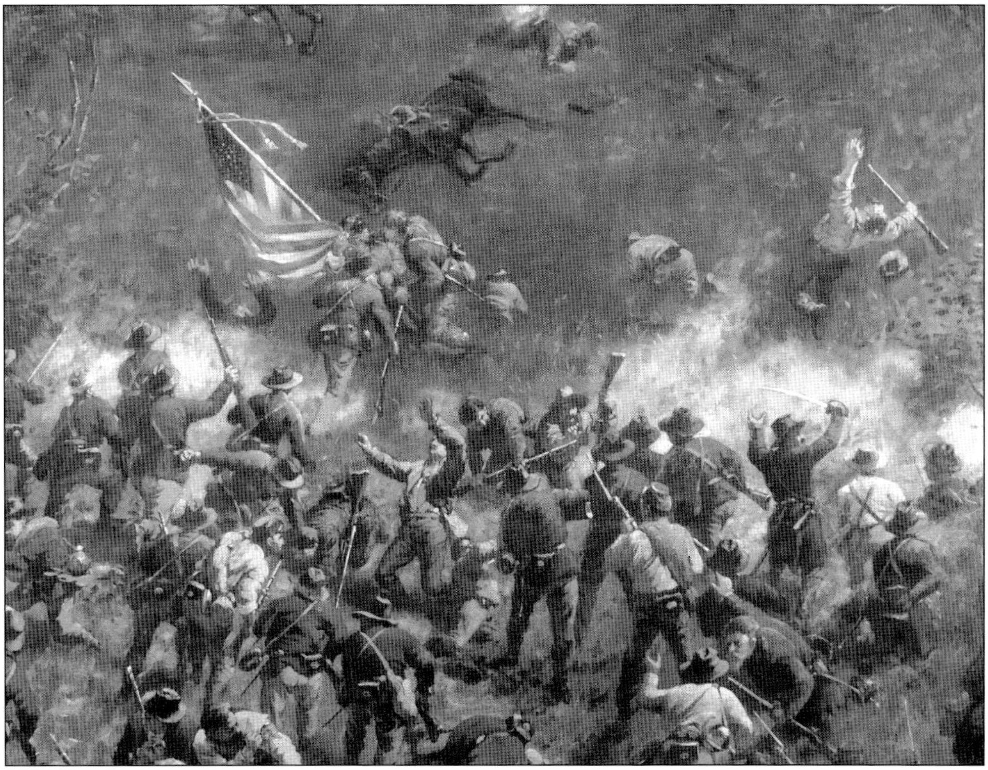

While street artists today paint scenes at enormous scale on the sides of buildings, the largest paintings of the 19th century were panoramas, and a highly significant survivor of the tradition is the 42-feet-high-by-371-feet-long cyclorama painting *The Battle of Atlanta*, recently restored and reinstalled at the Atlanta History Center after years housed in Grant Park. Created over five months by 17 German artists at the American Panorama Company in Milwaukee, the painting debuted in Minneapolis in 1886 (above). If the Cyclorama painting is the largest in Atlanta, one of the city's most significant, beautiful, and meaningful works of art is Rodin's *L'Ombre* (*The Shade*); it was originally sculpted in 1880, and seen right is a 1968 cast from the original mold. The statue was donated to the city by France following the 1962 Orly plane crash, which killed 106 Atlantans. (RMC.)

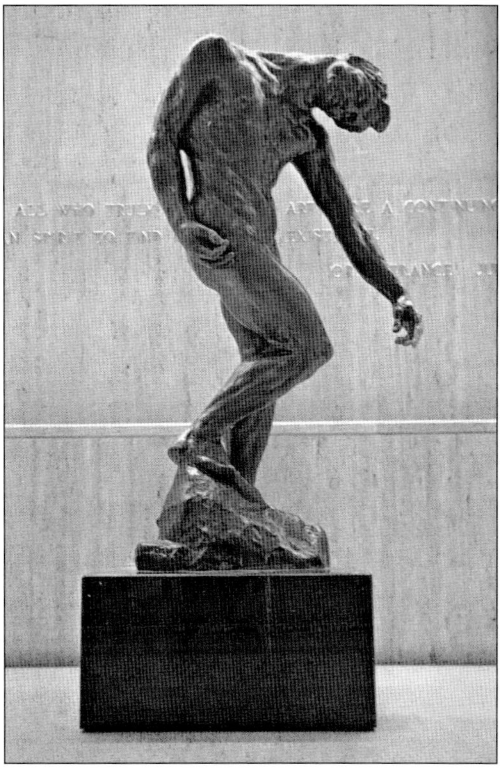

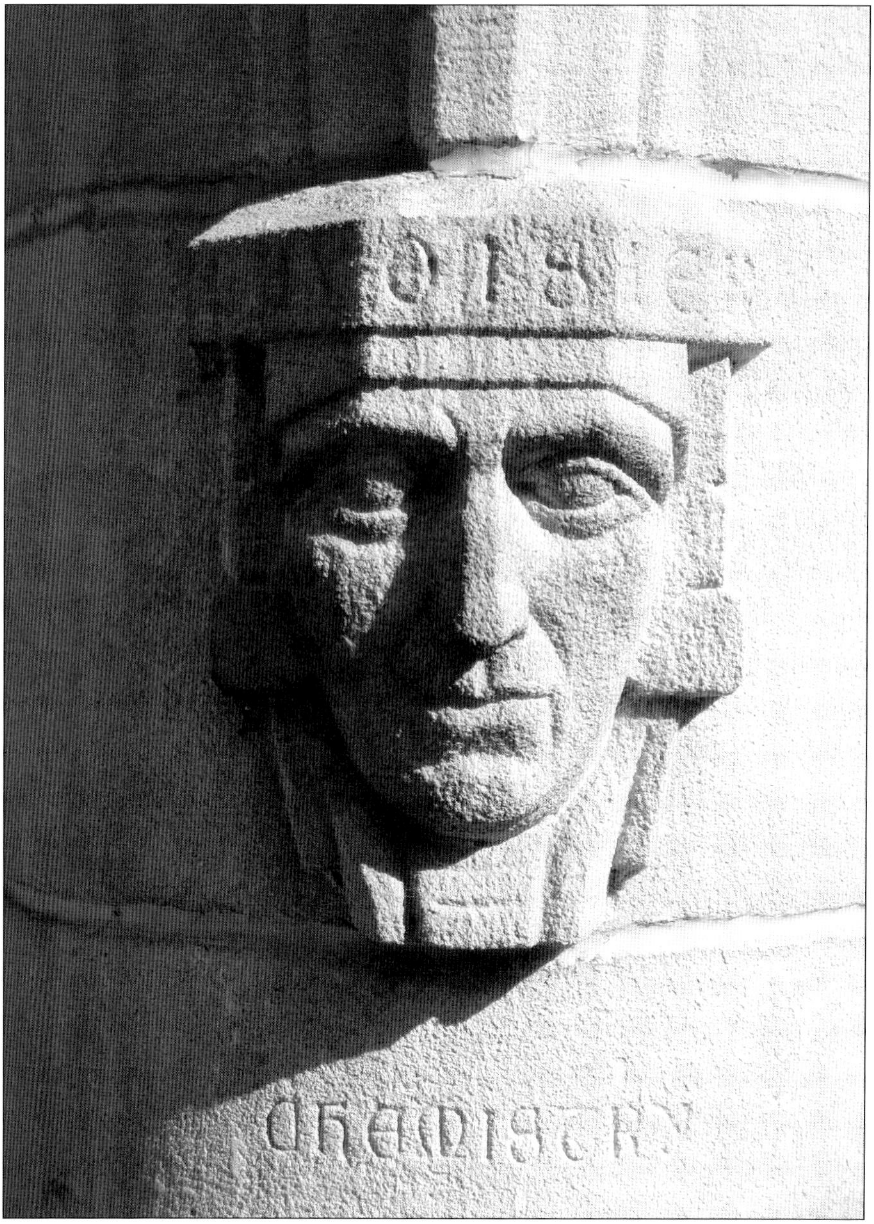

Julian Hoke Harris's 10 corbel heads that adorn the arcade of Brittain Dining Hall at Georgia Tech inaugurated the career of an Atlanta sculptor of national significance. He taught at Georgia Tech throughout his career and as an educator, he delighted in sculpture that was didactic—well designed and crafted but with meaning. Like his design for stained glass of the south window inside the hall, Harris's 10 corbels on Brittain Hall represent the curricular subjects in art, science, and engineering taught at Georgia Tech. Each discipline is paired with a notable historic figure, with three in engineering/mathematics: Leonardo da Vinci (civil, mechanical, and aeronautical engineering), Thomas Edison (electrical engineering), and Isaac Newton (mathematics and astronomy); three in art: Michelangelo (fine arts), Eli Whitney (textiles), and Della Robbia (ceramics); and four in science: Lavoisier (chemistry, above), Darwin (geology), Aristotle (biological sciences), and Archimedes (physics). (RMC.)

Two

JULIAN HOKE HARRIS

The work of Julian Hoke Harris (1906–1987) extends over half a century, from his architectural sculpture in the 1930s through the 1950s to the carving and casting of bronze busts and bas reliefs throughout the midcentury and to the design of medallions during his later career. He enrolled in Georgia Tech's architecture school because it offered classes in drawing he admitted, and graduated in 1928 with a BS in architecture. He apprenticed under Ollivier Vinour of the newly formed firm of Marye Alger and Vinour, at the time working on the decoration of the Fox Theatre. It was apparent early on, however, that Harris decided he did not want to practice architecture, although he worked for decades with architects, many of his former students from a career teaching sculpture and design at the architecture school at Tech. Instead, Harris would pursue a career as a sculptor, and beginning in the 1929–1930 school year, he enrolled at the Pennsylvania Academy of the Fine Arts, winning a scholarship after his first year. Immediately upon completion of his work in Philadelphia, Harris was back in Atlanta working on the corbels (opposite) for the new Brittain Hall.

While a student at the Pennsylvania Academy, Harris passed his architectural licensing exam (1932), and he would maintain his license throughout his career, although he never practiced as an architect. He also maintained his membership in the North Georgia Chapter of the American Institute of Architects, and in 1959, Harris designed the AIA Firm Medallion. His sculpture adorned buildings designed by some of the leading architects of the day: in Atlanta, Tucker and Howell, Paul Heffernan of Bush-Brown, Gailey, and Heffernan, Robert and Company, George H. Bond, and Stevens and Wilkinson; in Augusta, Kuhle and Wade; and in North Carolina, Wootin and Rowland. Whenever his architectural sculpture was listed on his curriculum vitae or resume, in show catalogs, or in brochures on sculpture, Harris was always precise and careful to credit the architectural firm who designed the buildings for which his sculpture was produced.

Julian Hoke Harris may be the only individual to be elected a Fellow in both the American Institute of Architects (1972) and the National Sculpture Society (1961). In 1954, the year the AIA awarded no gold medal to an architect, Harris was awarded an AIA Fine Arts Medal. His citation referred to Harris as "an architect who found in sculpture the means by which he could recapture that close interweaving of the two arts which was known to some great epochs of the past and which raises the two to heights unattainable by either art alone." (This quote was taken from the article "The Fine Arts Medalist for 1954, Julian Hoke Harris, Sculptor, Atlanta, GA" in the June 1954 issue of the *Journal of the AIA*.) In 1976, Harris was elected an associate member of the National Academy of Design, becoming a full academician in 1979. This national reputation places his sculpture among the most significant works of public art in Atlanta.

Harris's artistic contributions are conspicuous, therefore, and include noteworthy bas reliefs, panels, and sculptural ornament on public and institutional buildings. When traditional architecture became increasingly supplanted by modern buildings with their glass walls and volumetric and surface abstractions, architectural sculpture (affixed to facades, ornamenting cornices, or enriching entry portals) became passé, and commissions were scarce. As a sculptor, Harris continued to obtain requests for portraits for which he sculpted bronze busts and bas reliefs, and when he began to execute small commemorative medallions, he excelled in this medium as well. In 1977, for instance, Harris struck the official Jimmy Carter Presidential Inaugural Medallion; the following year, he designed the AIA Centennial (Ralph Walker) Medal, and for Georgia Tech, he created several medals including the student-administered Philip Shutze Medallion (not to be confused with the Shutze Award of the Southeast Chapter of the Institute for Classical Architecture and Art, awarded since 2007). In 1981, the inaugural Shutze Medal was awarded to Shutze himself and, in its second year, honored Julian Harris. His AIA Fine Arts Award perhaps best sums up his career as a "sculptor, teacher, collaborator, and champion of all the fine arts."

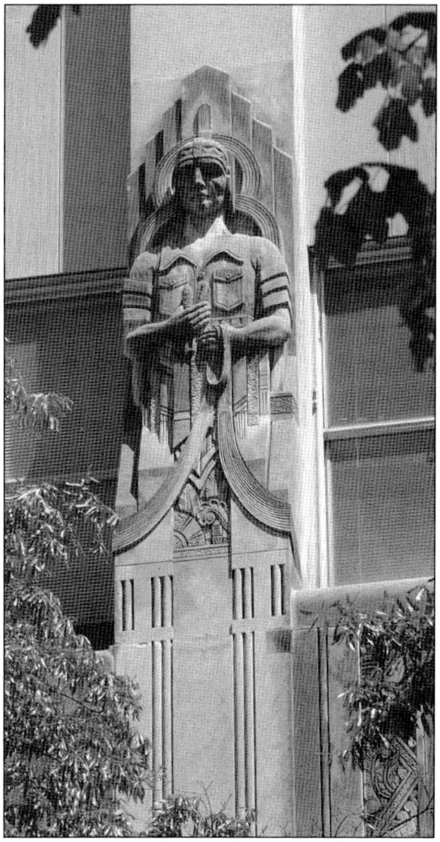

The archives at Georgia Tech include among Harris's archival materials two plaster model castings of the two figures over the entry to Marye Alger and Vinour's 1929 Art Deco Southern Bell Building (Peachtree Center Boulevard at Auburn Avenue). The authorship of these figures has remained a mystery, inasmuch as Harris was only just beginning his training in sculpture at the Pennsylvania Academy, and even if Harris designed the figures and made the plaster casts, another sculptor likely carved the actual figures. They represent a female telephone operator and male linesman. They are the finest figural works of Art Deco sculpture in the region. (RMC.)

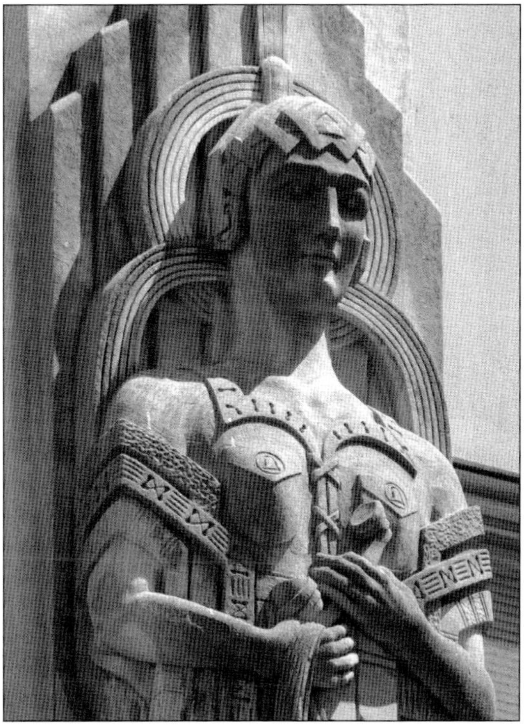

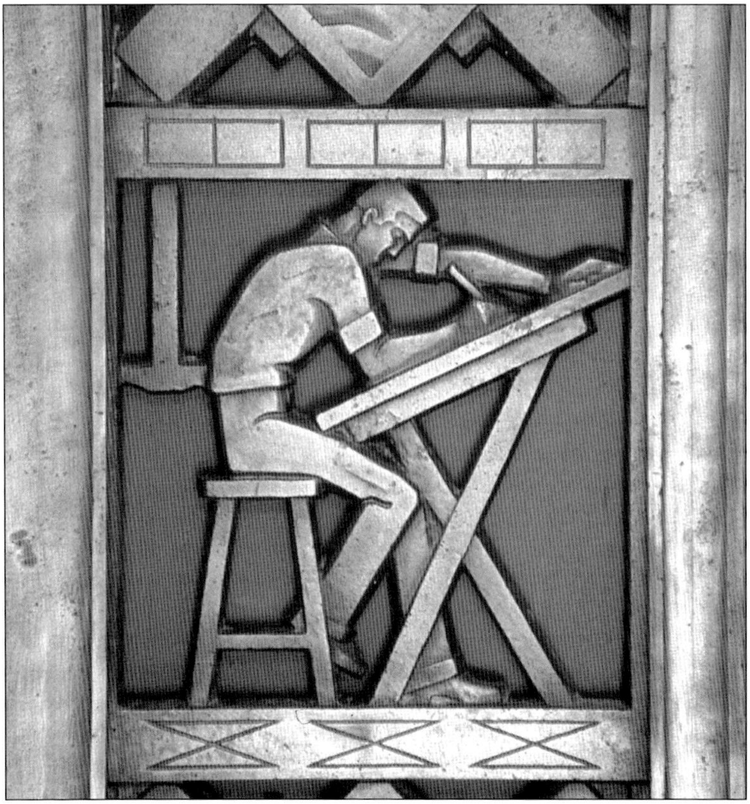

An early work for Georgia Tech (1934) is the set of bronze gates for the Navy ROTC program originally in the Armory (razed), now in the Stephen Hall Building. Thirty-five panels are filled with figures and scenes representing the curriculum and athletic activities at the school. Here, an architecture student is working at his drafting board; in other panels, eagles, ships, anchors, and a sailor sending semaphore reference the Navy. (RMC.)

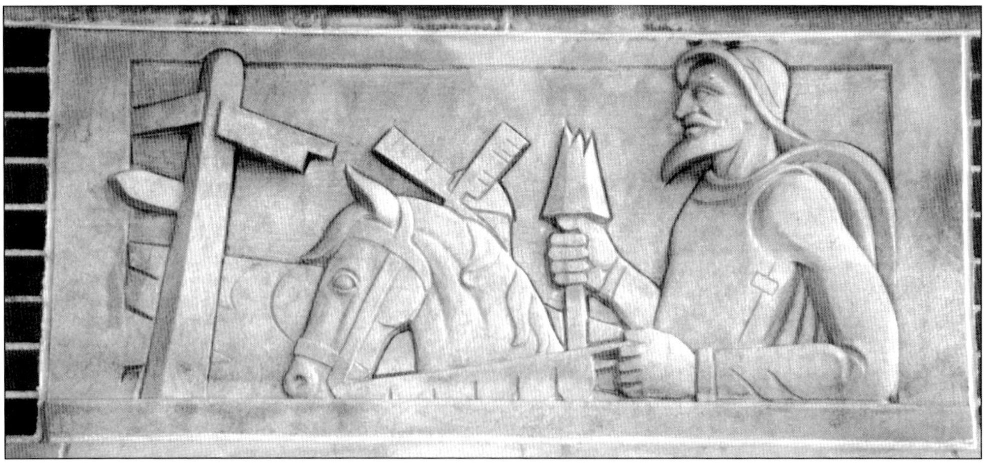

Two limestone panels on Howell and Harrison dormitories at Georgia Tech display Don Quixote's figure with a lance, windmills, and other references to the Cervantes dreamer. Carved in bas relief, they date to 1941, about the time Harris was appointed to complete Gutzon Borglum's 1915 Stone Mountain Memorial sculpture. But when Pearl Harbor was attacked, Harris spent May 1942 to February 1946 in the US Army, turning to different projects after the war. (RMC.)

Harris planned two large figures (retelling the Pygmalion myth) as sculptural ornaments for the blank exterior brick wall of the west elevation of Georgia Tech's 1951–1953 library. When the library donor balked at nude male figures and canceled the commission, the smaller scale maquettes that Harris had already crafted as studies were retained; one he kept, and the other was given to architect Heffernan and is today mounted in the Architecture Building lobby. (RMC.)

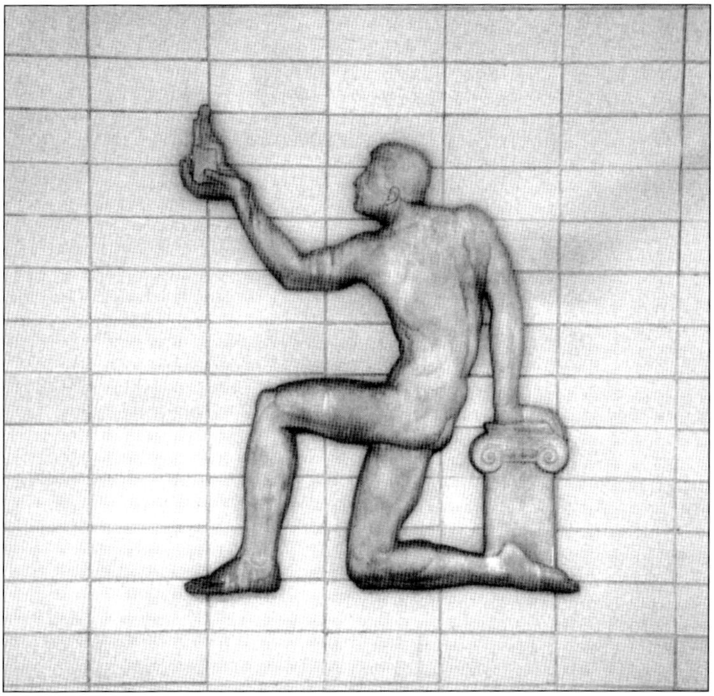

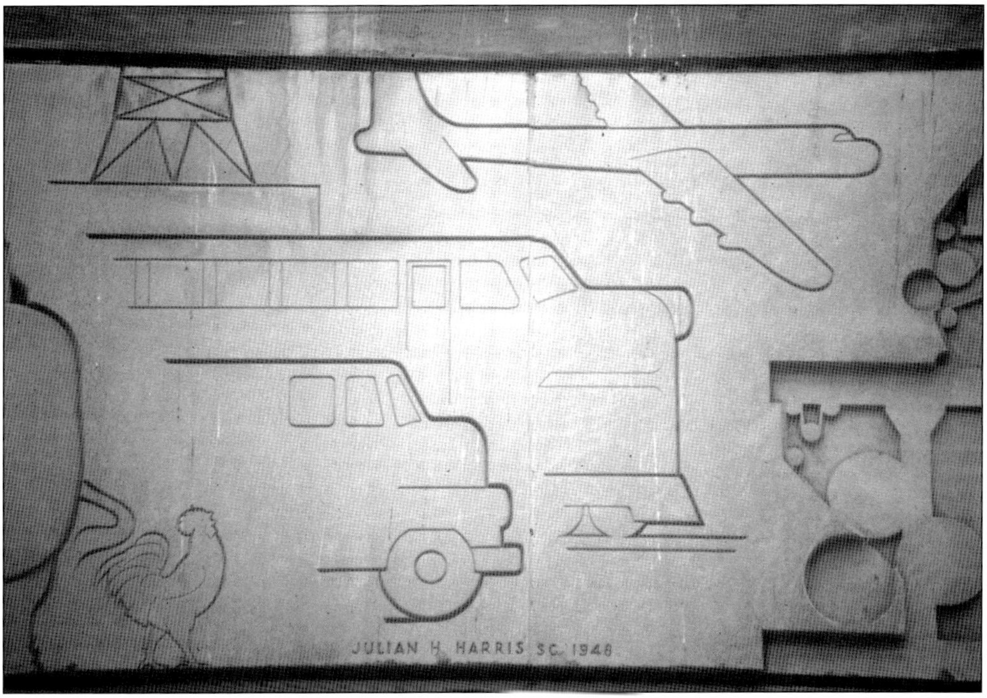

The history of the newspaper is the theme of a continuous panel originally on the Atlanta Constitution Building, also known as the Georgia Power Building (today in ruins on the corner of Alabama and Forsyth Streets). The panel is now mounted overhead as one descends the stairs into the Georgia World Congress/Mercedes Benz Stadium MARTA station. This 1948 panel shows transportation imagery typical of the Streamlined Moderne era. (RMC.)

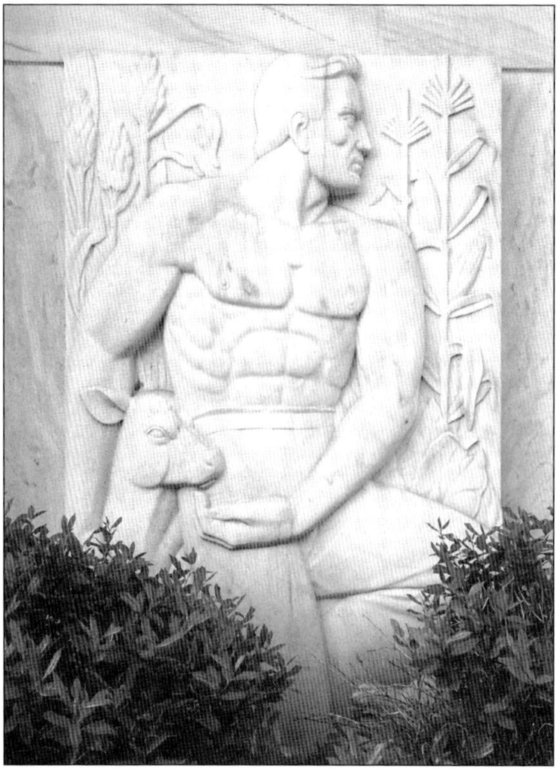

The Agriculture Building, wrapped in Georgia white Cherokee marble, is one of the several Modern Classic-styled state office buildings designed by A. Thomas Bradbury (1902–1999) and surrounding the Georgia capitol. The two panels flanking the entry, also featuring Georgia white marble, represent Horticulture/Farming and Animal Husbandry. They give evidence of Harris's admiration for classical sculpture and are among his best works. Georgia Tech's architecture school, where Harris taught part-time, offered classes in life drawing during this period, and the sculptor's masterful representation of the nude human figure is here evident. Figures stand out against the lower relief background plants which provide decorative patterns of corn stalks behind Husbandry, who holds a lamb and grapes and branches bearing fruit and blossoms behind the female figure of farming. (RMC.)

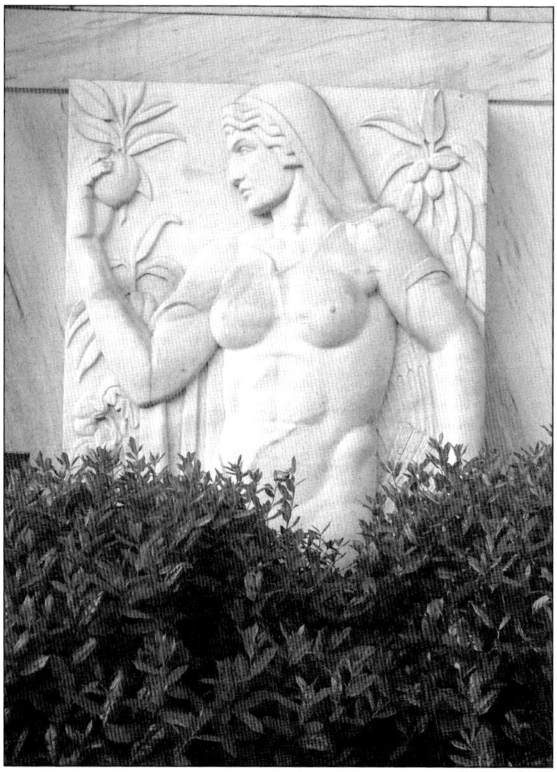

Col. Blake R. Van Leer (1893–1956), pictured right in Harris's bas relief portrait, was the fifth president of Georgia Tech. In 1956, Van Leer was pressured by the governor of Georgia to withdraw Georgia Tech's football team from the Sugar Bowl because the opposing team had an African American player. Van Leer is quoted as telling the board of regents, "Either we're going to the Sugar Bowl or you can find yourself another damn president of Georgia Tech." Two weeks after the game, Blake died of a heart attack. Tech dedicated the campus's 1959–1961 Electrical Engineering Building to Van Leer. Julian Harris sculpted bas relief portraits on building dedicatory plaques, as here—Van Leer's likeness, drawn from photographs and cast in 1964, is one of Harris's best—or below on the 1965 plaque dedicating the William Vernon Skiles Classroom Building. (RMC.)

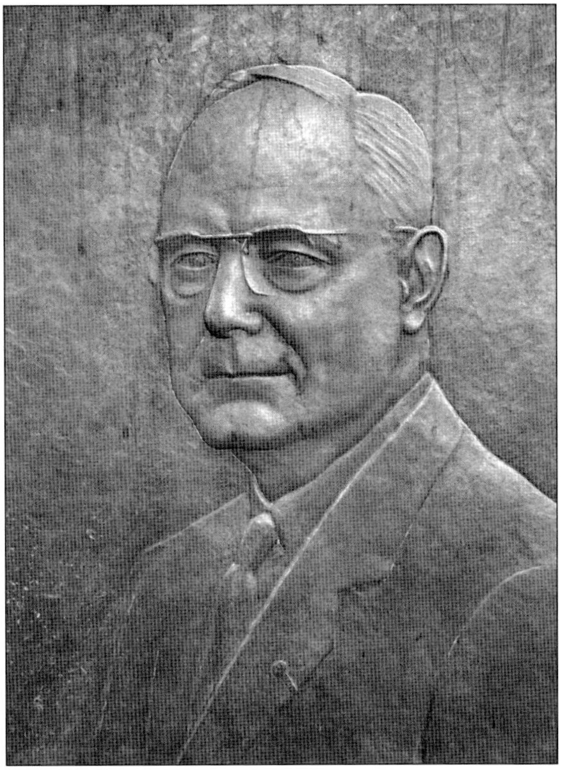

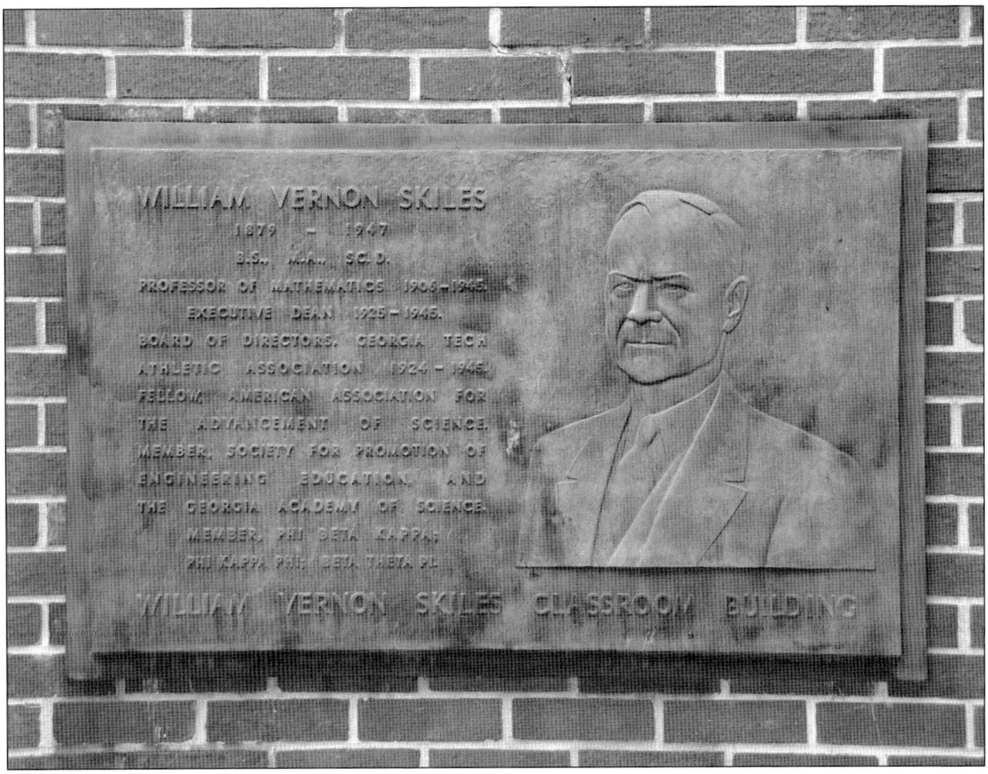

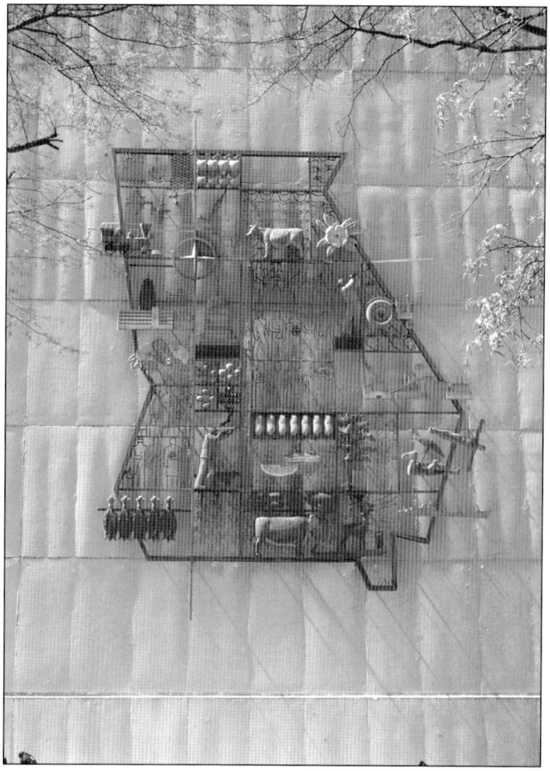

Between 1959 and 1961, Harris began to experiment with anodized aluminum, designing a large eagle in the material for the stripped façade of the First Federal Savings and Loan Building in Augusta (1959), an aluminum grill for the Whitfield County Courthouse in Dalton (1960), and a Calder-inspired mobile for Atlanta's Airport Terminal Building (1961); all three buildings are now razed. Harris's 1960 anodized aluminum grill map of Georgia, however, remains on the façade of the Commerce Building in downtown Atlanta. Applied metal sculptures reference Georgia agriculture and attractions, including (see detail of the southern region below) a cow and pigs, watermelons, tobacco, hunting, and peanuts, and elsewhere on the map a golfer near Augusta, the state capitol marking Atlanta, a railroad locomotive and airplanes near Marietta Dobbins Air Reserve Base, and sunbathers with beach umbrella near the Georgia coast. (RMC.)

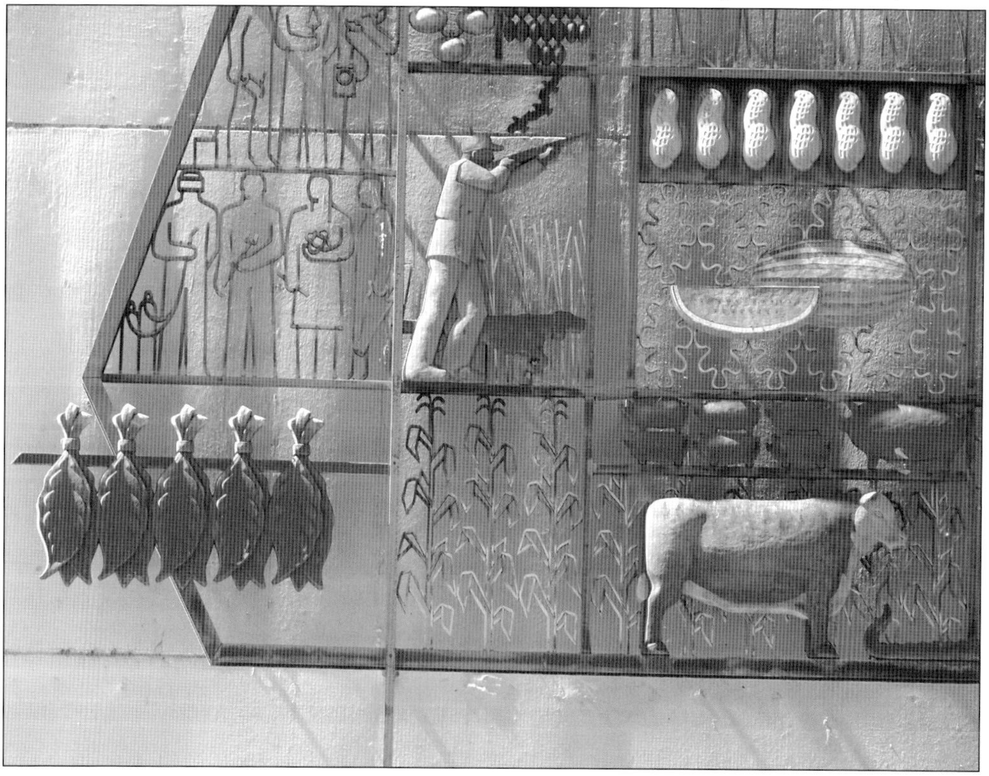

Harris also experimented with using a blowtorch rather than a chisel to cut stone and shape more abstract sculptures. His 1961 *Jet Age Madonna* in the garden of the First Presbyterian Church in Atlanta is a unique example of his cutting granite with flame. Perhaps influenced by the fluid and soft stone forms of Henry Moore or Barbara Hepworth, Harris's *Madonna* is a mere suggestion of a female figure, perhaps holding a child, but so reduced and abstract as to be almost nonrepresentational. Yet the humanity is not lost, as the stone appears to have been caressed into a maternal and protective object of devotion. (RMC.)

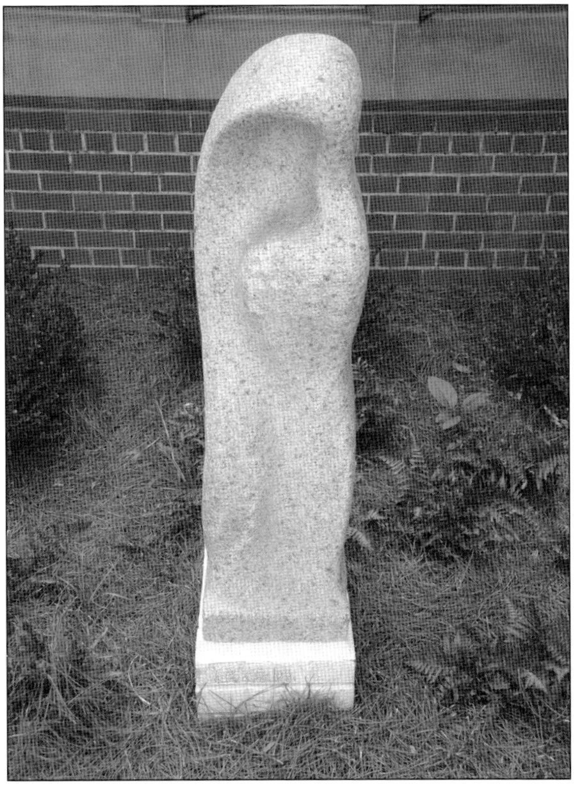

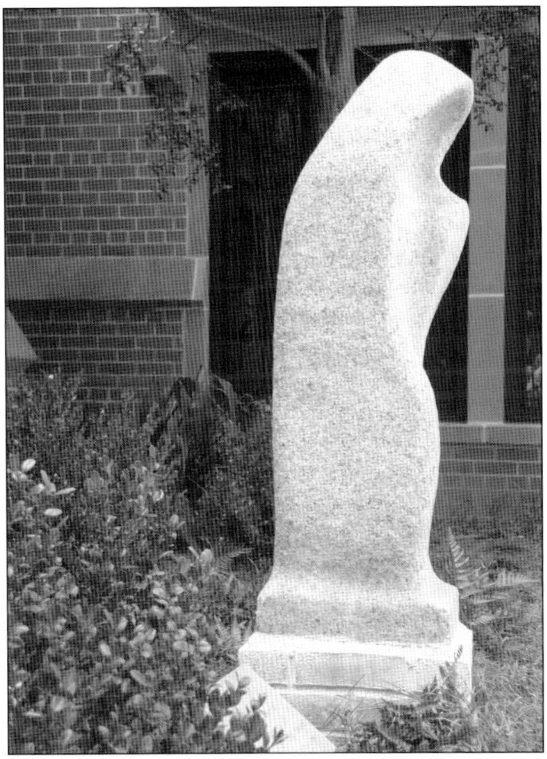

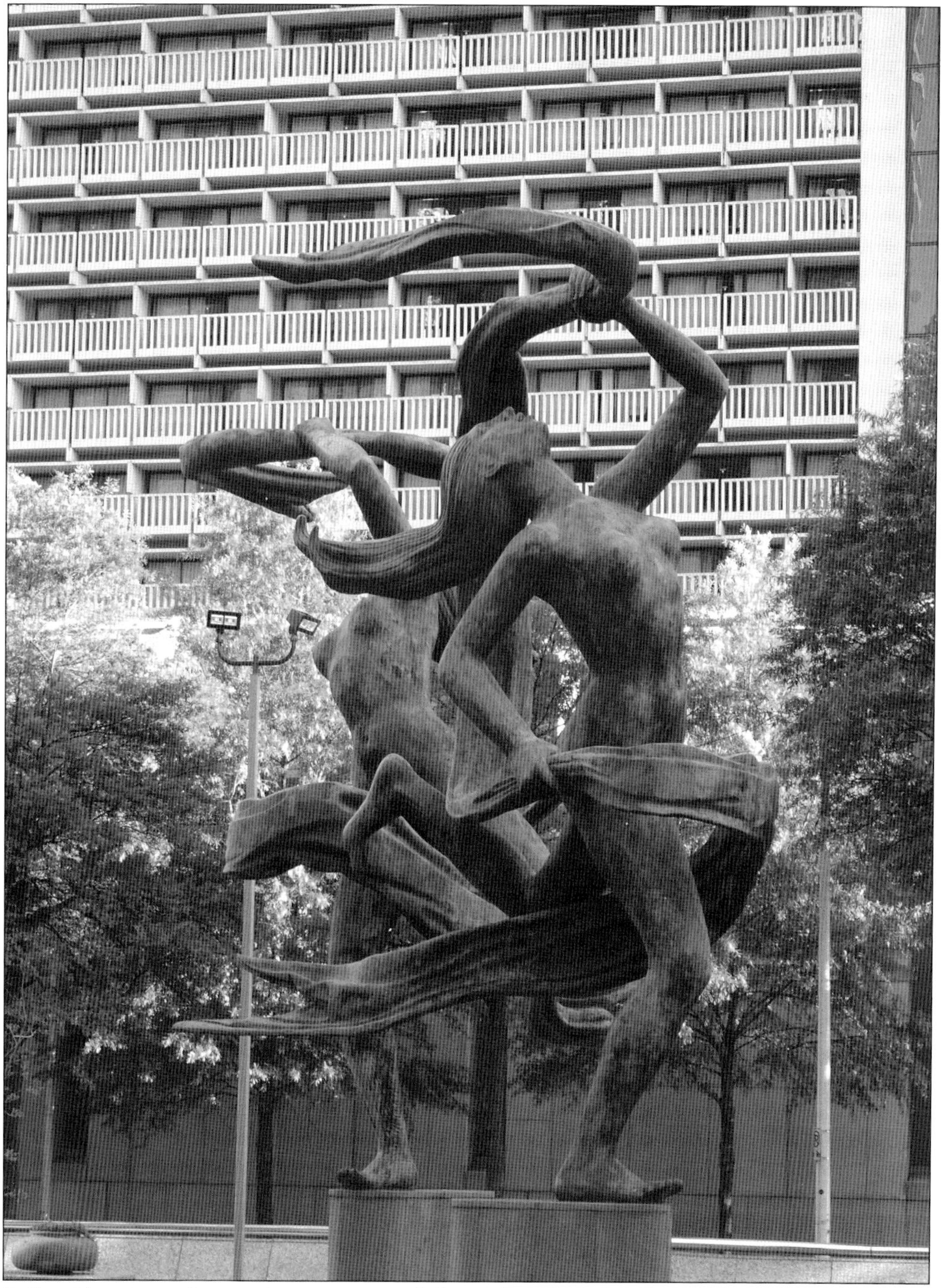

Ballet Olympia at the southwest corner of the architect's 1993 SunTrust Plaza, reflects John Portman's multidisciplinary approach to design, his willingness to appreciate other artists' work as complements to his architecture, and his broad view as an urbanist reshaping space. Here, Portman enlarged a bronze sculpture created by Paul Manship to 37 feet high, paired it with a matching bronze female dancer, and named it just prior to the Atlanta Olympic Games. (RMC.)

Three

JOHN PORTMAN

In 2009, Atlanta's High Museum of Art mounted a retrospective exhibit on the work of architect John Portman, and while his new skyscrapers and urban projects around the world were featured with stunning models, photographs, and drawings, it was the other art forms of this creative Renaissance man—his paintings, sculpture, and furniture—that offered new insights for many less familiar with the full body of his life work. We were introduced to Portman's private and public art beyond architecture, and so Portman's paintings and sculpture deservedly have a role to play in the present volume. The book *John Portman Art and Architecture* (UGA Press) accompanied the museum exhibit of the same name. Its intention was to bring Portman's *catalogue raisonné* up to date, illustrating major buildings from Entelechy I on and providing insights into the relationship of his Atlanta project to his international work. However, it was the present author's essay on Portman's paintings, sculpture, and furniture that sought to expand our understanding of Portman's art beyond his more familiar architecture. The roles of Southern sensibilities and tonalities and his interest in nature from the microcosmic to the cosmos helped define his art. One notes the exoticism and the artist's interest in the archaic, as well as Portman's "conversations with art history" extending to pop art, graphic art, calligraphy, and draftsmanship. As a city museum ought, the High introduced the art made public of one of the city's most prolific and creative favorite sons.

On the other hand, to a degree, Portman's paintings and sculptures are not public art, although much of it is visible in public spaces. Portman does not market his paintings or sculpture, and his art is not to be found in local commercial galleries. Although his paintings and sculptural pieces are not produced to be put on sale, many have found their way to public view on the walls of his architecture or in his urban spaces. Moreover, the smaller works make vital contributions to his larger vision as an architect. His furniture and paintings decorate his office interiors and hotel public spaces, while the large abstract sculptures punctuate his city plazas, bringing focus to streetscapes that serve to integrate his buildings with the city; each is a striking addition to the public spaces of his hotel lobbies, courtyards, and atriums.

More than that, the art and architecture as a whole is so interrelated that Portman's artistic expression in one medium constantly stimulated and informed his work in another. His beach house on Sea Island became a regenerative and nurturing museum/studio house for his aesthetic experimentation and the growth of new ideas. He was always impatient that architecture required time to come to fruition, and the watchful oversight of the long process required to develop an idea from an architectural concept to a built work created a situation akin to a traffic back-up of creative ideas—new possibilities were always anxious to break through, and a painting or sculptural work, he admitted, could simply be completed faster.

In all these mediums and disciplines, from a simple canvas to an entire urban center, the designer's process involved the articulation and abstraction of form, the shaping and organizing of space, and the expressive manipulation of light—those three fundamental elements of design: form, space, and light—were the artist's instruments. But a painting could be completed more quickly than a building, and Portman's creativity was bursting to express itself. After a productive weekend at his beach house, Portman would return to the Atlanta office on Monday and report that a new sculptural work had been completed or that this had been "a two painting weekend."

Portman's tallest building in Atlanta is One Peachtree Center, now named SunTrust Plaza. Its lobby is a museum of Portman's sculptures and paintings. Behind, in the Garden Offices Atrium, Portman-designed furniture, more paintings, and a focal abstract sculpture called *The Web* conspire to create a modern *Gesamtkunstwerk* set in the architect's secular three-aisled basilica. Scattered throughout the city, at Loudermilk Park in Buckhead, at his remodeled 230 Peachtree Building at the heart of Peachtree Center, and on the campus of Georgia Tech, are remarkable sculptural abstractions at large scale—indeed, at an urban scale, comprising a public art conceived by an architect.

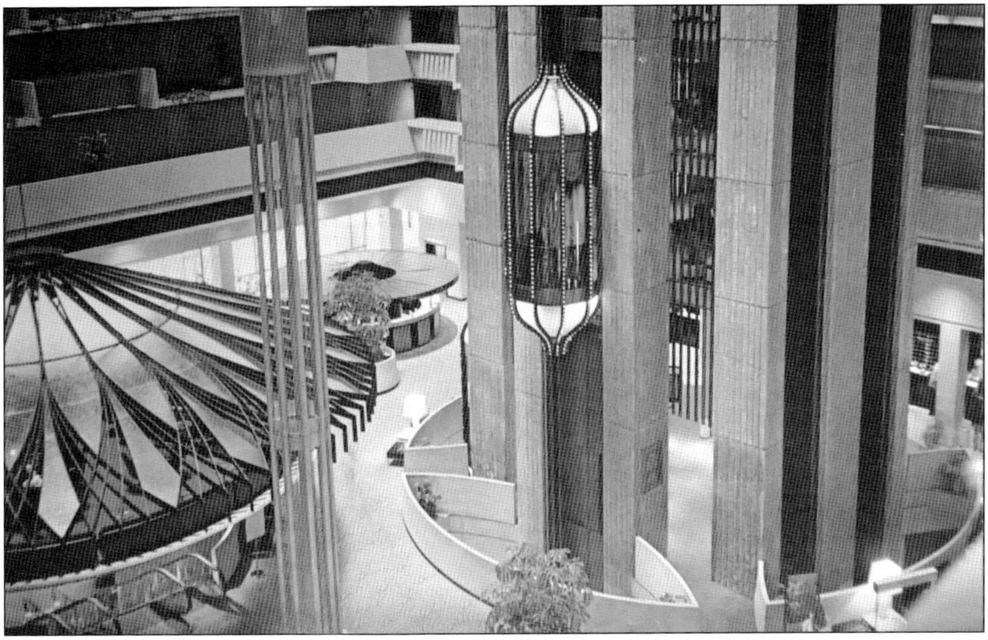

John Portman burst on the architectural scene in 1967 with his Regency Hyatt House (now Hyatt Regency Atlanta) whose jet-aged glass elevator cabs, 22-story atrium lobby, and rotating Polaris restaurant rooftop brought him international acclaim. Its atrium originally featured a raised circular bar under a vast sheltering umbrella and fan cobblestone flooring inspired by streets in Europe, both now gone. But what remains from the early interior are the formal patterns of balconies overlooking the unprecedented and exhilarating space of the atrium lobby—an architecture in itself sculptural and abstract. Still highlighting the interior (a now more antiseptic space since renovation) is the giant wire sculpture by Richard Lippold (1915–2002) titled *Floris Raris.* Commissioned in 1975, it rises 120 feet into the Portman space, exhibiting a classic instance of the architect's successful collaboration with artists in other mediums. (Above, courtesy Kenneth H. Thomas Jr.; below, RMC.)

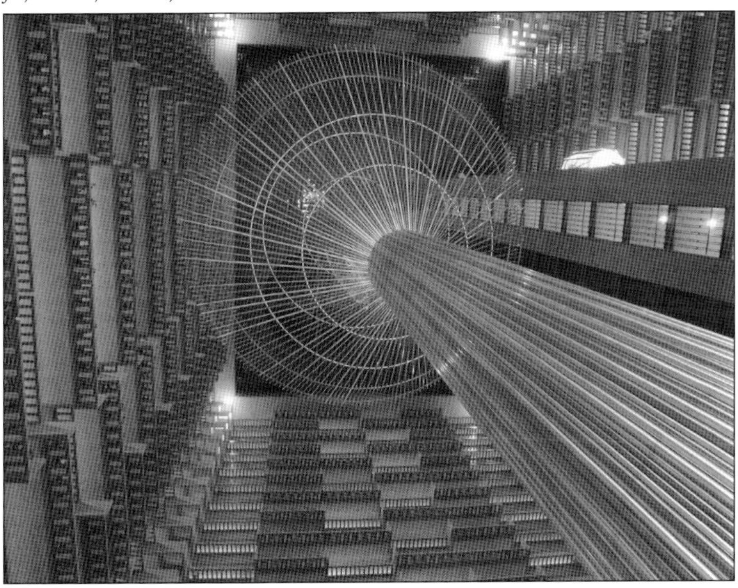

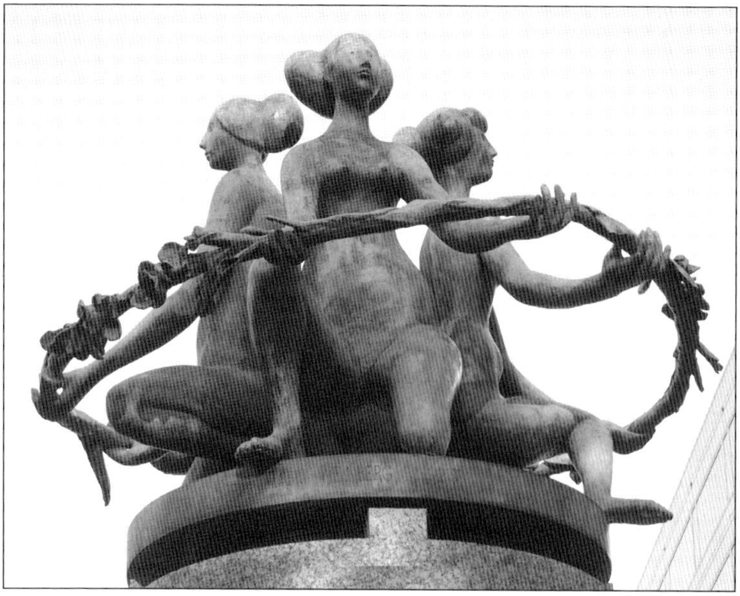

Among the artists Portman admired was Hartford native and 1951–1953 Prix de Rome winner Elbert Weinberg (1928–1991), whose sculpture *Rites of Spring* (1992) sits on a wall at the northwest corner of the public space surrounding SunTrust Plaza. Four female nude figures, squatting back to back in a circle and with their arms extended, hold a garland. (RMC.)

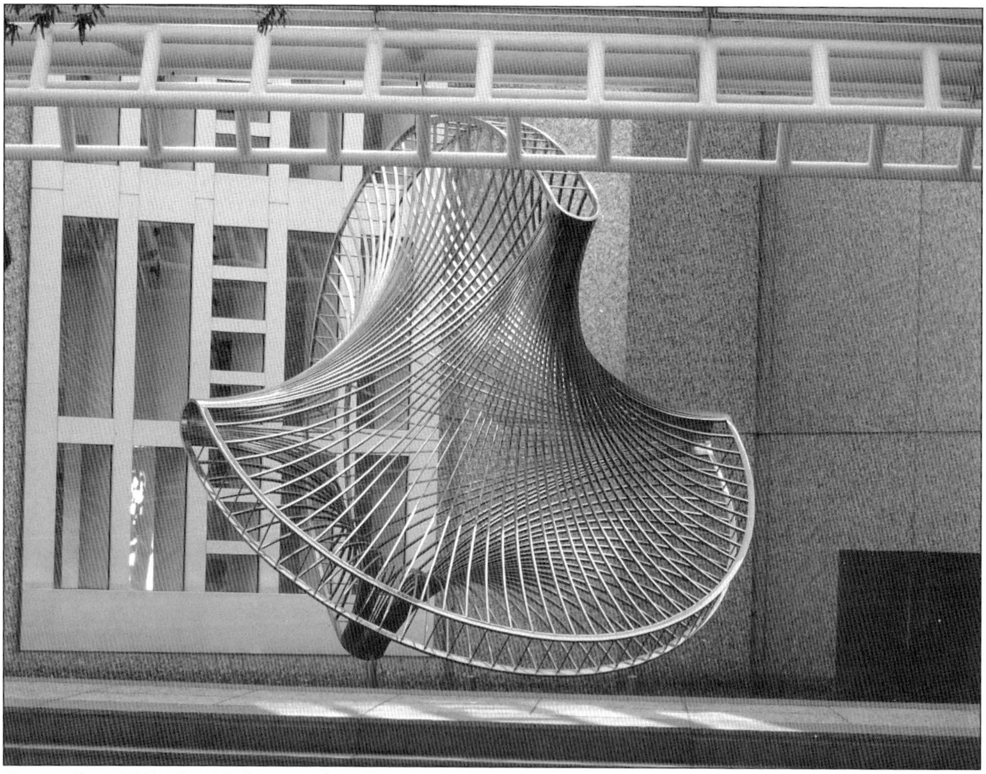

Created in 1971, the 12-foot steel sculpture *Early Mace* by Charles Perry (1929–2011) was originally located in Peachtree Center and moved to the base of the tower at SunTrust Plaza, its pedestal set in a pool of water. Fabricated of regularly spaced and curving steel rods, the changing perception of the Bézier parametric lines, as one moves past the sculpture, introduce a kinetic element and suggest Moiré patterns. (RMC.)

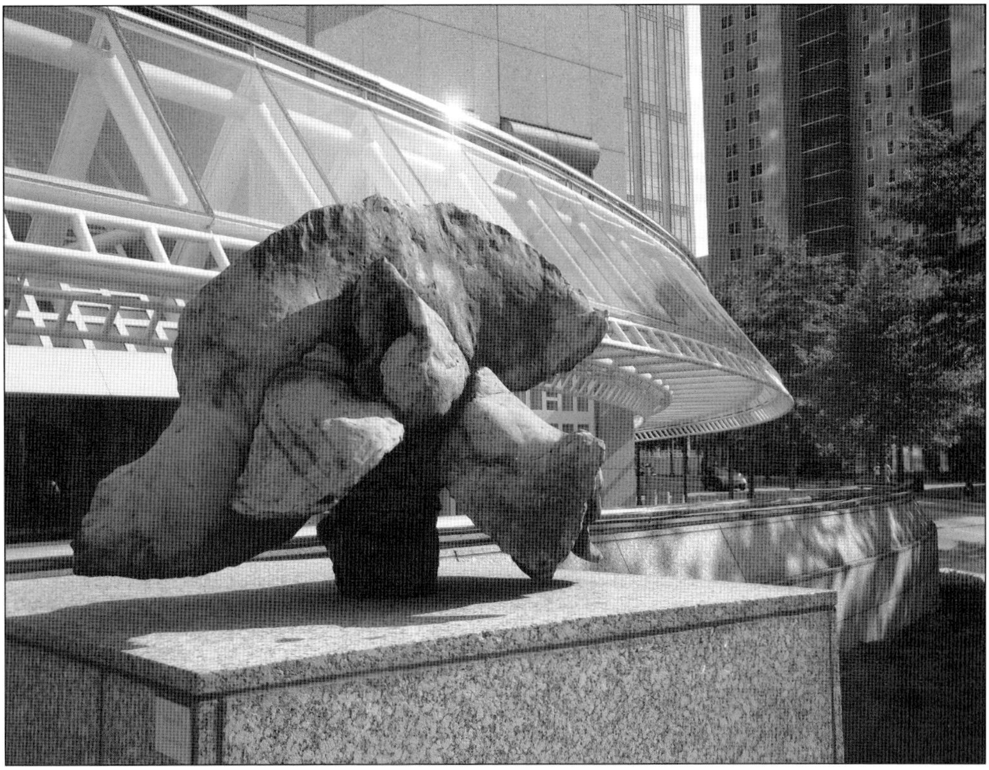

The fundamental fabrication of an organic form in sculpture's formative years resulted from human hands shaping wet clay, and the primitive, indeed archaic, forms of Portman's *Concord* on the SunTrust Plaza lower northeast terrace present sculpture in this most organic and prototypical form. Sculpture that evolved to abstraction or semi-realistic representations of Nature repeatedly interested Portman, as his *Dogwood* tree flower sculpture (above) suggests. Taken further, *Les Lions d'Atlanta* (the two pairs of rampant bronze male and female lions at Portman's One and Two Marriott Towers, flanking his Marriott Marquis Hotel) are more easily recognized as lions (below). Dating from 1987, they are the work of Brussels-born sculptor Olivier Stebelle. (RMC.)

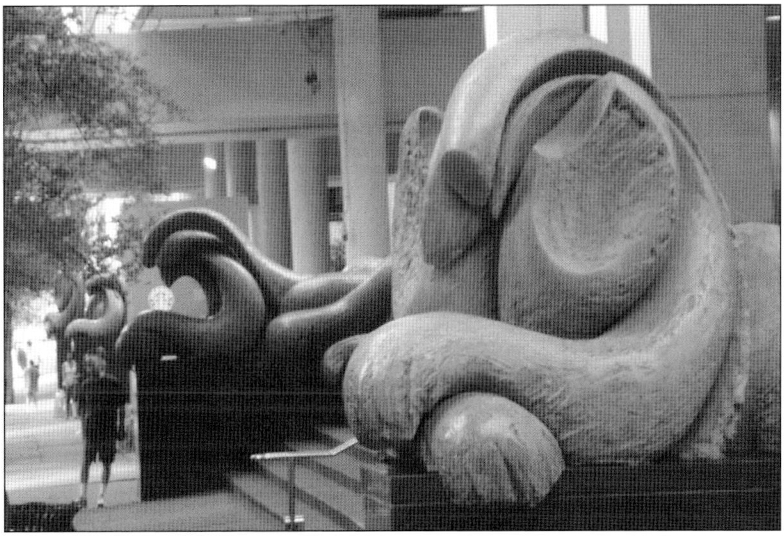

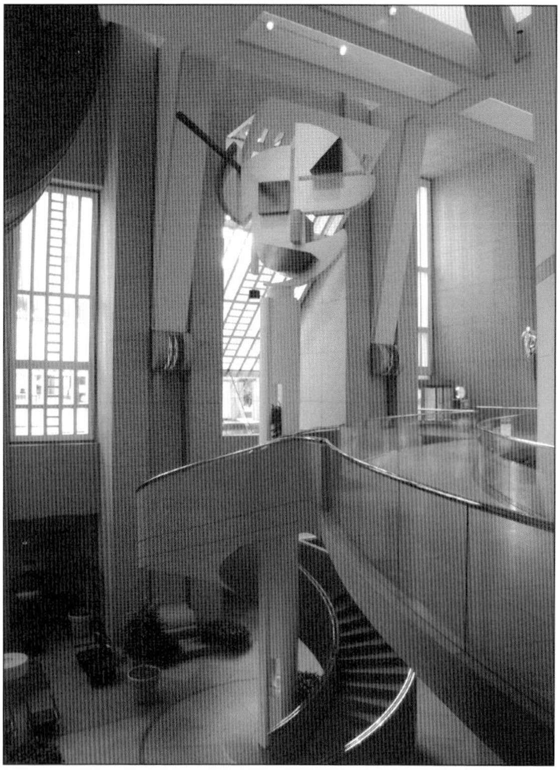

Portman employed sculpture to ornament the lower lobby and to join the levels of the two-story lobby of SunTrust Plaza. Two dominant works on columns are titled *One Eyed Jack* and *Three Moose Fighting*, each rising within the curves of a spiral staircase, and both dated 1993. *One Eyed Jack* (left), composes pie-slice painted aluminum planes of background white accented with primary red, yellow, blue, green, and black appearing as though a two dimensional Mondrian De Stijl painting had been deconstructed and recombined as a three-dimensional "counter construction" conceived by Portman as a Cubist fabricated head with a face derived from a playing card jack with one eye showing. *Three Moose Fighting* (below) is all antlers—a three-dimensional collage of interlocking forms, hooked and embattled but contained within an energy field atop the supporting column. (RMC.)

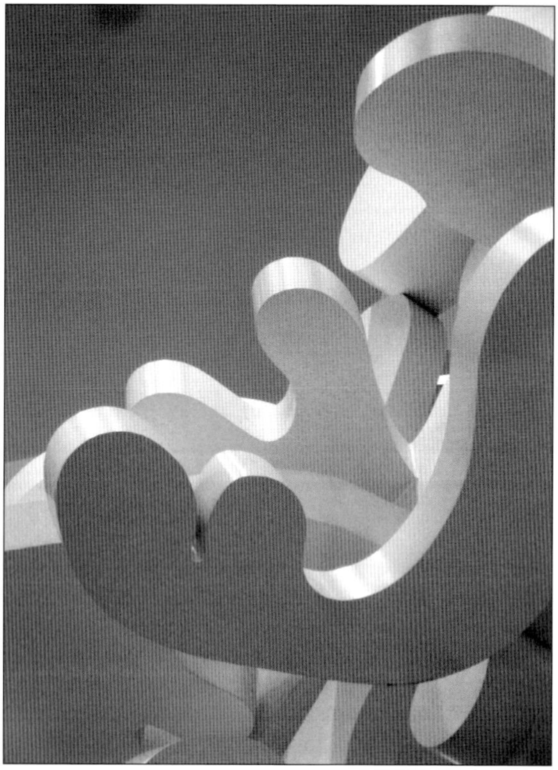

Recalling Michelangelo's so-called unfinished *Sforza*, also known as *Rondanini, Pietà* (1564), with its appearance of unpolished, still raw stone "becoming" finished art, in 1992, Portman crafted for the center of the SunTrust Plaza elevator corridors, a painted aluminum *Venus* (right), suggestive of the *Venus de Milo* emerging from unfinished stone. Here, Portman embodies the Aristotelian concept of Entelechy, an artistic idea in the act of becoming finished statuary. Nearby in the lobby is Portman's *Blueboy: Homage to Dubuffet* of the same year (below), shaping similar torso forms in fabricated aluminum wrapped in blue, black, and white paint in the spirit of Jean Dubuffet (1901–1985). After 1962, Dubuffet produced a series of works whose palette was limited to red, white, black, and blue, and in the late 1960s, the French artist turned increasingly to sculpture, often in painted polystyrene, here referenced by Portman. (RMC.)

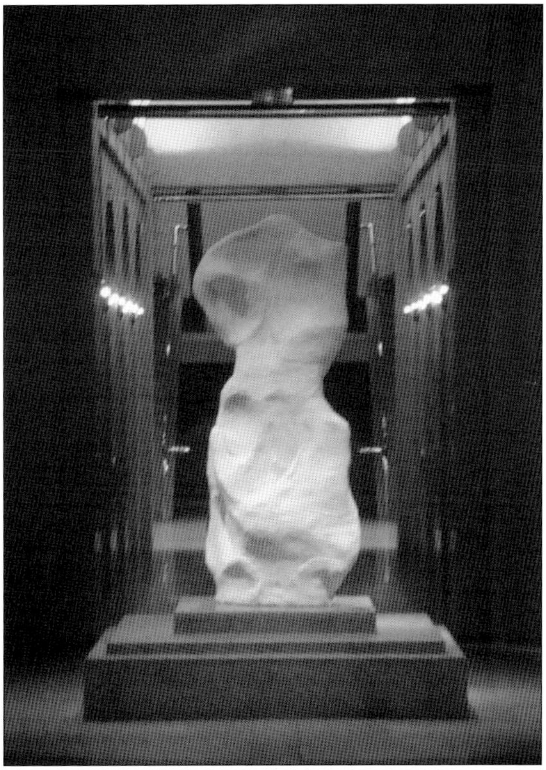

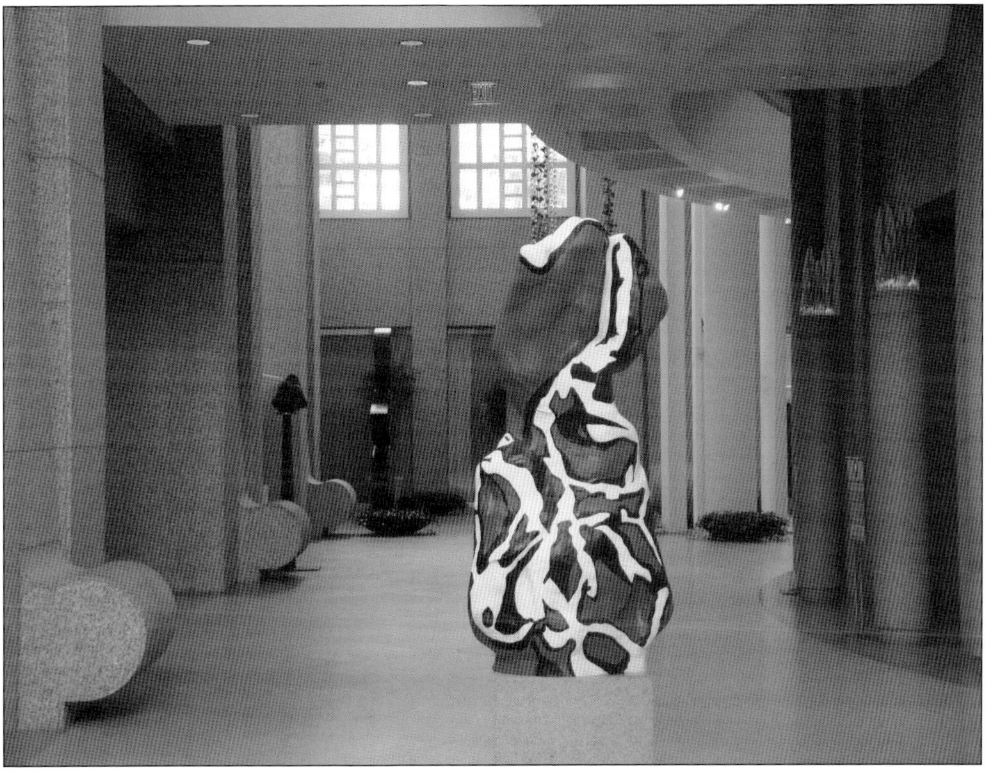

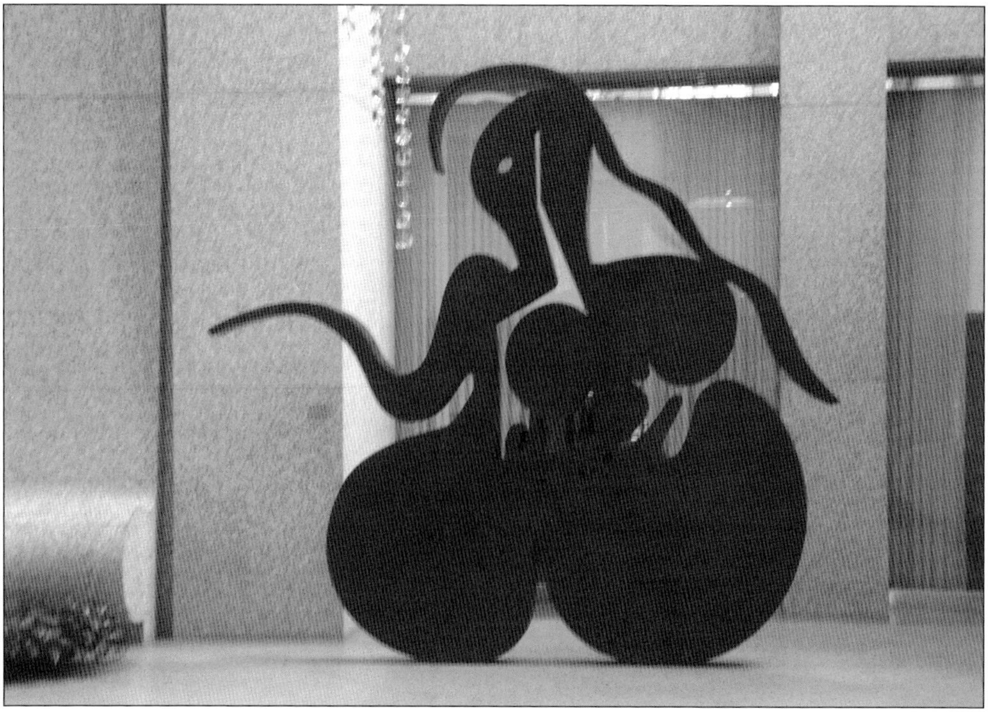

Portman's "conversations with art history" continued with his appreciation for the paper cut-outs of Henri Matisse and his "drawing with scissors." Portman's 1989 *Madonna and Child* (above) recalls the stencil-like cut-out forms of Matisse's *Blue Nudes* series of 40 years earlier, which embraced the flatness of paper but retained planes of white between the dancing and posed blue figures to suggest formal dimension and depth. Portman's *Madonna and Child*, fully in black, offers a similar stencil outline of hard-edge minimalism while referencing traditional poses of Mother and Child sculpture, although here, the child appears less in his mother's arms than in the womb. In 1986, Portman created monochromatic rectangular panels with stencil cut-outs, including his fabricated aluminum *Dooley's Dance* at the Sea Island Beach House and *Red Hot* (fabricated aluminum), seen below, displayed at Peachtree Center with similar stencil panels in black. (RMC.)

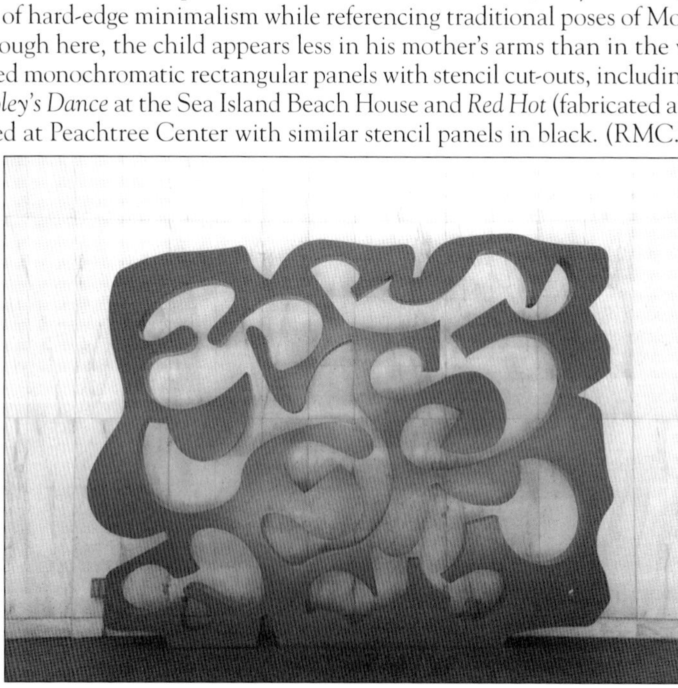

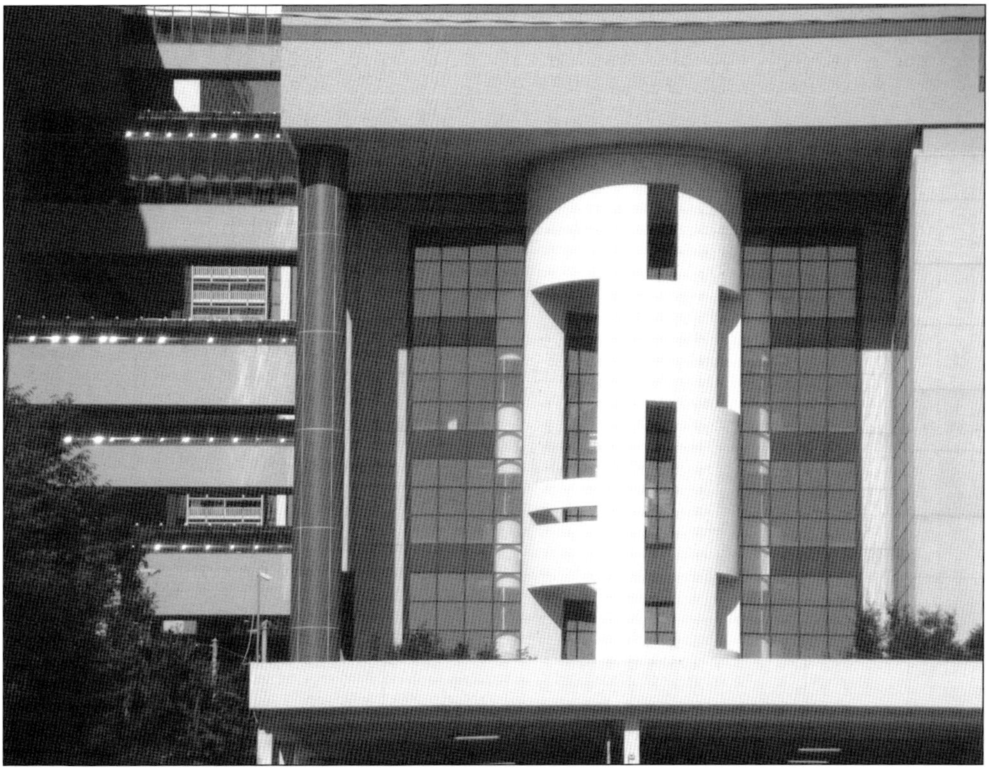

At Portman's AmericasMart Atlanta (2008, above), whole sections of the building take on sculptural form at a superscale; seen here is a white cylinder perforated with narrow openings through which the blue glazing of the building behind is visible. The column at left is painted primary red. The columnal forms recall the articulated cylindrical stacks at the entry to Portman's ADAC (Atlanta Decorative Arts Center) Building (below). ADAC (Portman's high-end furniture and decorative arts exhibition center in Buckhead) opened in 1961 and has been expanded five times since—in 1970, 1979, 1982, 1985, and 1986. As part of a 2007 renovation of ADAC, the sculptural group of perforated Corten steel cylinders titled *South Music* was commissioned by Portman and created by Spanish sculptor Angel Orensanz (1940–), below. (RMC.)

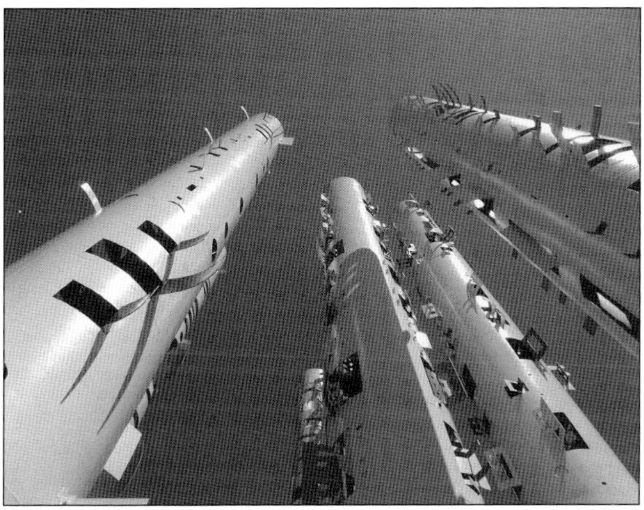

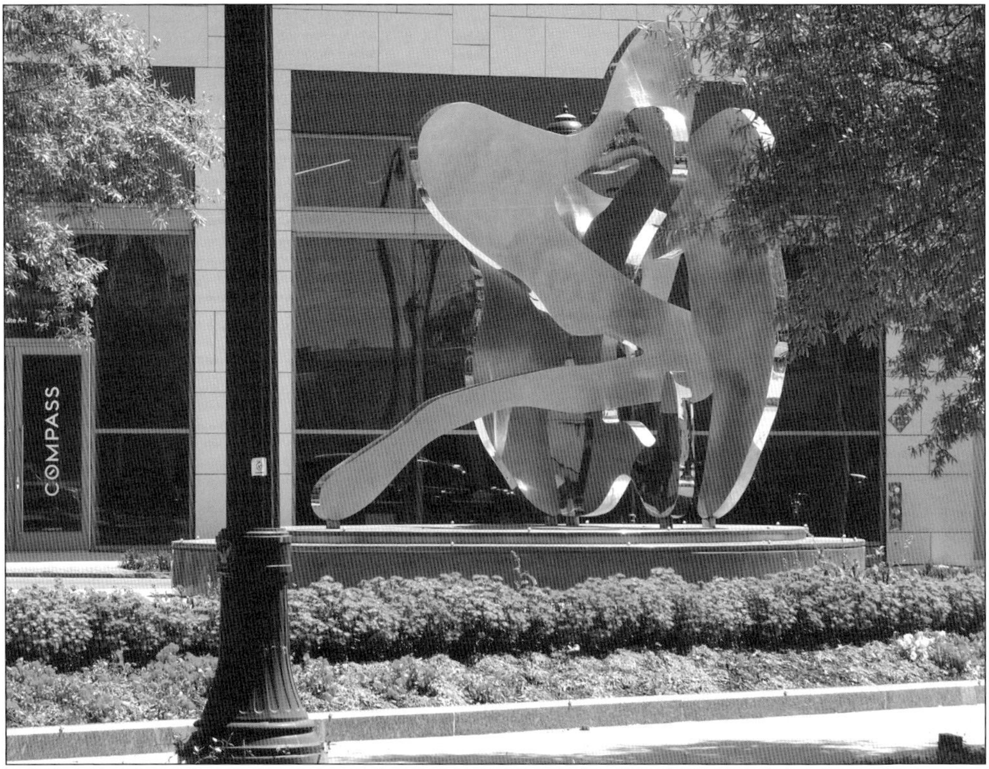

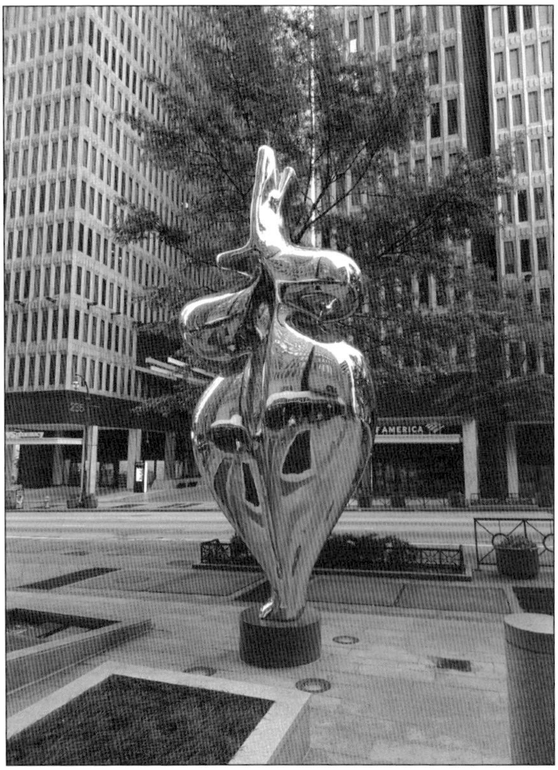

R. Charles Loudermilk (1927–), for whom Triangle Park, in the heart of Buckhead, was renamed in 2009, is a prominent civic leader, philanthropist, and founder of the Buckhead Coalition. He asked John Portman to design a sculpture for the Charlie Loudermilk Park, and the 12-foot stainless-steel *Aspiration* (above) was completed in 2015, symbolizing their shared commitment to Atlanta and to Buckhead's "continuing emergence . . . as an important community in its own right." The following year, in 2016, in downtown Atlanta, Portman unveiled *Belle* (left), an 18-foot tall stainless-steel figure inspired by the female form and reflecting on its gleaming surfaces Portman's surrounding architecture. Sited in front of his redeveloped 230 Peachtree in the heart of Peachtree Center, "the lovely lady *Belle*, is representative of my love for Atlanta," the architect said in 2016. (RMC.)

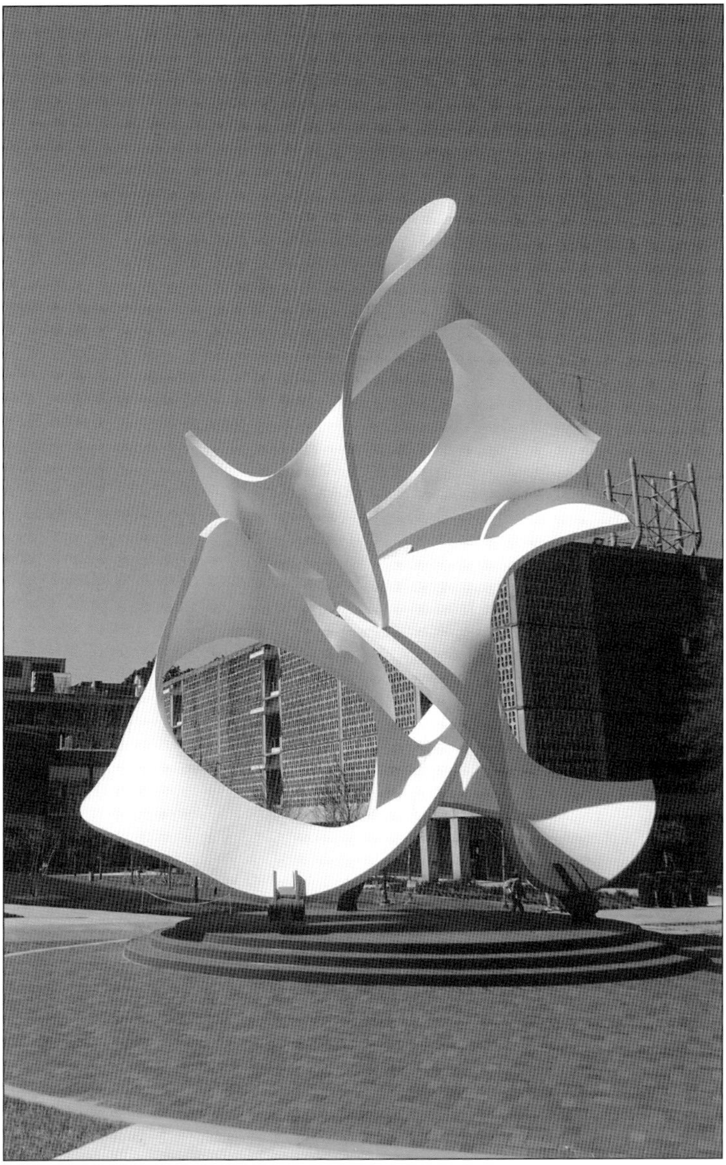

John Portman's association with Georgia Tech has been longstanding, and it is perhaps fitting that his final work of public art is on Tech's campus. Portman has remarked, "Georgia Tech is a jewel in Atlanta's crown, and the College of Architecture . . . played a pivotal role in shaping my life." Portman received his bachelor's degree in architecture from Tech in 1950, and in 2012 was awarded an honorary doctorate degree. He has endowed the John Portman dean's chair in the College of Architecture and created the Portman Prize for architectural students (awarded at Kennesaw State University, Georgia Tech, and Harvard), the latter intended "to encourage students to develop a holistic design approach that ties big ideas to small details." The prize "is awarded through competition by a distinguished jury chaired by the Portman Visiting Critic who also participates over the semester as a roving design studio critic and public lecturer." Portman's 38-foot-tall by 36-foot-wide sculpture *KR+C* symbolizes the "Knowledge and Research plus Creativity" that fuels Georgia Tech. The sculpture is constructed of fiberglass by a Georgia company that specializes in custom speed boat fabrication. (RMC.)

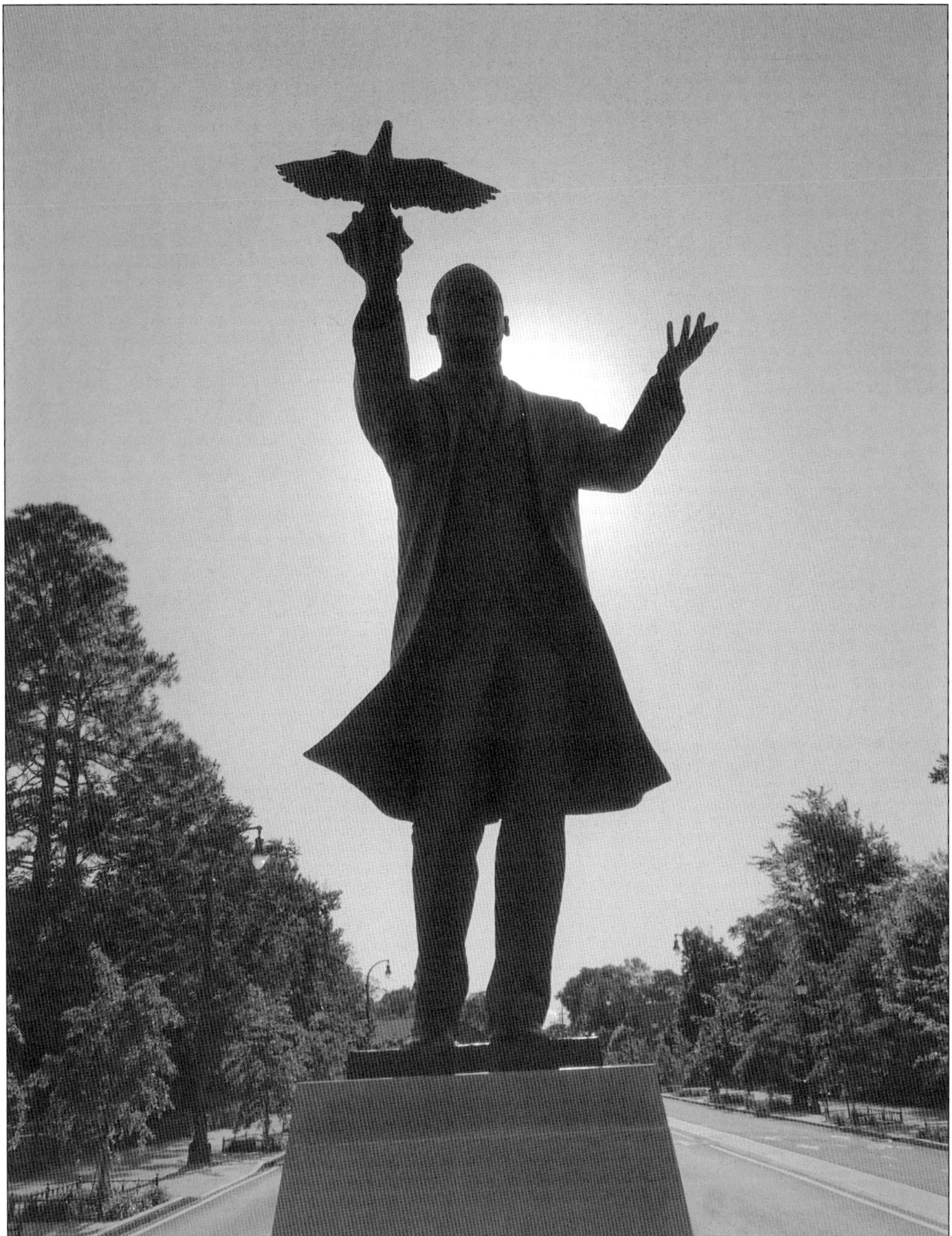

The 12-foot sculpture of Martin Luther King Jr. inscribed with "Hope Moving Forward" is the first of seven planned installations for the "MLK Innovation Corridor Project," a redevelopment plan for MLK Jr. Boulevard west of Northside Drive near Mercedes Benz Stadium. The sculpture by Jamaica-born Atlanta resident Basil Watson (1958–) was unveiled during the week of Martin Luther King Jr.'s birthday holiday in 2021 and was dedicated by the City of Atlanta. Watson was inspired by King's remarks (the last 10 words inscribed on the back of the monument), "Darkness cannot drive out darkness; only light can do that. Hate cannot drive out hate; only love can do that." (RMC.)

Four

Civil Rights Art

Although Little Rock, Birmingham, Montgomery, Selma, Jackson, and Memphis witnessed major events in the civil rights movement, Atlanta in many ways has been the spiritual home of the movement. Atlanta is the birthplace of Martin Luther King Jr. (1929–1968) and the home of Ebenezer Baptist Church and Hunter Street Baptist Church, where "Daddy" King (MLK Sr., 1899–1984), his son Martin, and Ralph David Abernathy (1926–1990) preached nonviolence. It was in Atlanta that a collection of traditionally black colleges found in Dr. Benjamin Mays (1894–1984), a mentor who laid the intellectual foundation for the American civil rights movement and who at Morehouse College nurtured students including Julian Bond (1940–2015), a Freedom Rider, social activist, and pioneer black politician. It was in Atlanta's Paschal's Restaurant, in the family rooms and basements of homes of black leaders, and on Sweet Auburn Avenue that civil rights goals, perspectives, and strategies were shaped. And it was in Atlanta, as bus boycotts spread throughout the South following the famed Rosa Parks (1913–2005) incident in Montgomery (1955), that King and Abernathy formed the Southern Leadership Conference on Transportation and Nonviolent Integration, the progenitor of the national SCLC (Southern Christian Leadership Conference), headquartered on Auburn Avenue in Atlanta. And in more recent years, Atlanta was the longtime home of John Lewis (1940–2020), a Freedom Rider who became a statesman during an era when few politicians are worthy of the appellation; Lewis represented Georgia, but in a larger sense, embodied universal civil rights values, as a member of the US Congress from 1987 until his recent death in 2020.

These leaders and others of local and national significance are memorialized in public art in Atlanta: in monuments and statues and on murals throughout the city. Whereas the Kings (both Martin and Coretta), Abernathy, Rosa Parks, and Lewis may be more familiar names, Atlanta church leaders were right alongside these pioneer leaders of the civil rights movement, including Rev Joseph Lowery (1921–2020), Rev. Joseph E. Boone (1922–2006), Rev. James Orange (1942–2008), and Rev. Hosea Williams (1926–2000), as well as Andrew Young (1932–), C.T. Vivian (1924–2020), Maynard Jackson (1938–2003), and the "mayor of Auburn Avenue," John Wesley Dobbs (1882–1961). These men are the founding fathers of the civil rights movement and the subjects of murals, monuments, and sculptures across the city. And the women of the movement, including community leaders and activists for related social causes, are in evidence in Atlanta's public art as well: in the herstory murals painted on the walls of schools and masonry buildings throughout the city celebrating Ella Baker (1903–1986), Stacey Abrams (1973–), or Kamala Harris (1964–), as well as murals about social causes such as Sofahood's "art for the marginalized" exemplified in her *All Power to the People* mural, or the "hero" murals dedicated to the SCLC women and Evelyn Gibson Lowery (1927–2013), or to reproductive justice activist Dazon Dixon Diallo (1965–), or to LGBTQ activist Joan Garner (1951–2017). Other contemporary dimensions of the social justice movement are reflected in Black Lives Matter, George Floyd (1973–2020), Justice for Jamarion [Robinson] (1990–2016), and black pride murals.

This dimension of Atlanta's public art is perceived as especially "art of the people" and the urban mural is the most populist of art forms. Originally condemned as manifestations of urban blight by the strident and illegal tagging of buildings by graffiti artists, much of the street art of Atlanta shows remarkable talent. Images of individuals are often well-observed, compositions are well studied, and execution is commendable. The scale of the art is relative to the burgeoning scale of the modern metropolis, finding ancestry, perhaps, in 19th-century panoramas but stimulated by large-screen motion picture projection screens that make subject content "bigger than life." The parallel of cinemas, in Australia for instance, projecting movies from an interior projection booth to an outside garden wall or adjacent building façade may not be known to many of today's muralists, but images of civil rights leaders loom large on the side of local barbershops and grocery stores, bars, and warehouses, creating an accessible public art in every urban neighborhood of the city. Commemoration of past leaders in art is no longer limited to statues in public parks and portraits in public museums, but the city itself becomes an outdoor museum, in which photorealistic portraiture and social messaging as well as commemorative tribute are in evidence through mural art, the public art of everyman.

In many ways, Mohandas Gandhi (1869–1948) was the spiritual leader of the worldwide peaceful protest and civil rights movement. Gandhi referred to his form of nonviolence as "satyagraha," meaning "truth-force" or "love-force." Martin Luther King Jr. embraced Gandhi's philosophy, and in 1960, in *"Pilgrimage to Nonviolence": On Gandhi's Legacy*, King wrote, "I came to see for the first time that the Christian doctrine of love operating through the Gandhian method of nonviolence was one of the most potent weapons available to oppressed people in their struggle for freedom." He acknowledged further that "while the Montgomery boycott was going on, India's Gandhi was the guiding light of our technique of nonviolent social change." Sculptor Ram Sutar (1925–) designed the statue of Gandhi, which was unveiled in 1998. The sculpture stands near the entrance to the visitors center at the Martin Luther King Jr. National Historic Site. (RMC.)

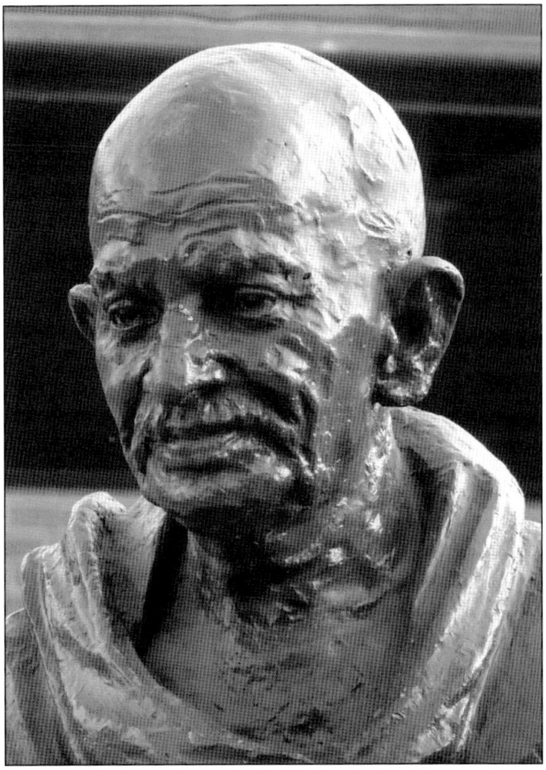

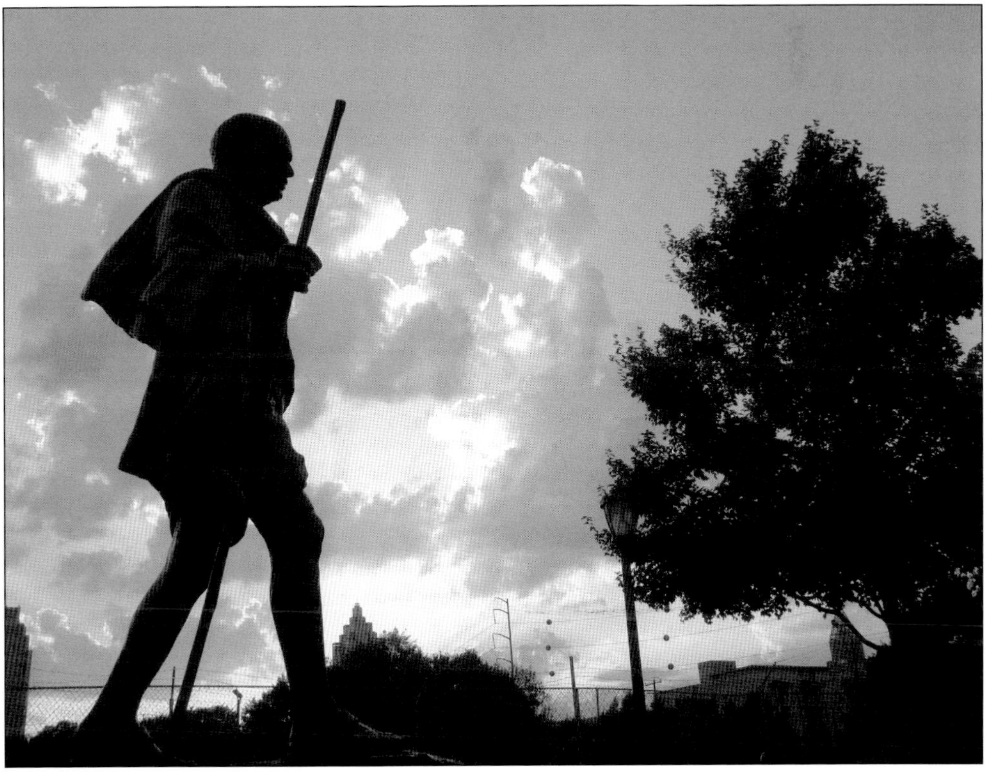

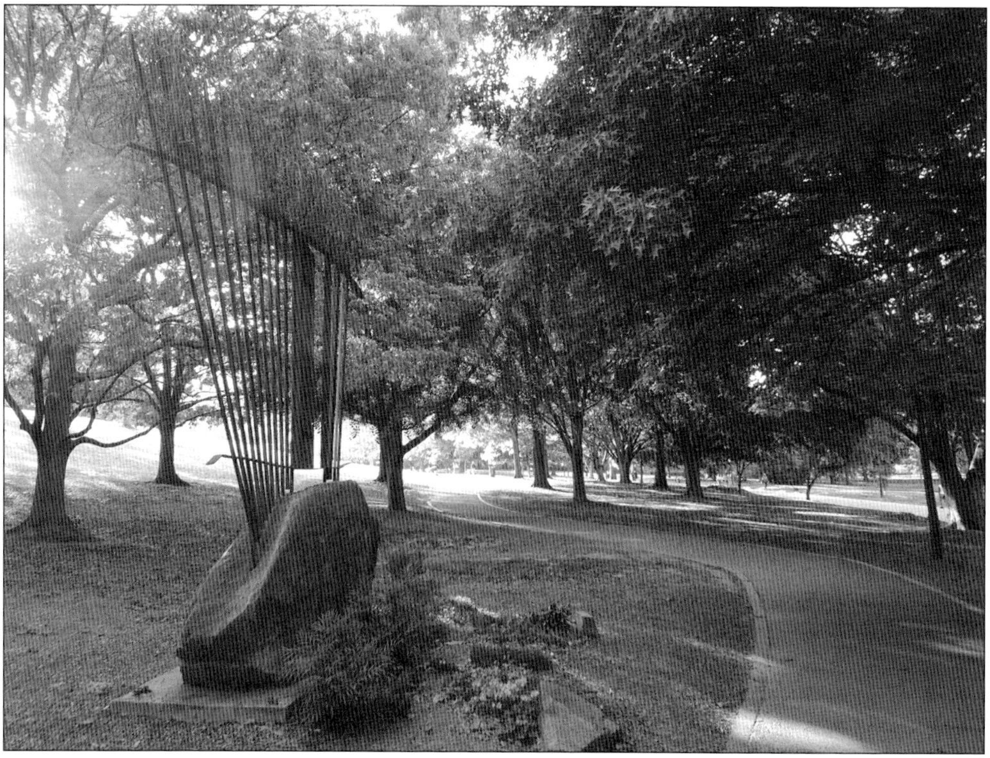

The protests of Nelson Mandela (1918–2013) against apartheid in South Africa gained worldwide attention. He served 27 years in prison before South African president F. W. de Klerk released him in 1990. A sculpture by David Hammons (1943–) in Piedmont Park, *Free Nelson Mandela* (above), was created in 1987. A 12-foot-high fence radiates from a granite rock and is capped with barbed wire. Within is a working gate, padlocked shut while Mandela was in prison but unlocked after Mandela's release, using the key that the artist had left with Atlanta city officials. The gate remains open today. Another Mandela tribute of note is the Ubuntu mural by India Bullock at Zunzi's South African-inspired restaurant (below). Next to his portrait, Mandela is quoted as, "In Africa we have a concept known as UBUNTU—the profound sense that we are only human through the humanity of others." (RMC.)

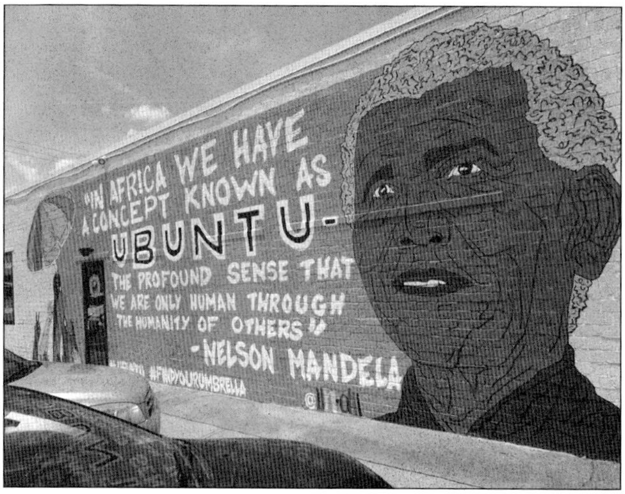

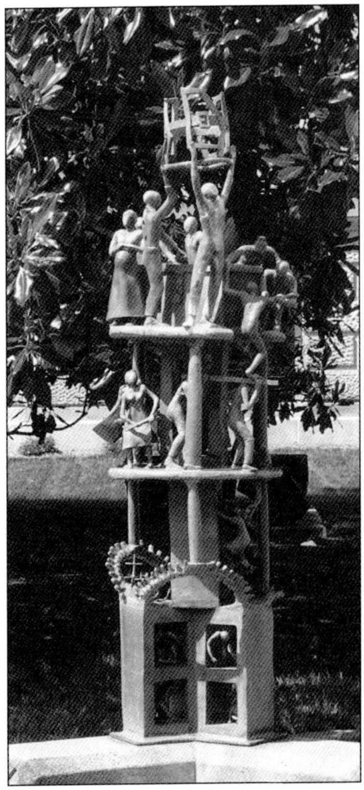

An early episode in Georgia's struggle for equal rights is commemorated in a bronze sculpture by John Thomas Riddle (1933–2002) titled *Expelled Because of Color.* Its plaque records its dedication "to the memory of 33 black state legislators who were elected yet expelled from the Georgia House because of their color in 1868." The sculpture, unveiled in 1978, was commissioned two years earlier by the Georgia Legislative Black Caucus. It documents "black Georgians' struggle from the slave ship to the State House," represented in a tower of episodic scenes often depicting figures struggling and confined in claustrophobic spaces within the stacked blocks. The sculpture is located on the grounds of the state capitol. (RMC.)

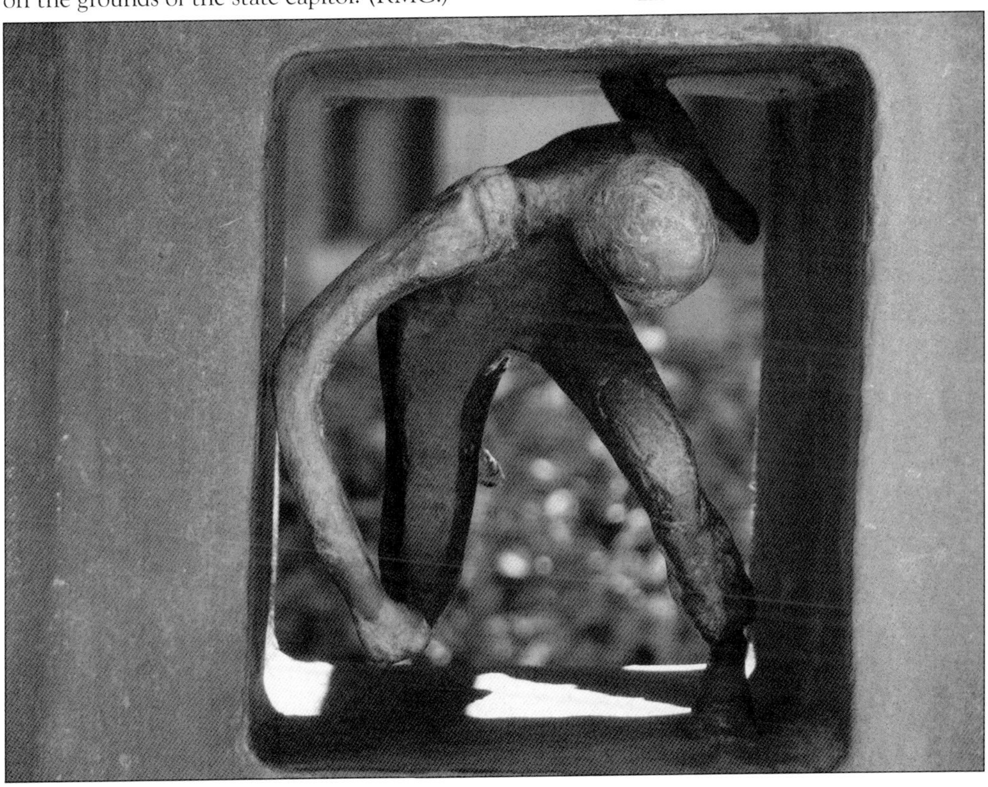

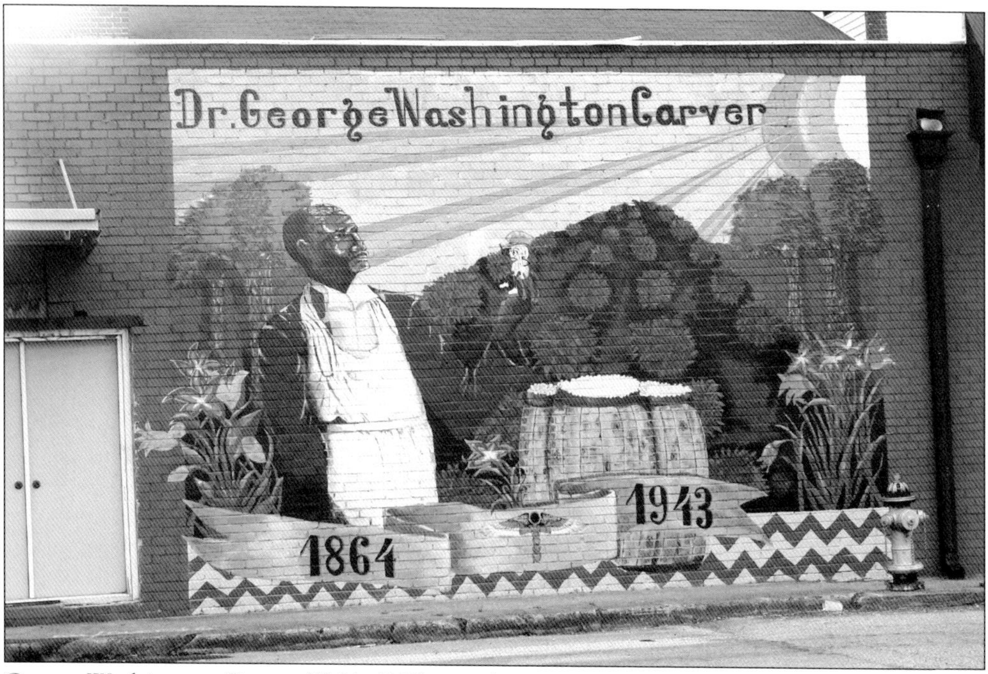

George Washington Carver (1864–1923) was the most prominent African American scientist of the early 20th century. An inventor and specialist in agricultural science, Carver promoted the rotation of planting of alternative crops to cotton, such as peanuts and potatoes, in order to prevent soil depletion. Carver taught for 47 years at Tuskegee Institute in Alabama where he is buried. The mural by an unknown artist is on the side of Sadiq's Bistro in Atlanta. (RMC.)

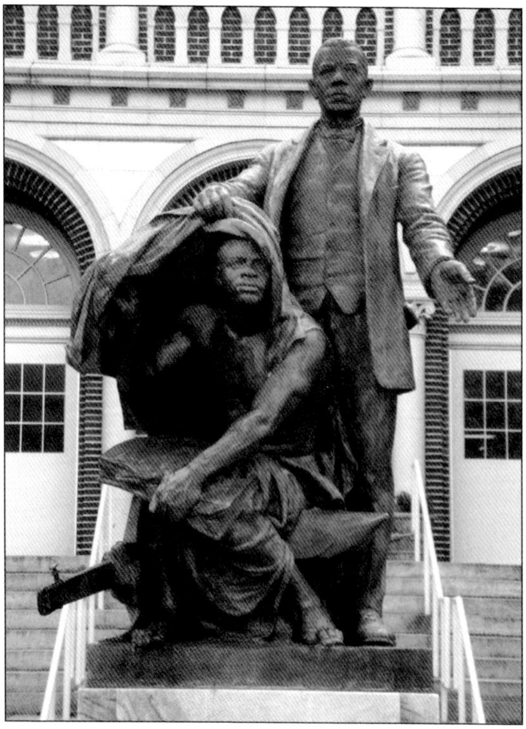

Booker T. Washington (1856–1915), born into slavery, was the first principal and president of Tuskegee Institute and the namesake of Atlanta's first high school for blacks. In front of the school stands the 1927 sculpture by Charles Keck (1875–1951) *Lifting the Veil of Ignorance*, a duplicate of the original at Tuskegee, lauding Washington's leadership, as inscribed on the piece, for "point[ing] the way to progress through education and industry." (RMC.)

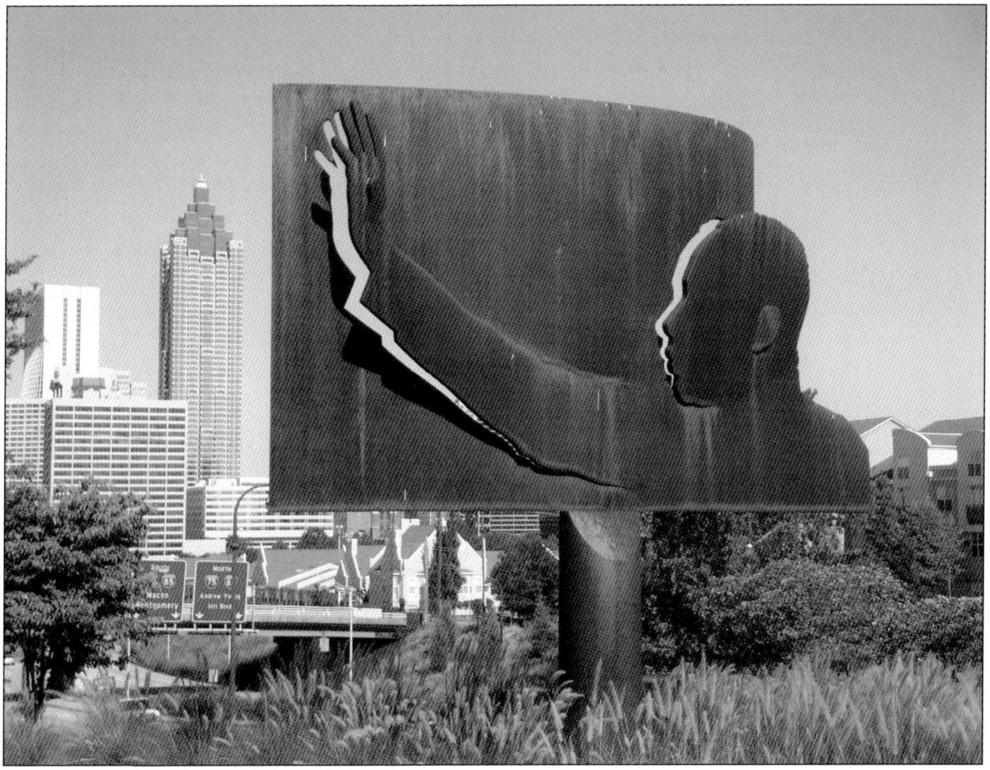

Barcelona artist Xavier Medina Campeny (1943-) was commissioned to sculpt *Homage to Martin Luther King Jr.* as a gift to Atlanta from the Catalonian host city of the 1992 Summer Olympics. A sheet of Corten steel is sliced and bent to reveal a profile outline of King. The sculpture is sited at the downtown entry to Freedom Parkway and serves as a welcome to the Martin Luther King Jr. Historic District and National Park. (RMC.)

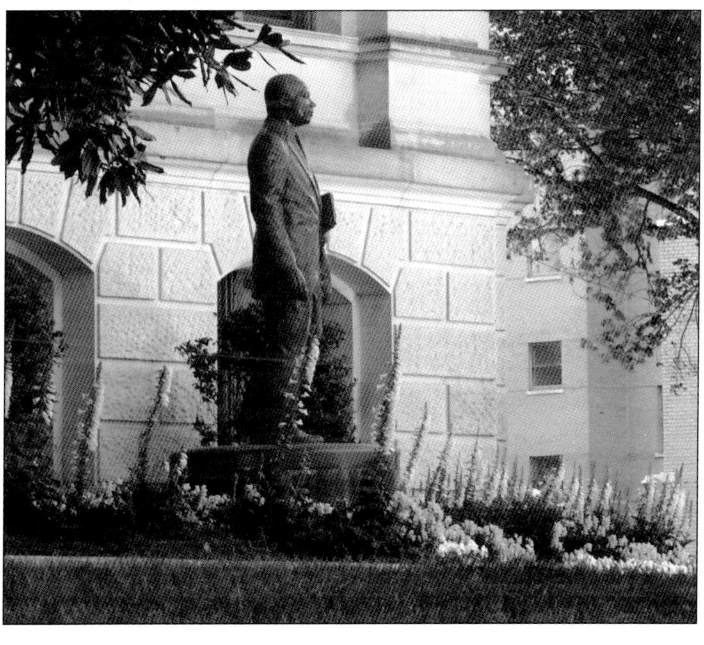

While other statues of Martin Luther King Jr. are found in Atlanta (at the MLK Jr. International Chapel at Morehouse College and on MLK Jr. Drive, for instance), Marty Dawe's 2017 bronze and granite sculpture of King is sited significantly on the grounds of the state capitol, where other statues and monuments document previous historic figures who supported racial segregation (see pages 19–21). (RMC.)

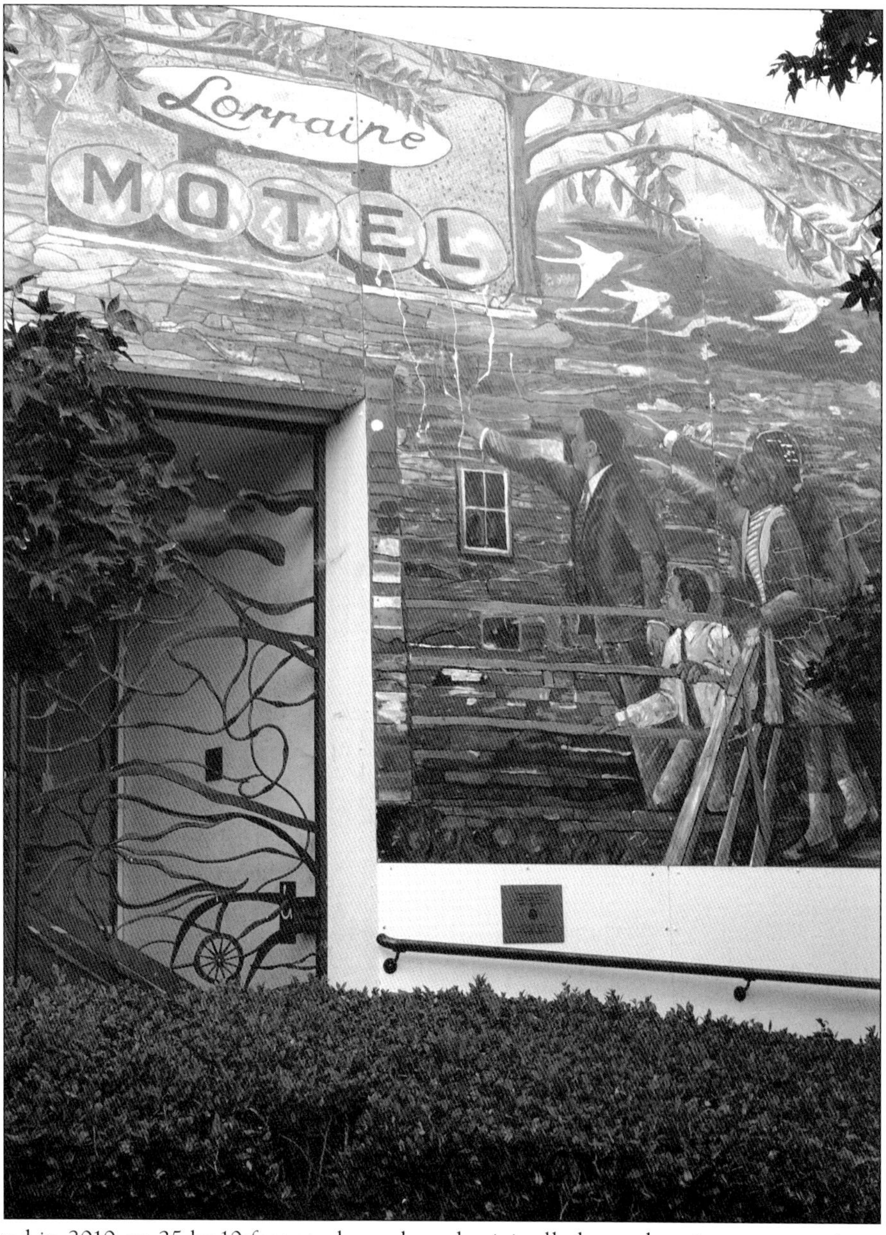

Painted in 2010 on 25-by-10-foot steel panels and originally located against a natatorium since razed, the Martin Luther King Jr. Memorial Mural (now in storage) by Louis Delsarte (1944–2020) was conspicuously sited along the entry path east of the Martin Luther King Jr. National Historic Site Visitor Center. It is hoped it will be returned to public view. Employing colors reminiscent of German expressionist painting and indeed recalling the Harlem Renaissance (to which he was exposed as a youth growing up in an artistic home in New York), Delsarte created a "filmstrip of King's life . . . like a running account, an allegory of the people who made up his world." Recognizable in the mural are Rosa Parks, Bobby Kennedy (1925–1968), Malcolm X (1925–1965), and Ralph David Abernathy. Local volunteers assisted the artist in the execution of the mural, which is said to have taken a year and a half to research and refine. Delsarte was a professor of arts and humanities at Morehouse College. (RMC.)

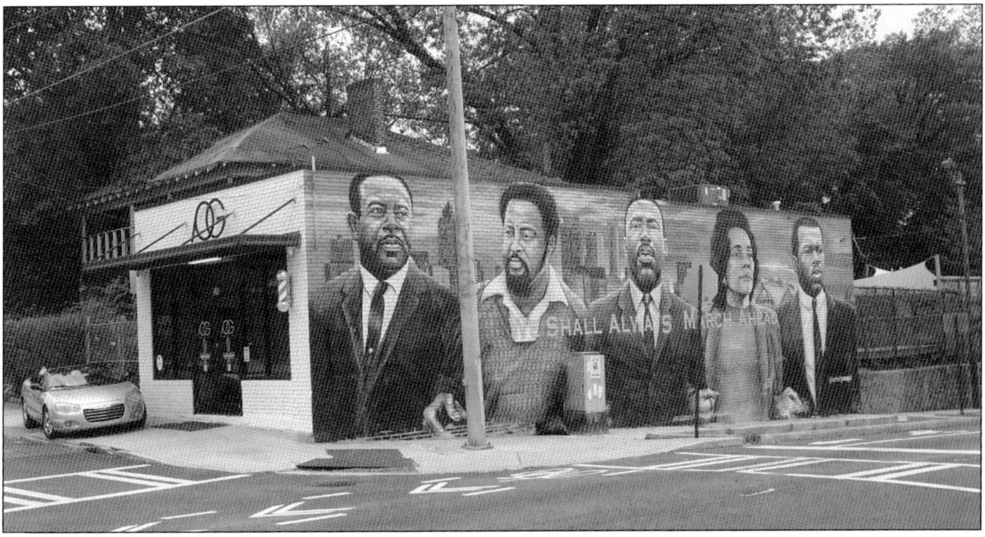

The property at 320 Sunset Avenue NW should be a destination "must" for everyone interested in the public art of the civil rights movement. On the long side of Privado Grooming hair salon is a mural by Muhammad Yungai (1974–) titled *We Shall Always March Ahead*, depicting five giants of the civil rights movement arm in arm; from left to right are Ralph David Abernathy, Hosea Williams, Martin Luther King Jr., Coretta Scott King, and John Lewis. (RMC.)

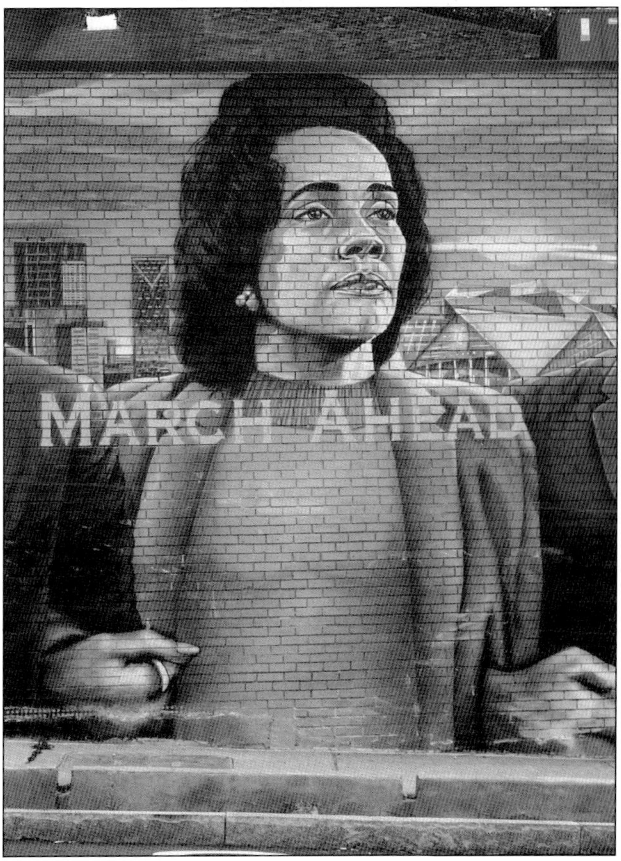

Coretta Scott King (1927–2006), "the First Lady of the Civil Rights Movement," is pictured here in one of the few renderings of her in Atlanta street art. After her husband's assassination, Coretta founded the King Center and sought to make MLK Jr.'s birthday a national holiday (signed into law by President Reagan in 1983). At her death, she was the first African American to lie in state in the Georgia state capitol. (RMC.)

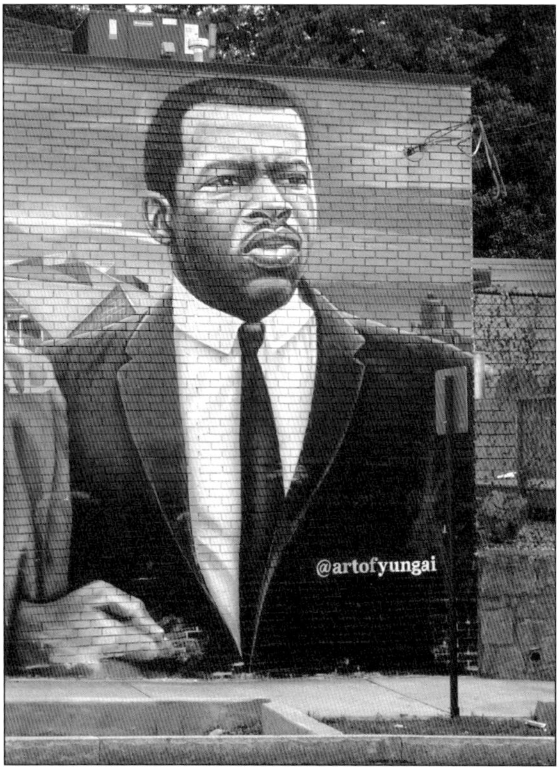

On the far right of Yungai's mural is John Lewis, who outlived the other four civil rights leaders. A loyal King "lieutenant," Lewis began his activism as a student; he was one of the original 13 Freedom Riders and a founding member, and later chairman, of the Student Nonviolent Coordinating Committee (SNCC). In 1986, Lewis was elected to Congress and served 17 terms until his death in 2020. (RMC.)

On the left side of Yungai's mural are Rev. Ralph David Abernathy, pastor of West Hunter Street Baptist Church, and Rev. Hosea Williams, a member of King's trusted inner circle. Williams was considered by King his chief field lieutenant, the organizer of countless SCLC-sanctioned nonviolent protests. Abernathy was cofounder (and after King's death, president) of the SCLC and led the Poor People's Campaign in Washington. (RMC.)

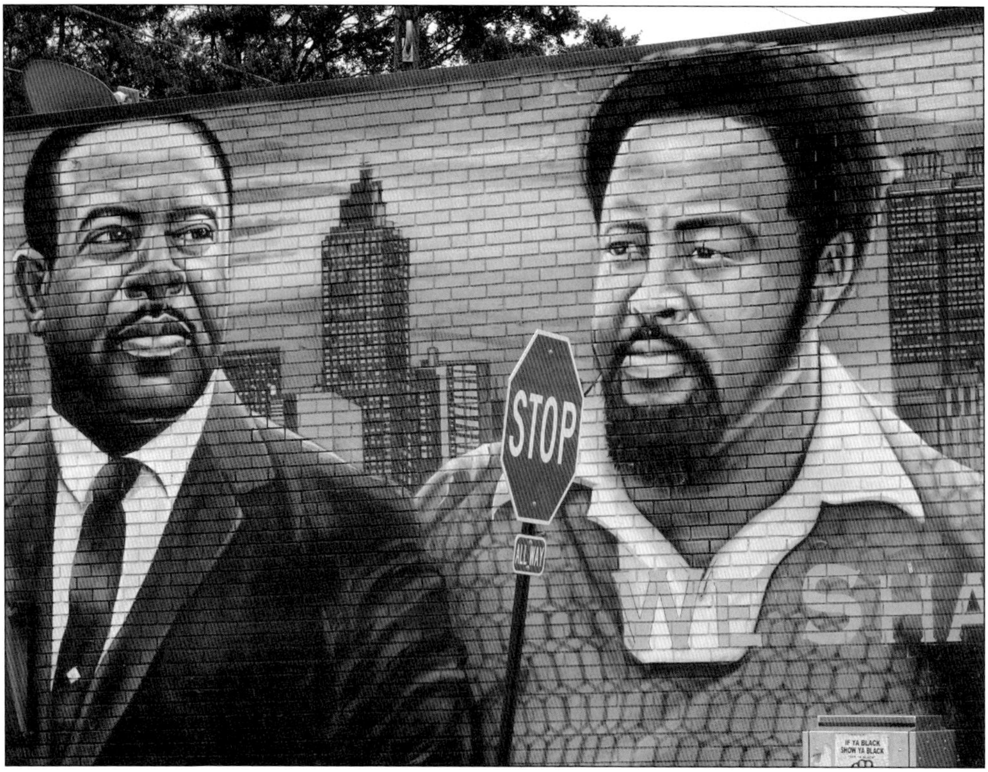

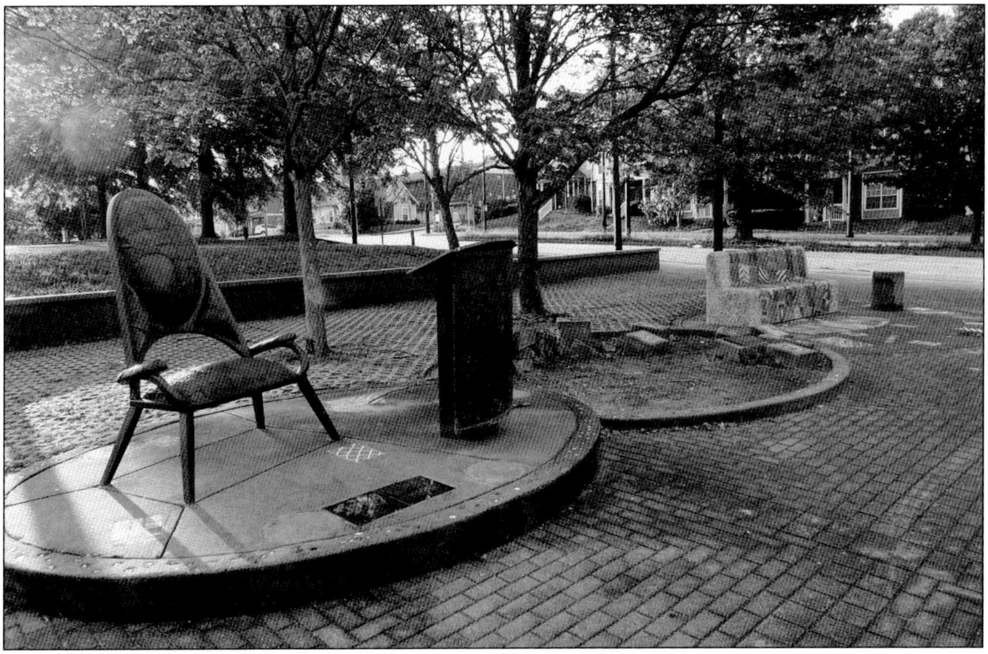

We Will Not Forget is the title given to the 1996 Abernathy Memorial by Emma Amos (1937–2020) in the Mechanicsville neighborhood of Atlanta. The monument features a bronze pulpit chair and lectern referencing Abernathy's religious life both in Montgomery, where he served for 10 years (1951–1961) as senior pastor of First Baptist Church, the largest black church in the Alabama capital, and afterward at West Hunter Street Baptist Church in Atlanta, where he preached for 29 years and organized the congregation's move to the former West End Baptist Church on the boulevard that now bears his name. At the Abernathy Memorial, another feature of the sculpture, a crumbling wall, was also symbolic of his life: his accomplishments in breaking down barriers. Finally, a concrete sofa, covered with a mosaic quilt, represents his family life. Abernathy was a friend and mentor of Martin Luther King Jr. (RMC.)

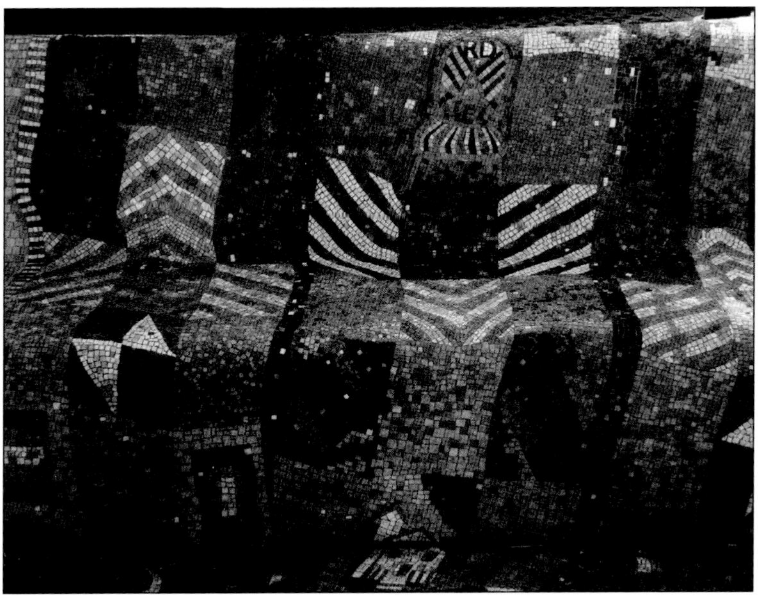

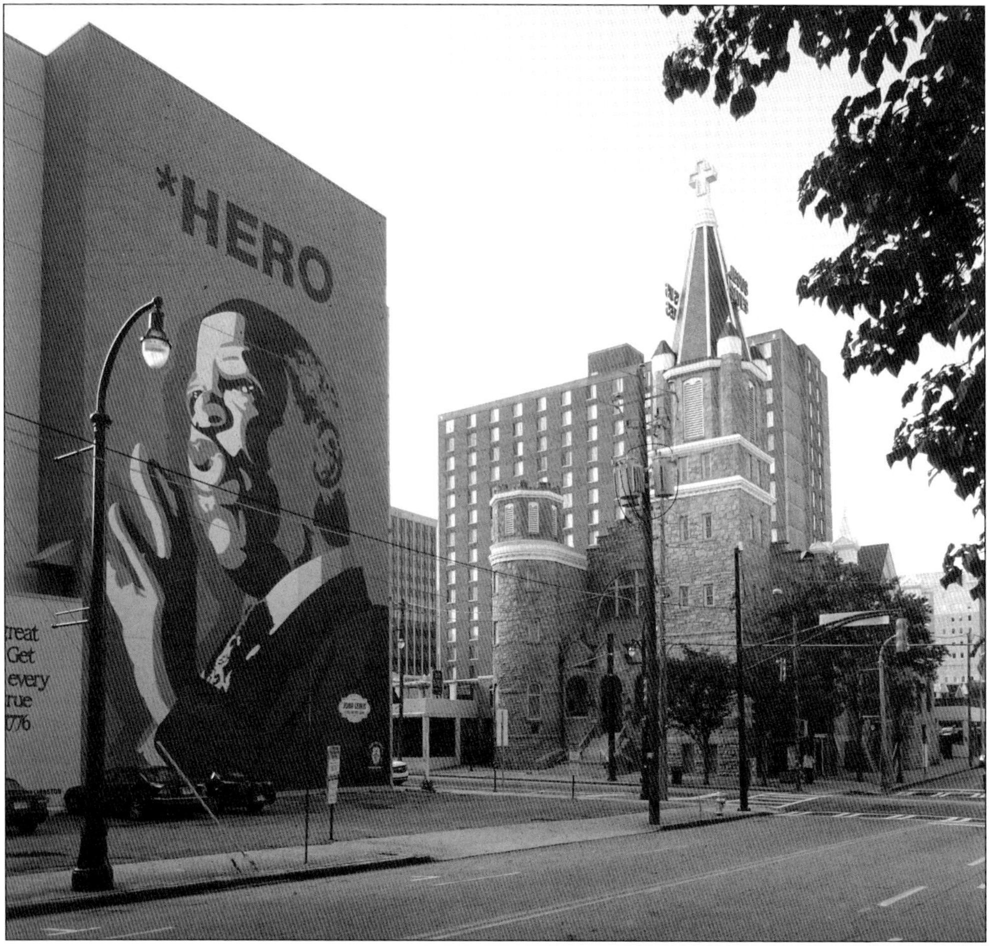

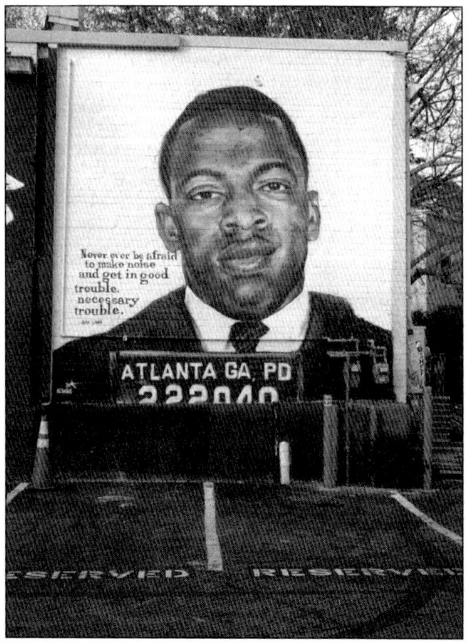

A young John Lewis is depicted in a mural (right) by Jarrett Becke (1980?–) in Little Five Points, referencing Lewis's arrests as a student activist and Freedom Rider (see page 66). An older Lewis is a hero in the giant Sweet Auburn district mural (above) by The Loss Prevention, a collective of artists and volunteers including Sean Schwab (1976–), founded in 2008. Lewis helped organize the 1963 March in Washington and, in 1965, was the first of three Selma-to-Montgomery marchers crossing the Edmund Pettus Bridge on Bloody Sunday, where he was beaten by state troopers and local police and seriously injured. Later, Lewis helped register nearly four million minority voters, served briefly in the Carter administration as associate director of ACTION, and then served during the early 1980s on the Atlanta City Council. Between 1986 and his death in 2020, Lewis represented Georgia's 5th District in the US Congress. (RMC.)

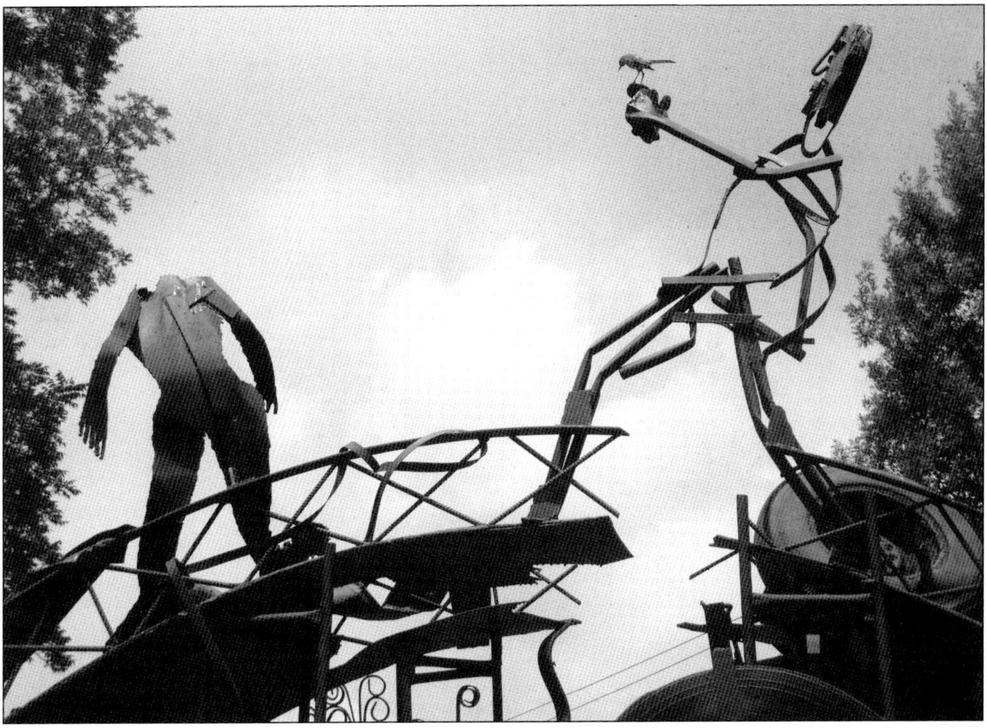

In 1997, Thornton Dial (1928–2016) created *The Bridge* (above), dedicated to both John Lewis, commemorating his Edmund Pettus Bridge episode, and to CAUTION (the Coalition Against Unauthorized Transportation In Our Neighborhoods). Supported by Lewis, CAUTION and most of Atlanta opposed the building of the Jimmy Carter "presidential parkway," drawing a red line at the Dekalb County line where a six-lane bridge was begun, and "the Road" was seen to threaten the Olmsted parks beyond (a landmark district). The Road was stopped by court order, and the portion built in Fulton County was later named the John Lewis Freedom Parkway. A mural (below) by NNEKKAA (also known as Neka King (1992–), C. Flux Sing (1976–), and Sean Fahie (1983–), depicts, from left to right, John Lewis, C.T. Vivian, and Rev. Joseph Lowery. The mural is located at Kubuni Afrique, a seamstress and alterations store in West End. (RMC.)

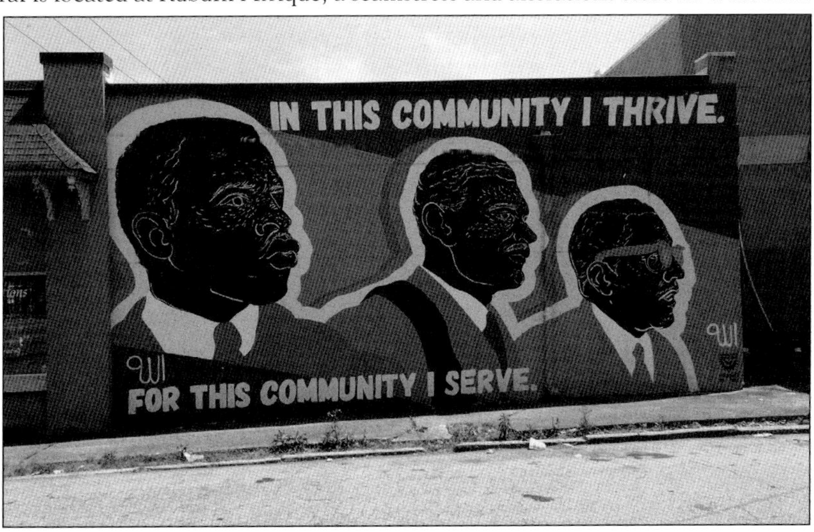

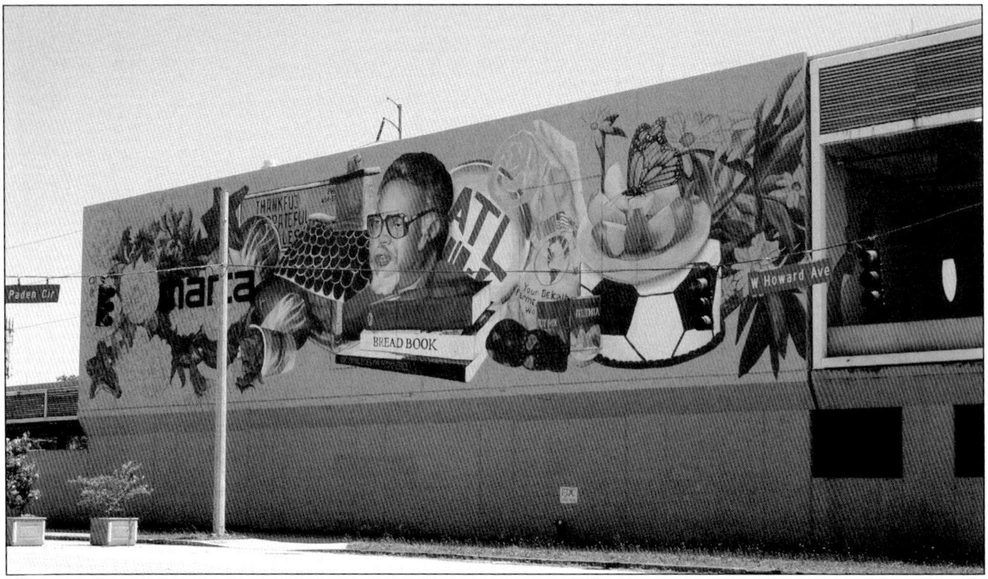

In 2019, the East Lake MARTA station paid tribute to Hosea Williams and his home neighborhood in a giant mural by the Argentine muralist Nicolás Romero Escalada (1985–), also known as eversiempre. Inspired by the work of Martin Luther King Jr., Williams was the founding president of one of the largest social services organizations in North America, the Hosea Feed the Hungry and Homeless, which his daughter, as new CEO, expanded after his 2020 death. (RMC.)

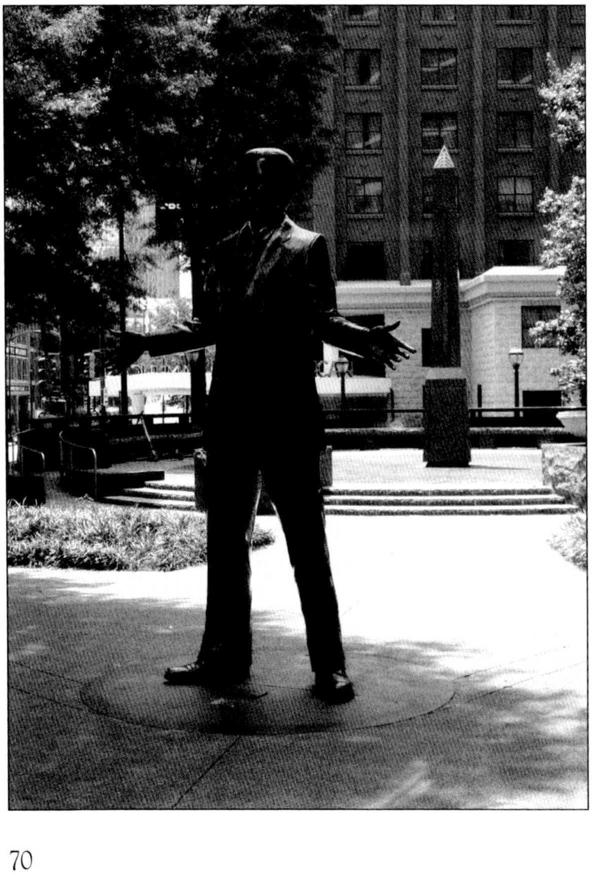

Andrew Young Plaza in Peachtree Center contains Charles Mitchell's 1981 bronze and limestone German sundial, a 2008 obelisk by African American sculptor Curtis Patterson (1944–), and a bronze statue of Andrew Young, created in 2008 by Johnpaul Harris (1945–) and funded by Charles Loudermilk (see page 54, above). Not on a pedestal, Young is set on the ground, with his arms spread to welcome visitors, as a "man of the people." (RMC.)

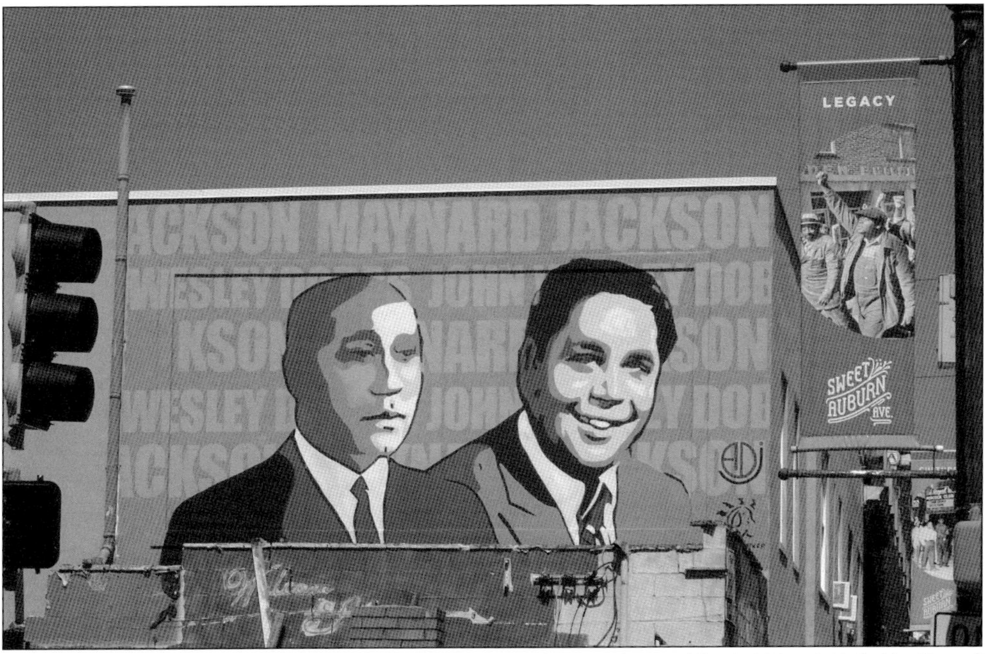

The mural by PetieParker (1983–) of two mayors, John Wesley Dobbs (1882–1961, left), Grand Master of the Prince Hall Masons and cofounder of the Atlanta Negro Voters League, who was nicknamed the unofficial mayor of Auburn Avenue, and his grandson, Maynard Jackson (1938–2003, right), who, in 1973, was elected the first African American mayor of Atlanta, appears like a billboard overlooking Auburn Avenue opposite the 1996 sculpture/plaza by Ralph Helmick (1952–) dedicated to Dobbs. (RMC.)

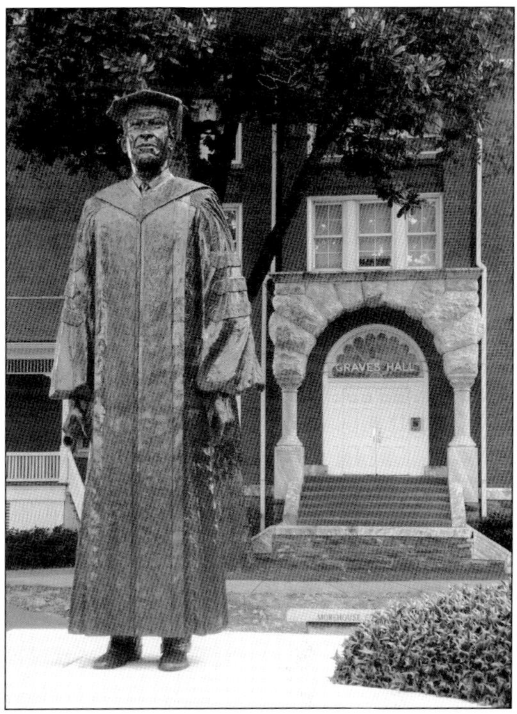

Benjamin Mays (1894–1984) was president of Morehouse College from 1940 to 1967 and is said to have laid the intellectual foundations of the civil rights movement, mentoring students such as Martin Luther King Jr., Julian Bond, and Maynard Jackson. After King's "I Have a Dream" speech at the 1963 March on Washington, Mays gave the benediction, and when King was assassinated in 1968, Mays delivered the eulogy, saying "No man is ahead of his time." (RMC.)

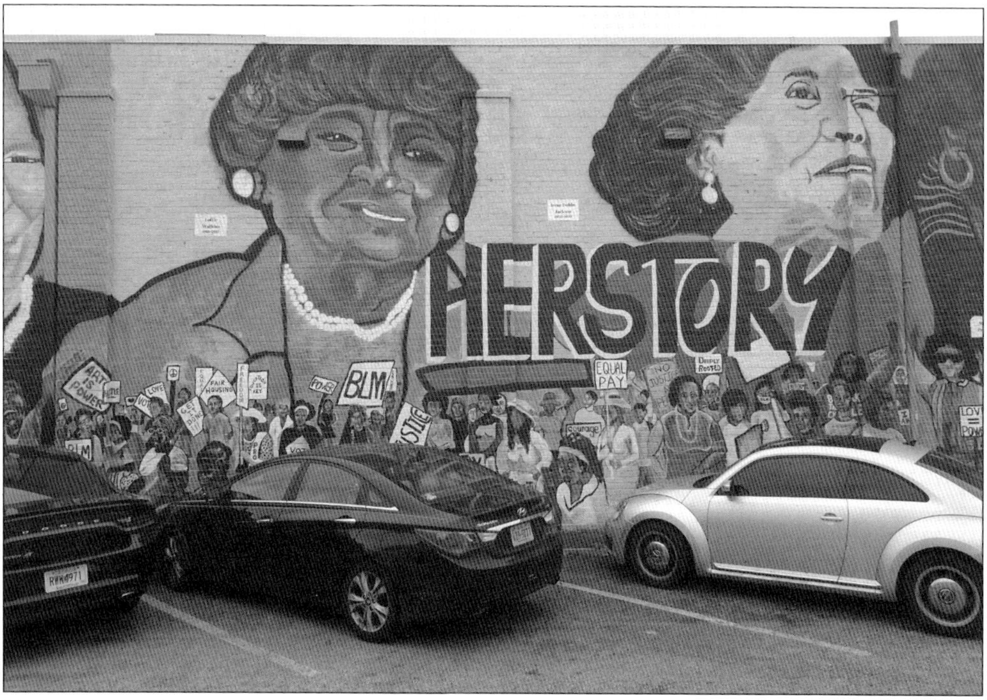

With a play on the word history, Ashley Dopson (1983–)'s herstory mural titled *Heroine* is a tribute to female community leaders who were active locally in business, social causes, and the struggle for racial equality. The detail seen here depicts Lottie H. Watkins (1918–2017, left) who was the first African American real estate broker in the Atlanta area, and Irene Dobbs Jackson (1908–1999, right), a Spelman College professor who helped desegregate Atlanta's public libraries. (RMC.)

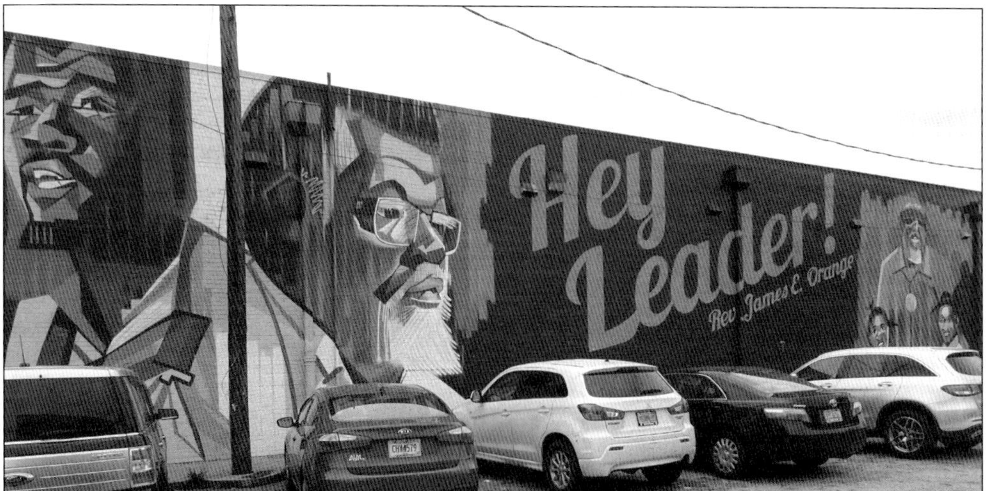

Rev. James Orange (1942–2008), also known as "Shackdaddy," participated in civil rights marches organized by King and Abernathy and served as a project manager for the SCLC. Physically a formidable man (six foot three and over 300 pounds), he was, according to Andrew Young, "a gentle giant." His message of nonviolence was especially aimed at young gang members. In 1968, Orange was at the bottom of the steps of the Lorraine Hotel when Martin Luther King Jr. was killed. (RMC.)

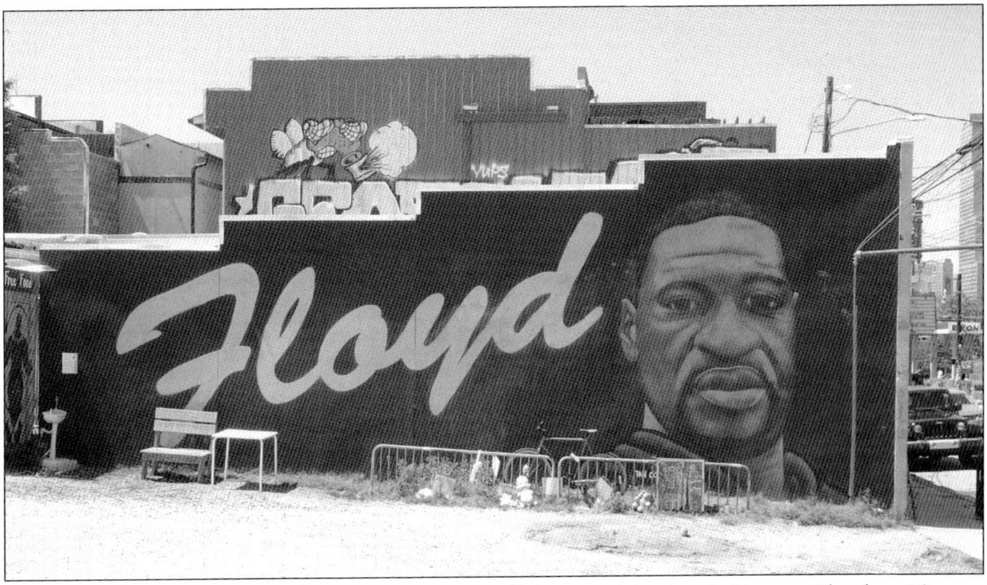

The most familiar name in the contemporary call for social justice is George Floyd, a 46-year-old black man who was arrested by Minneapolis police officer Derek Chauvin, who, after Floyd was handcuffed and lying prone on the ground, knelt on his neck and caused Floyd's death. In a subsequent trial, officer Chauvin was convicted of second-degree unintentional murder, third-degree murder, and second-degree manslaughter. Minneapolis agreed to pay the Floyd family $27 million to settle a wrongful death lawsuit. Throughout the period of news coverage, murals dedicated to George Floyd appeared in cities nationwide, including Atlanta. The mural on Edgewood Avenue with Floyd's portrait and the single word "Floyd" is typical. In East Atlanta, Renda Writer (1978–) created a repeat pattern of "George Floyd" signatures in rows, which, with the building's window as the starfield, recalls the American flag. (RMC.)

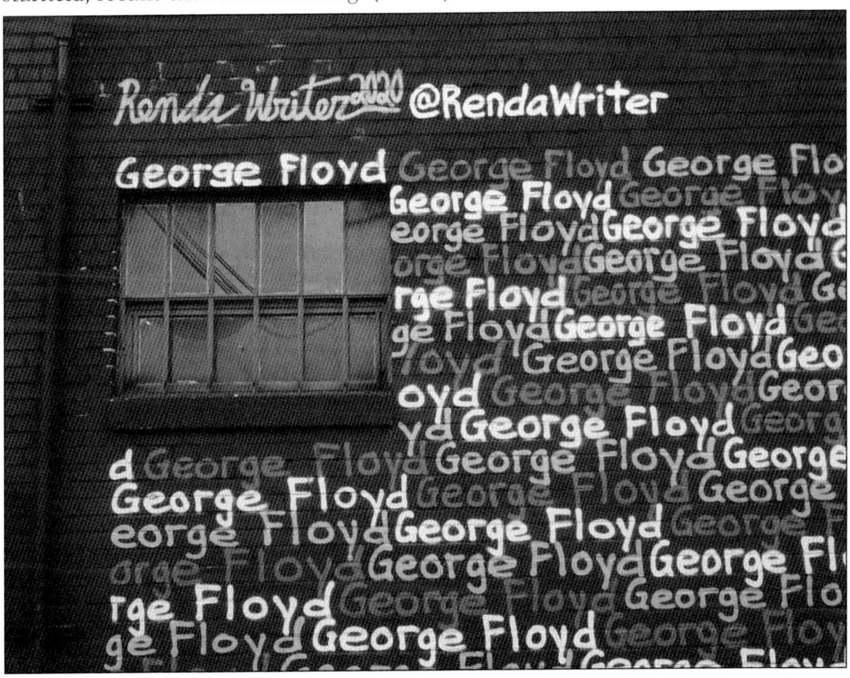

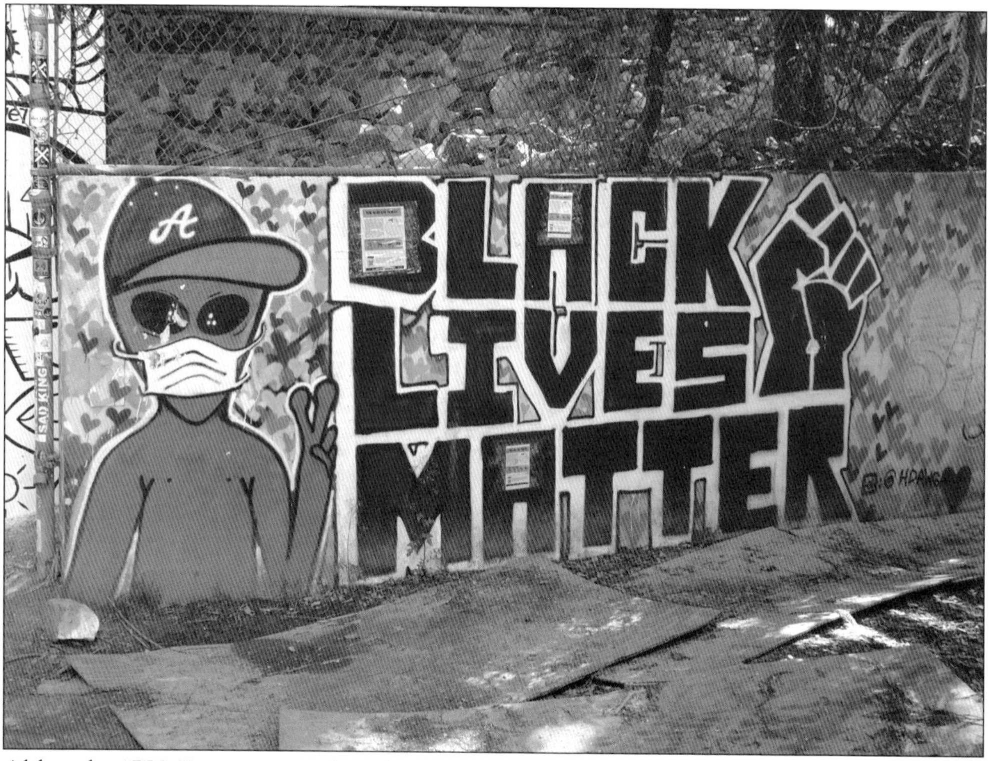

Although a "BLM" tag is easy and quick for graffiti artists, the BLM message spelled out in 16 letters and at large scale has appeared in several locations across Atlanta: at the Drew Charter school, in front of Decatur High School in Decatur, and on the east Beltline trail at Angier Springs Road. Figurative murals appear under bridge abutments and as part of larger murals in schools and on commercial buildings. The BLM mural (above) is by "H Dawg" (1989–), depicting an ATLien in a baseball cap who appears frequently in H Dawg and who is here wearing a COVID mask and declaring that "Black Lives Matter." On the East Beltline (below), among works by various artists, is *Black Boy Joy* by Erica Chisolm (1993–), who admitted her belief that "black men are robbed of their right to feel joy early." (RMC.)

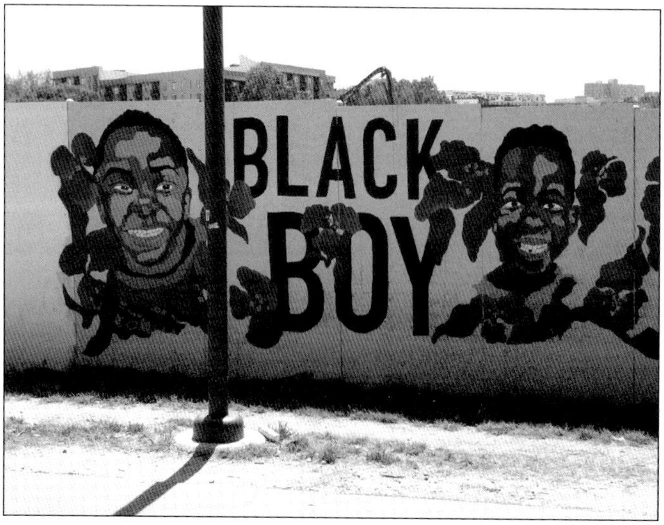

Artist Sofahood (1998–), who describes herself as "a black and Afro-Latinx, visibly and loudly queer . . . passionate leftist . . . short-haired, agender yet woman-identifying artist," adopts as the title of the above mural the 1960s motto of the Black Panthers "All Power to the People." Thus inheriting by association a spirit of rebellion and protest, Sofahood "create[s] content for the marginalized." Her 2020 mural for Adult Swim and Living Walls is at 439 Edgewood Avenue SE. (RMC.)

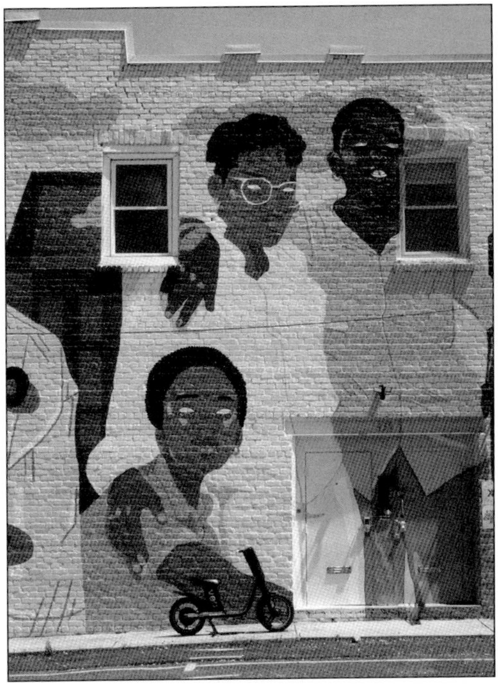

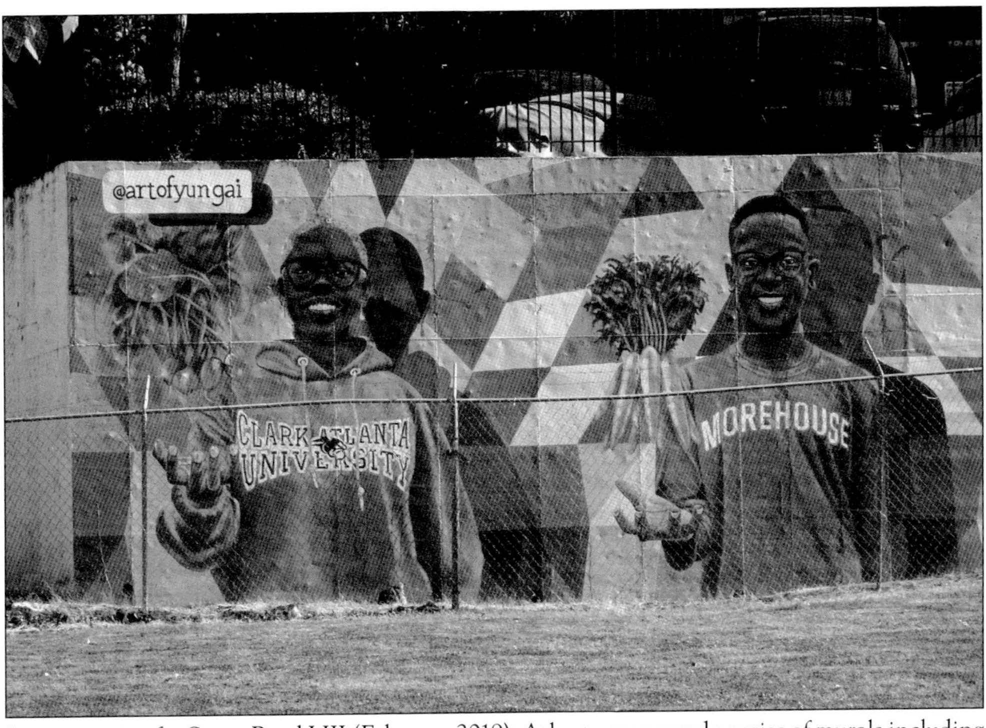

In preparation for Super Bowl LIII (February 2019), Atlanta sponsored a series of murals including three commissioned from Muhammad Yungai. With this one, Community Roots recognizes the importance of the city's historically black colleges and universities to urban farming, both undervalued and great for the community. With murals in several Atlanta schools, Yungai's "personal mission" has been "to introduce young black students to the greatness of their history." (RMC.)

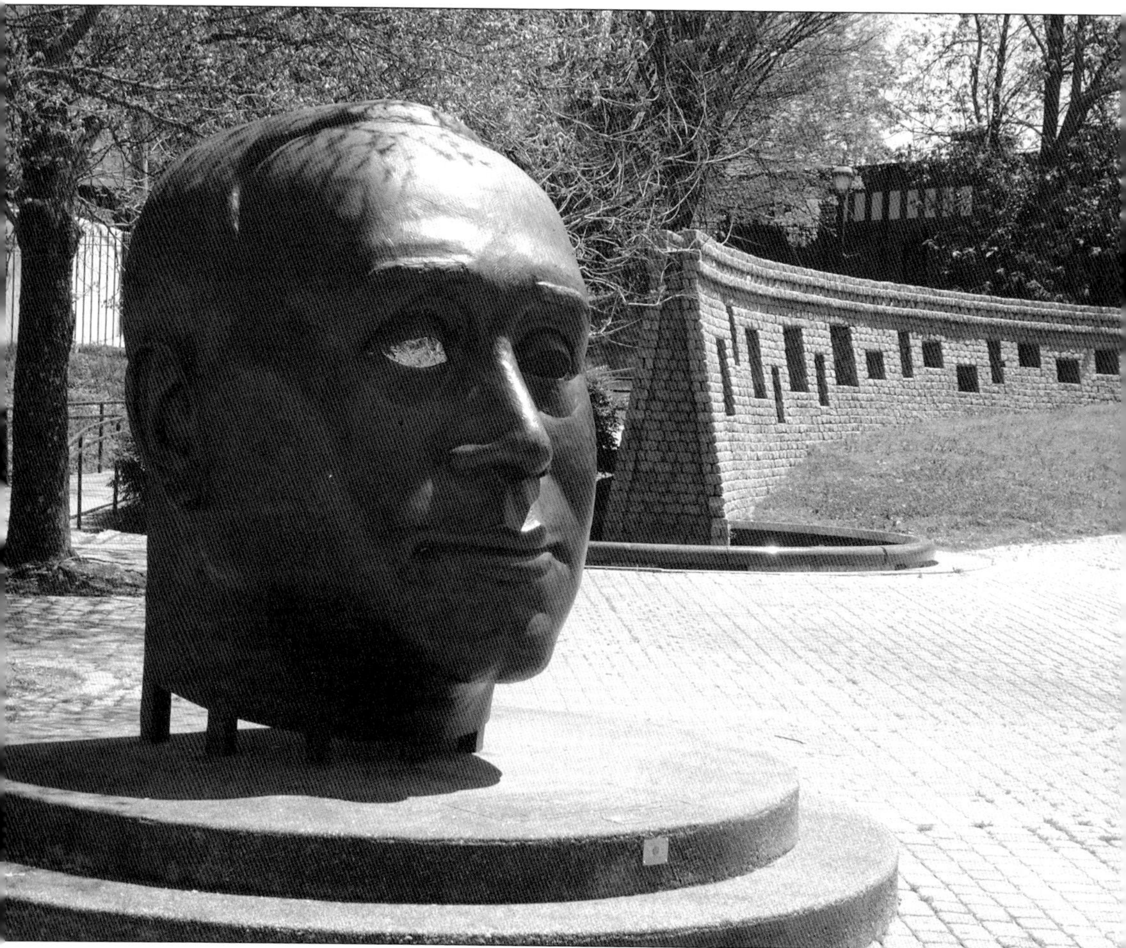

Ralph Helmick's 1996 silicon bronze monument *Through His Eyes* pays tribute to civil rights leader John Wesley Dobbs (see page 71), a leader in voter registration and civil rights political thought and a famous orator who coined the phrase "Sweet Auburn." He famously said, "Bucks, ballots, and books are the key to African American freedom." The "portrait mask" depicting Dobbs is inspired by the 12th-century Nigerian life-sculpture tradition and includes text and quotes inscribed on the interior of the mask, from where Auburn Avenue can be literally viewed "through his eyes." Installed for the 1996 Atlanta Olympics, the monument is set on a plaza, whose background stone wall and stair railings display profiles and silhouettes of African symbols. (RMC.)

Five

African Influence

For almost half a century (since 1974 with the election of Maynard Jackson), the city of Atlanta has been governed by an African American mayor. The majority of the population is "black or African American" (50.95 percent according to the latest census bureau data), more than 10 percent more than the white population of 40.9 percent. To the degree that street art, public murals, and outdoor sculpture in public places is the people's art, it is no wonder that much of Atlanta's public art shows African influence, reflecting the African diaspora and the community of African American artists at work in the city. The African diaspora may be defined as the worldwide collection of communities descended from native Africans or people from Africa predominantly in the Americas. The term most commonly refers to the descendants of West and Central Africans who were enslaved and shipped to the Americas via the Atlantic slave trade between the 16th and 19th centuries, While slavery is not the specific subject of murals or public sculpture, African influence and (as the last chapter has indicated) a strong African American civil rights movement legacy, is in evidence in the city's public art.

In recent years, attendees at high school and college graduation ceremonies have noticed African American students wearing a Kente stole, and while onlookers may observe that the colors appear to suggest African influence and are more typically worn by black student graduates and African American faculty, many observers may know little about the custom, its meaning or, indeed, about African influence on American culture in general or about African art in particular. Similarly, while some public art in Atlanta "looks African"—certain street murals in particular—an impression that the art has African influence may be as vague and uninformed as the notion that a painting "looks Southern" or as generalized an idea as labeling art "traditional," "modern," or "American." Moreover, questioning whether a graduate student who is not black can or ought to wear a Kente cloth stole may be comparable to asking whether a Caucasian painter might display African motifs in his painting or might be trespassing on a heritage, rather than paying homage to it, if or when African influences were in evidence. The Spanish artist Pablo Picasso's masterpiece *Les Demoiselles d'Avignon* (1907) is both modern (considered the first Cubist painting) and distinctly African in influence. If asked to identify the meaning of the painting, the budding Cubist Picasso might talk abstractly about simultaneity of point of view or simply inform the viewer that the picture portrays five nude female prostitutes in a brothel on Carrer d'Avinyó, a street in Barcelona. Neither assessment nor Picasso's Spanish birth discounts the genuine African influence on the imagery.

So public art in Atlanta under African influence is not only about painting and sculpture but may include textile design, that is, the admittedly attractive fashion of the donning of Kente stoles at graduation, and, as with a painting, we might ask the meaning and significance of the practice. In the case of the "African" academic regalia, the Kente stole signifies the student's difficult journey to learn about themselves and their heritage; it symbolizes the graduate's connection to, or sympathy for, the history of the African diaspora. Although the custom today is to mark an important occasion, historically, Kente cloth was worn in a toga-like fashion by royalty among ethnic groups such as the Ewe and Ashanti people of the Akan kingdom, what is today Ghana in Western Africa. Indeed, the word "kente" means "handwoven cloth" in the Twi language of the Akan people.

Although some universities, as they do with other academic regalia, adopt colors or patterns to distinguish the graduate's subject major or some extracurricular activity, historically, the colors of the Kente cloth conveyed symbolic associations and meaning: gold signified status/serenity, yellow represented fertility, green meant renewal, blue suggested a pure spirit/harmony, red meant passion, and black suggested a union with ancestors and a sense of spiritual awareness. Exposed to this practice of Kente stoles and to other expressions of African American tradition and custom, the public at large is learning more about African art and customs and may readily come to appreciate African influences on street art, urban murals, and some outdoor sculpture.

Atlanta's public institutions are contributing to this increased awareness. In 2014, Georgia Tech launched Africa Atlanta, a series of public events culminating in the loan of art and artifacts from the Royal Museum for Central Africa in Tervuren, Belgium, in an exhibition that examined 500 years of cultural exchange between the Kongo, Europe, and the United States. The objects on view showed the rise of the Kongo as a major Atlantic presence and the transmission of Kongo culture through the transatlantic slave trade into American art. Kongo across the Waters was on view at the Jimmy Carter Library and Museum before moving on to Princeton University.

All the while, the High Museum continued to expand its collection of African art, including a diversity of forms from ancient to contemporary periods. "To highlight cultural bonds throughout the Black Atlantic world and beyond," the High collects the work of African and African American artists. From Africa itself, the "heart and soul" of the collection consists of extraordinary examples of masks and figurative sculptures, enriched by exceptionally fine textiles, beadwork, metalwork, and ceramics. Masks may be the most familiar artifact of African art culture to the general public. They were worn during ceremonies ranging from religious to harvest/rain dances. During an African mask ceremony, the dancer may go into a deep trance in order to communicate with the ancestors. Masks may be worn vertically to cover the face, as a crest resting on the head, or as a helmet that encases the entire head. A 2013 mural by Maria2 on Euclid Avenue in Atlanta shows influence from such mask traditions (see page 89).

Beyond any influence of African art on African American painters and sculptors working in Atlanta, the transference to public spaces of indigenous African sculpture, in particular Zimbabwe art, has exposed Atlantans to the most recognized contemporary sculpture emerging from Africa today. On permanent display between concourses T and A at Atlanta's Hartsfield Jackson International Airport is the exhibit Zimbabwe Sculpture: a Tradition in Stone, featuring sculptures by some of Zimbabwe's best-known recent sculptors. Since antiquity, local Zimbabwe artists have been using the steatite/soapstone deposits of the eastern Zimbabwe mountain ranges to produce works of art. Some contemporary sculptors such as Lambeck Bonjisi carve hard green serpentine stone—*Caring Mother* is an example at the airport. Georgia Tech's art collection includes three Zimbabwe pieces including *The Great Zimbabwe Bird* (the bateleur, a short-tailed eagle that is the national symbol of Zimbabwe).

As one observes Atlanta's public art, particularly the work of the large group of African American muralists, one might rightly ask, what is black about black art? What constitutes the African heritage, immediate or distant, reflected in the art of this predominantly black city? Do people hear American jazz when they view a Corey Barksdale (1972–) mural, knowing that so many of the classic jazz musicians and singers were African American? Are the colors African inspired? It is true that a school mural by Fabian Williams or Muhammad Yungai is intended to contribute to a young black boy or girl's awareness of an ancestry, which may seem distant to a 10-year-old now, but is part of black history—part of their DNA. Yungai has said that his work "is really about empowering young black people first, and [also] the black community itself." The roots run deep, to Africa itself.

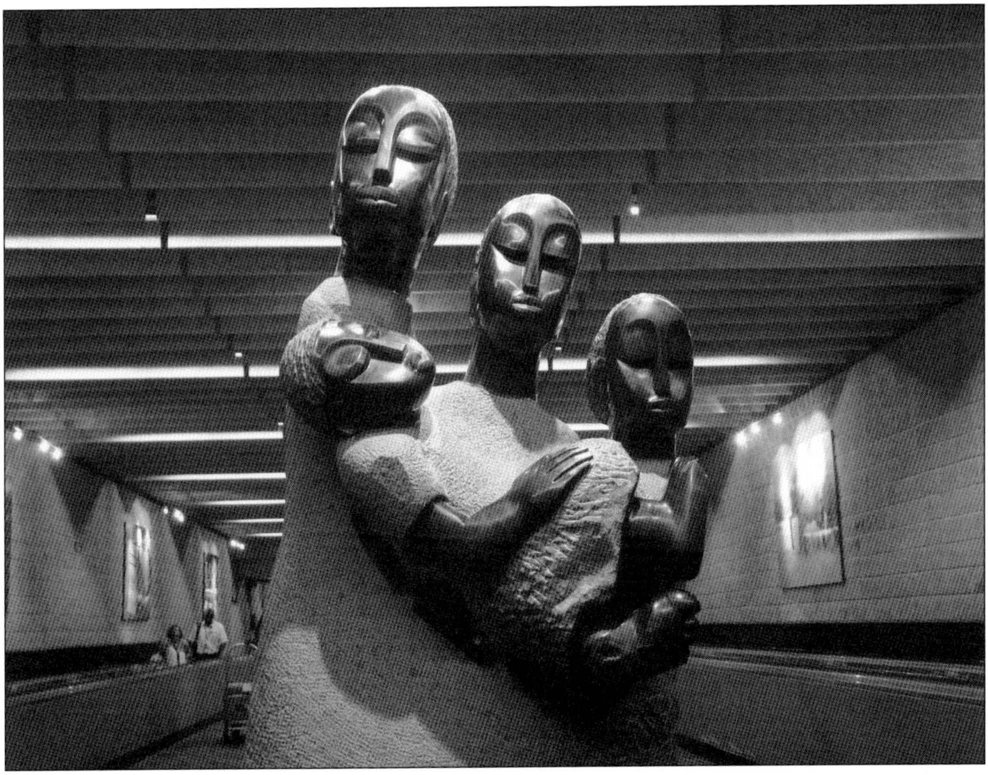

Generation Pyramid (above) depicts four generations of a family and is carved from springstone by Gedion Nyanhongo (1967–), the son of a sculptor. Gedion is part of a tradition of impressive Shona sculpture from Zimbabwe and has two pieces on permanent exhibit at the Atlanta airport. His subjects present to viewers "the traditional values of the importance of community, positive and respectful human relationships, the sacredness of life." Through his art, Gedion intends "to seek, evoke, and inspire these same values in their own family and cultures." *Caring Mother* (right) was carved from green serpentine stone by sculptor Lambeck Bonjisi (1973–2004) and is also part of the airport exhibition of Zimbabwe sculpture. (RMC.)

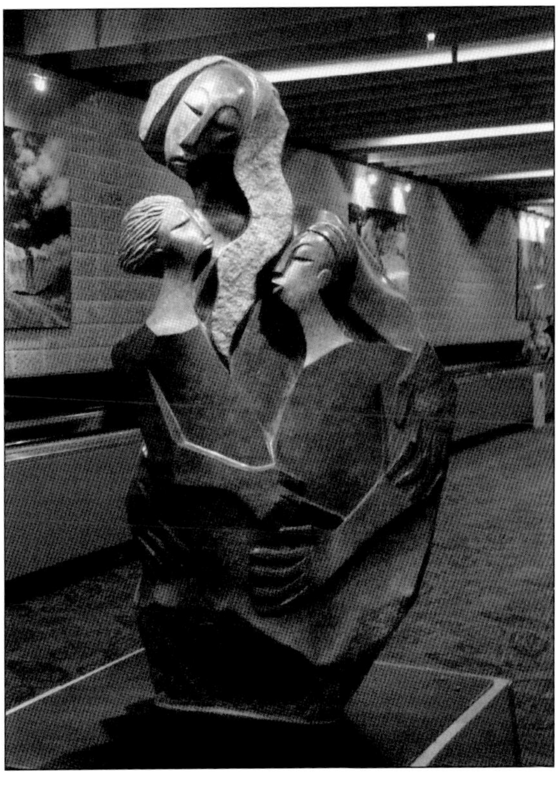

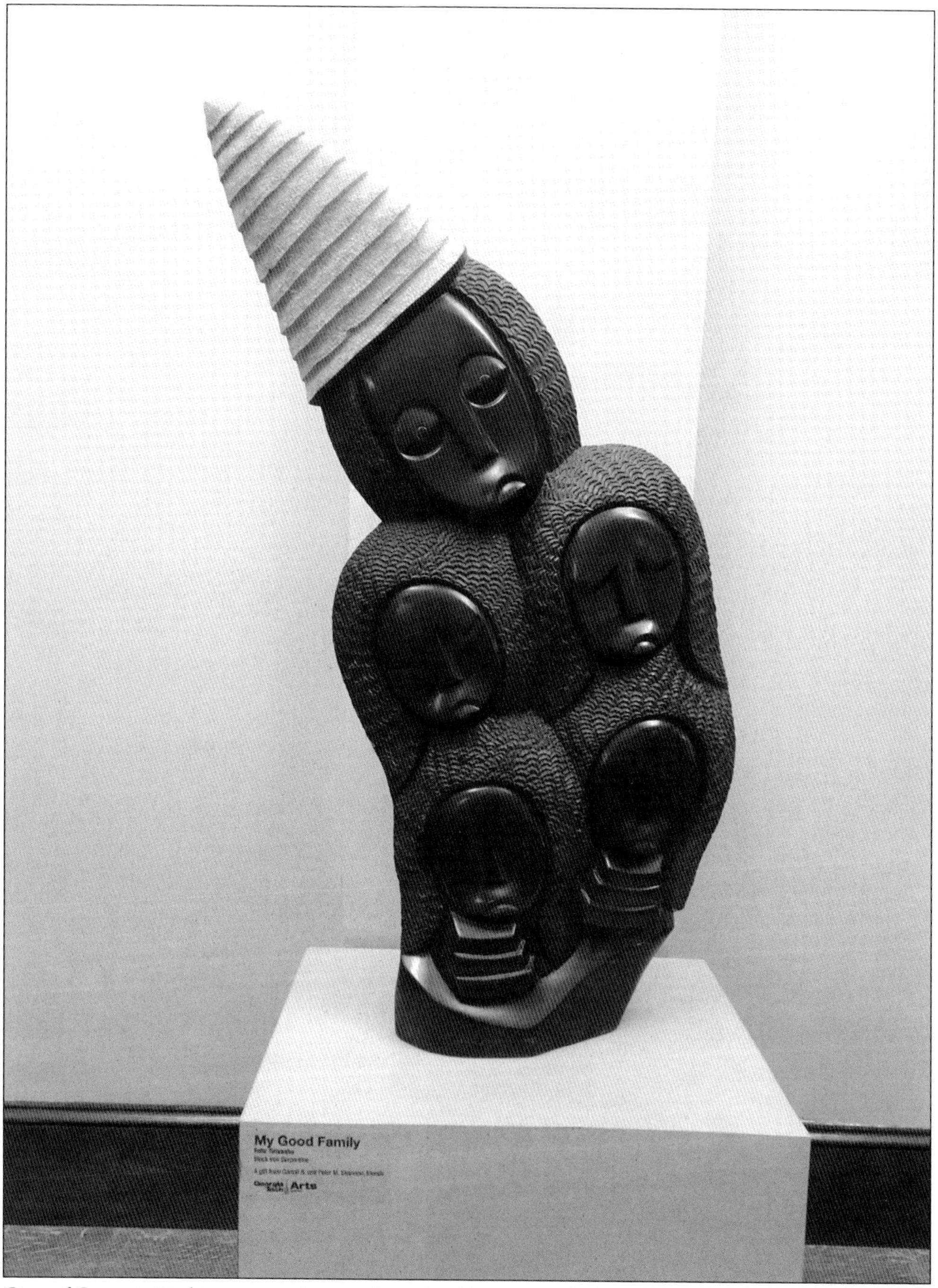

One of Georgia Tech's stone sculptures from the Shona people (an ethnic group native to Southern Africa and found primarily in eastern Zimbabwe) is this work titled *My Good Family*. Three Zimbabwe works were gifts to the university from the collection of Pete and Carroll Shannon; *My Good Family* is displayed in the Savant Building on campus. (RMC.)

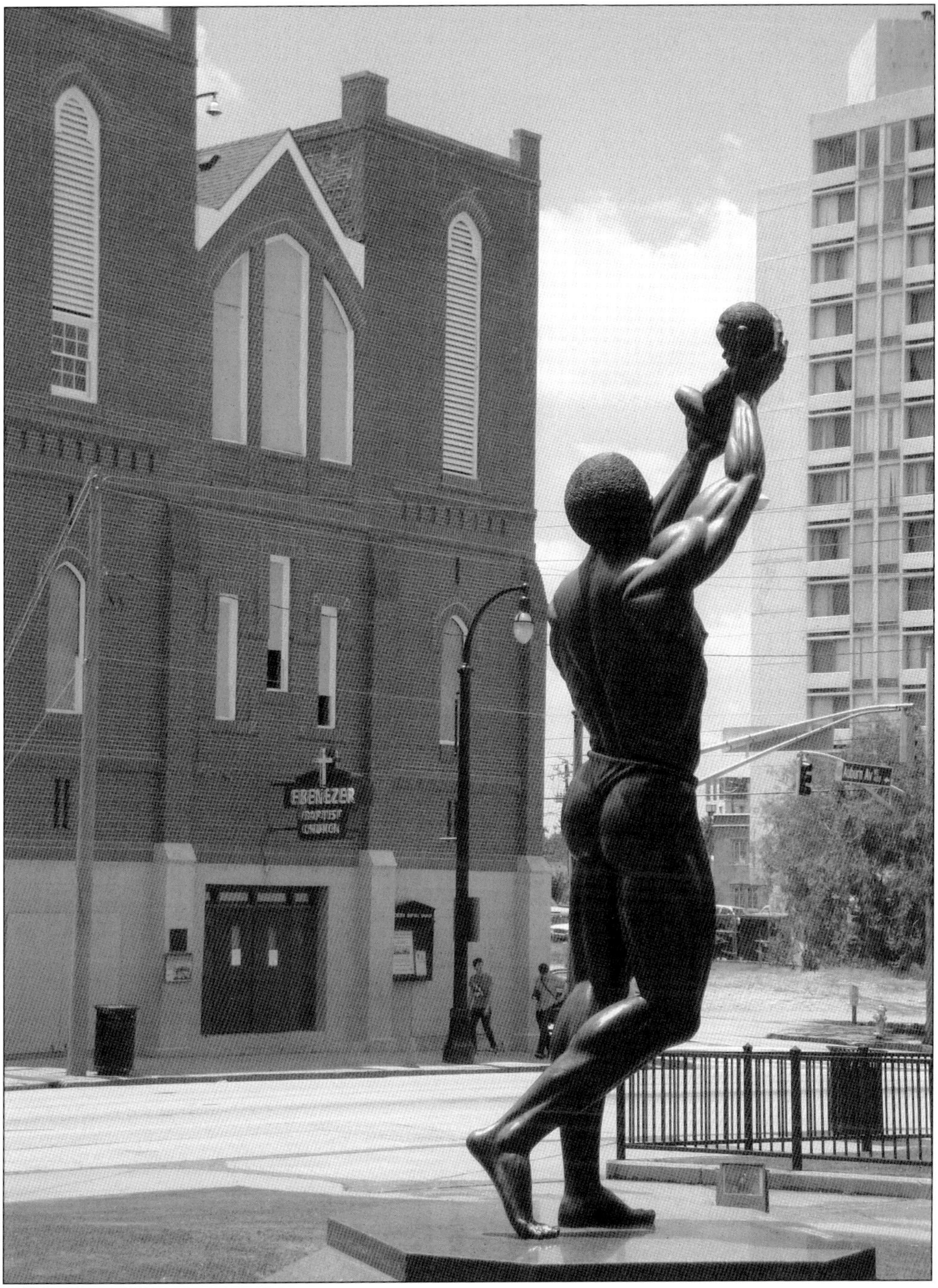

The sculpture *Behold* is based on an African ritual and depicts an allegorical figure of Kunta Kinte lifting his newborn toward the sky, a scene known to many familiar with Alex Haley's 1976 book and 1977 television miniseries, *Roots*. The bronze work of Patrick Morelli (1945–) stands on a granite pedestal across from Ebenezer Baptist Church and was received in 1990 by Coretta Scott King as a gift to the King Center, dedicated to Martin Luther King Jr. "for his moral courage and nobility of spirit." (RMC.)

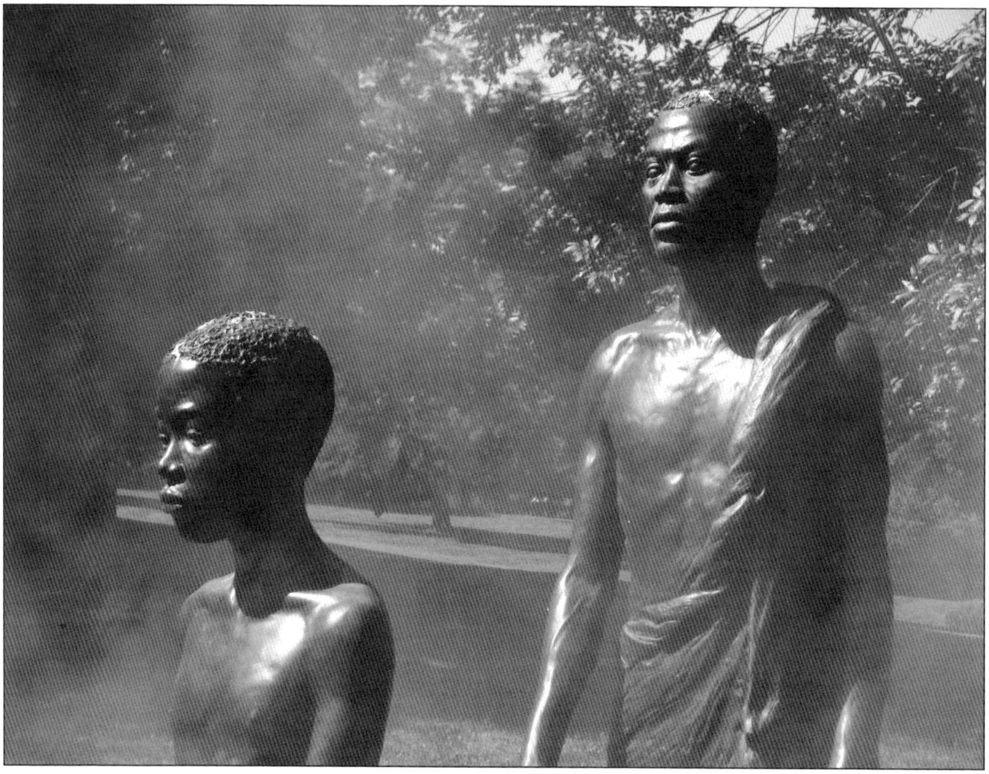

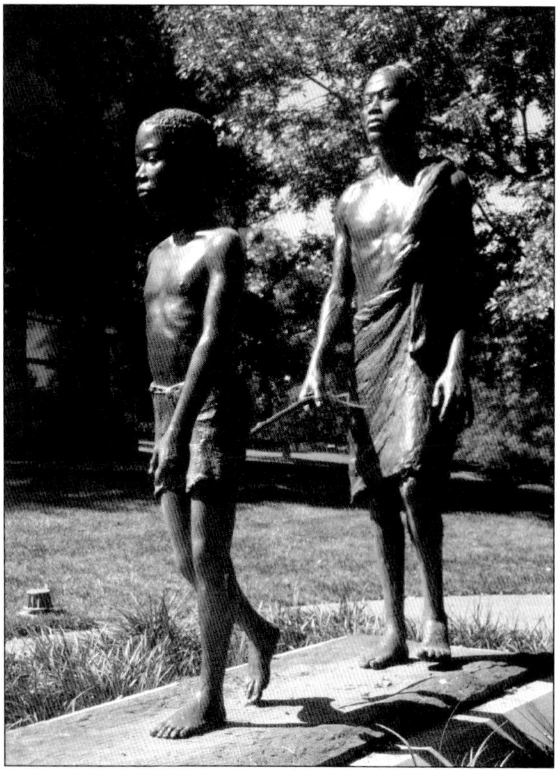

The 1996 sculpture *Sightless Among Miracles* is the work of R.T. Wallen (1942–) of Juneau, Alaska, and the first major artwork in the Carter Center gardens. A gift of John and Rebecca Moores, who founded the River Blindness Foundation in 1990, the sculpture recognizes the humanitarian role of Jimmy and Rosalynn Carter in substantially eradicating this ancient scourge, 99 percent of whose cases take place in Africa. Onchocerca volvulus is a parasitic (filarial) worm that is part of the helminth group of parasites afflicting as much as one-third of the world's population. River blindness, or onchocerciasis, is caused by the parasite. *Sightless Among Miracles* depicts a child leading a blind elder, an all-too-familiar image witnessed over hundreds of years in affected regions of Africa and Latin America (where the disease arrived with the slave trade). (RMC.)

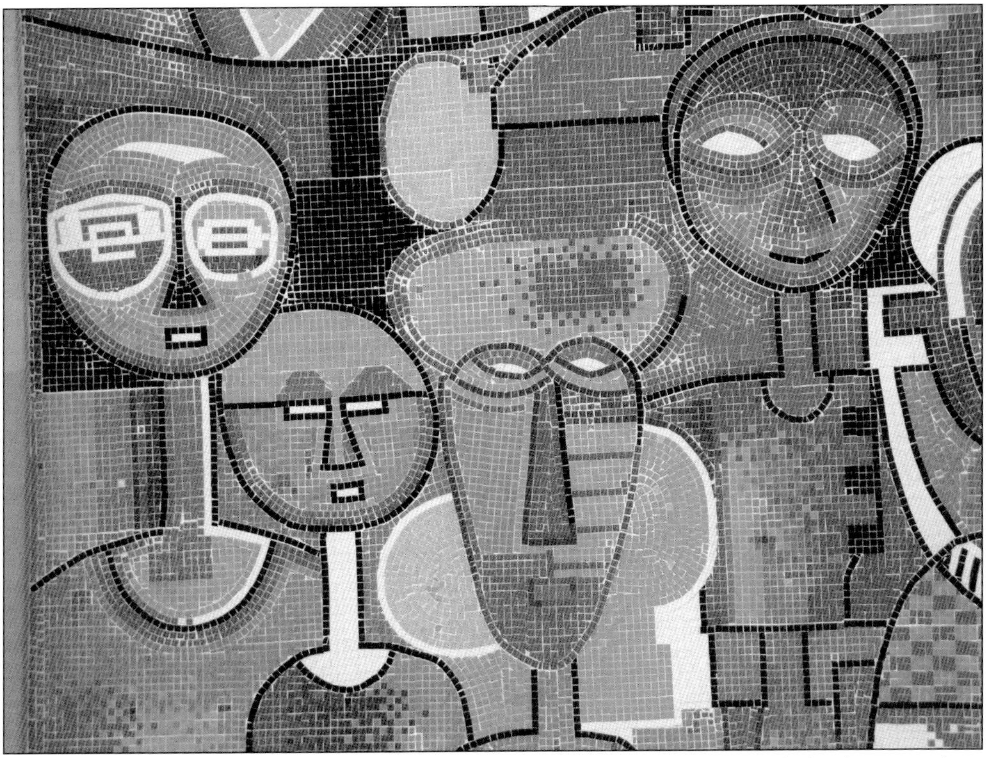

The 1960s experimental workshops of the Osogbo School of Art in Nigeria helped to introduce a distinctive style of modern African art to western cultures. This colorful mosaic in Howell Park (West End) is by Chief Jimoh Buraimoh (1943–), one of the school's most influential artists. As is characteristic of the school, much of Buraimoh's work intermingles traditional Yoruban styles and western culture. While actively painting in oils and executing etchings, Chief Buraimoh's signature works are his bead paintings and mosaics, of which this mosaic in Howell Park is representative. Titled *Meeting of the Elders*, the glass mosaic and concrete wall was installed in 1997 and has images front and back. (RMC.)

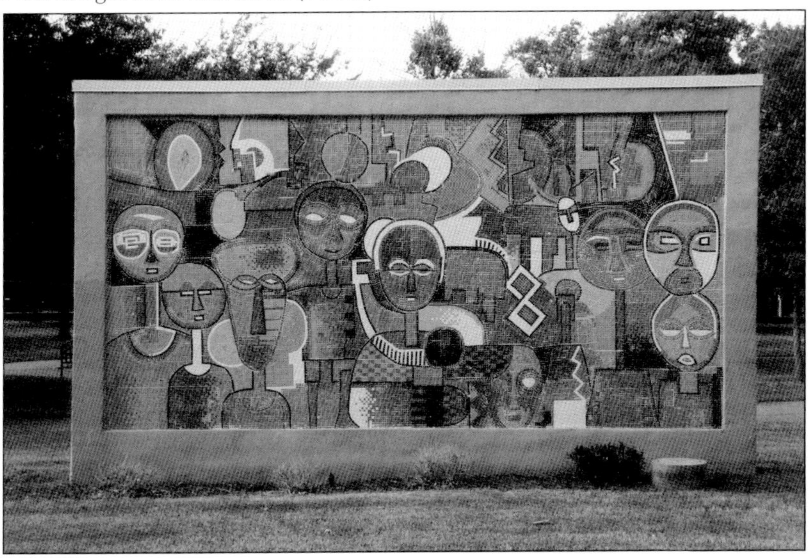

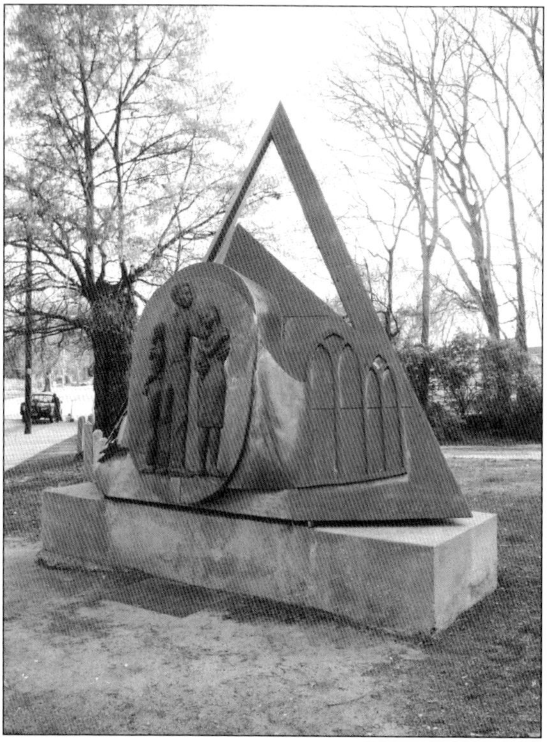

Two sundials by Ayokunle Odeleye (1951–), both recently restored, reference African American and African traditions. Odeleye's steel and bronze *Spirit, Family, Community* (1996), a functioning sundial at Hank Aaron Drive SE at Haygood Avenue SE, honors the family ties and contributions of the neighborhood community by featuring a bas relief depicting a family of four, as well as references to community life, such as church windows on a side panel. (RMC.)

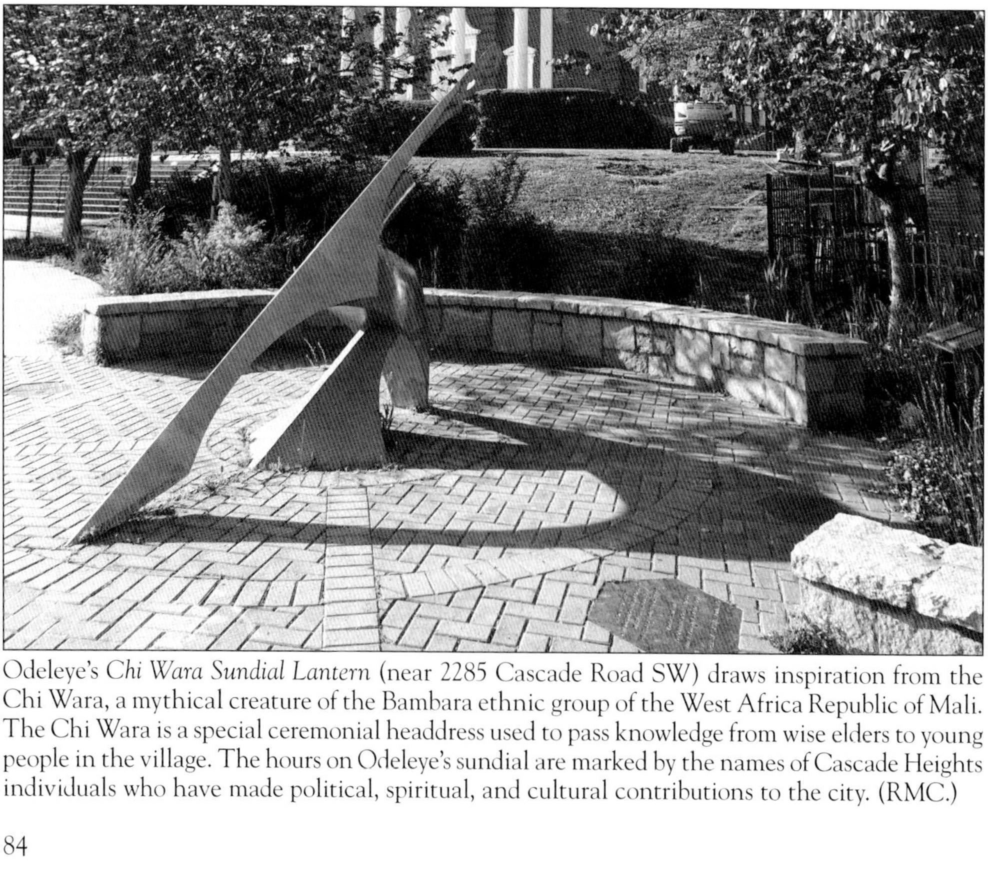

Odeleye's *Chi Wara Sundial Lantern* (near 2285 Cascade Road SW) draws inspiration from the Chi Wara, a mythical creature of the Bambara ethnic group of the West Africa Republic of Mali. The Chi Wara is a special ceremonial headdress used to pass knowledge from wise elders to young people in the village. The hours on Odeleye's sundial are marked by the names of Cascade Heights individuals who have made political, spiritual, and cultural contributions to the city. (RMC.)

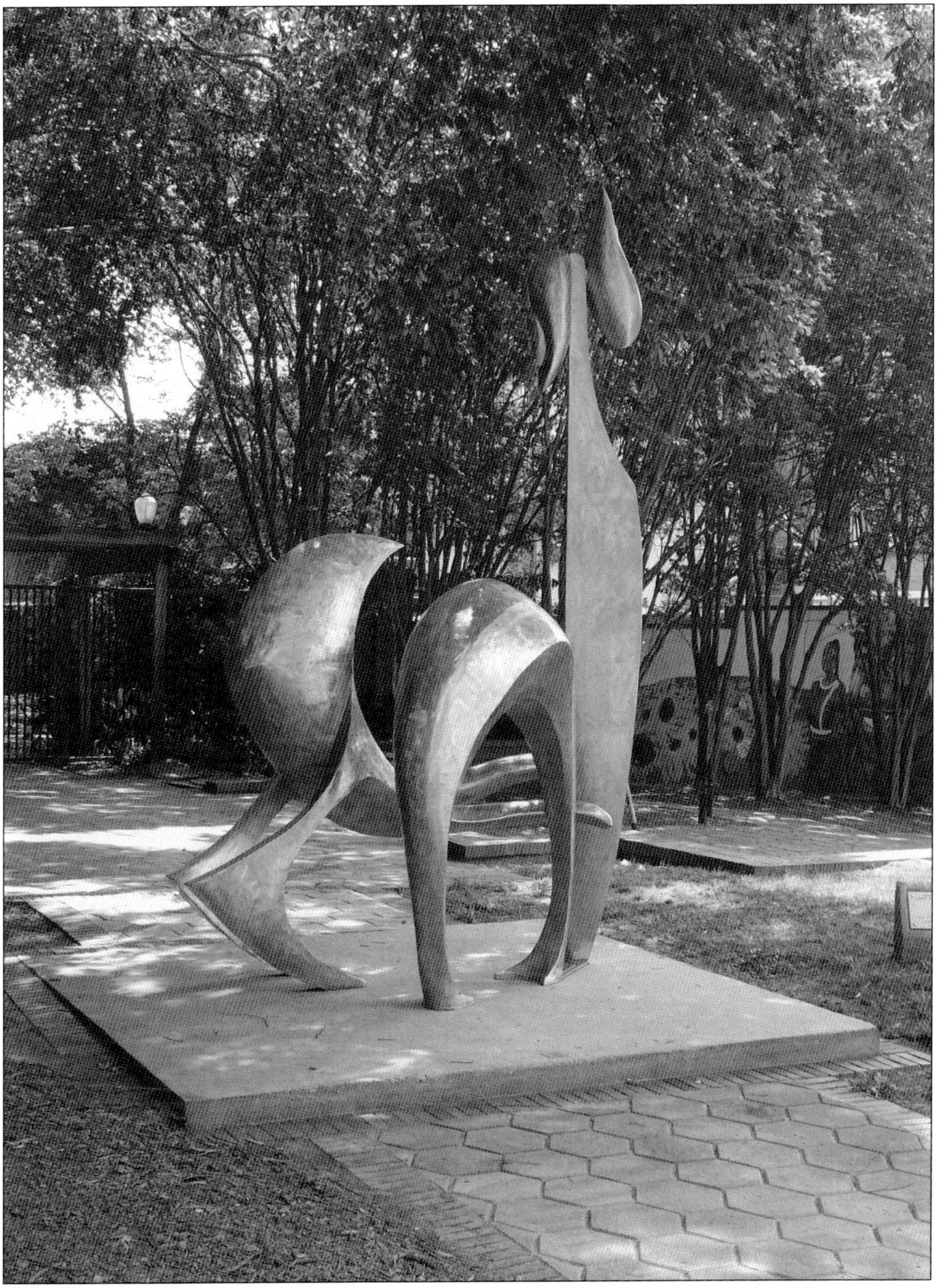

A third piece of public art by Ayokunle Odeleye, who teaches art at Kennesaw State University, is titled *Ancestral Totem*. Located in Calhoun Park (at the corner of Auburn Avenue and Piedmont Avenue NE), *Ancestral Totem* is an abstract stainless-steel sculpture again recalling imagery from traditional African arts by featuring an abstracted mask as an element of the sculpture. Among Odeleye's woodcraft works is the lectern in Ebenezer Baptist Church. (RMC.)

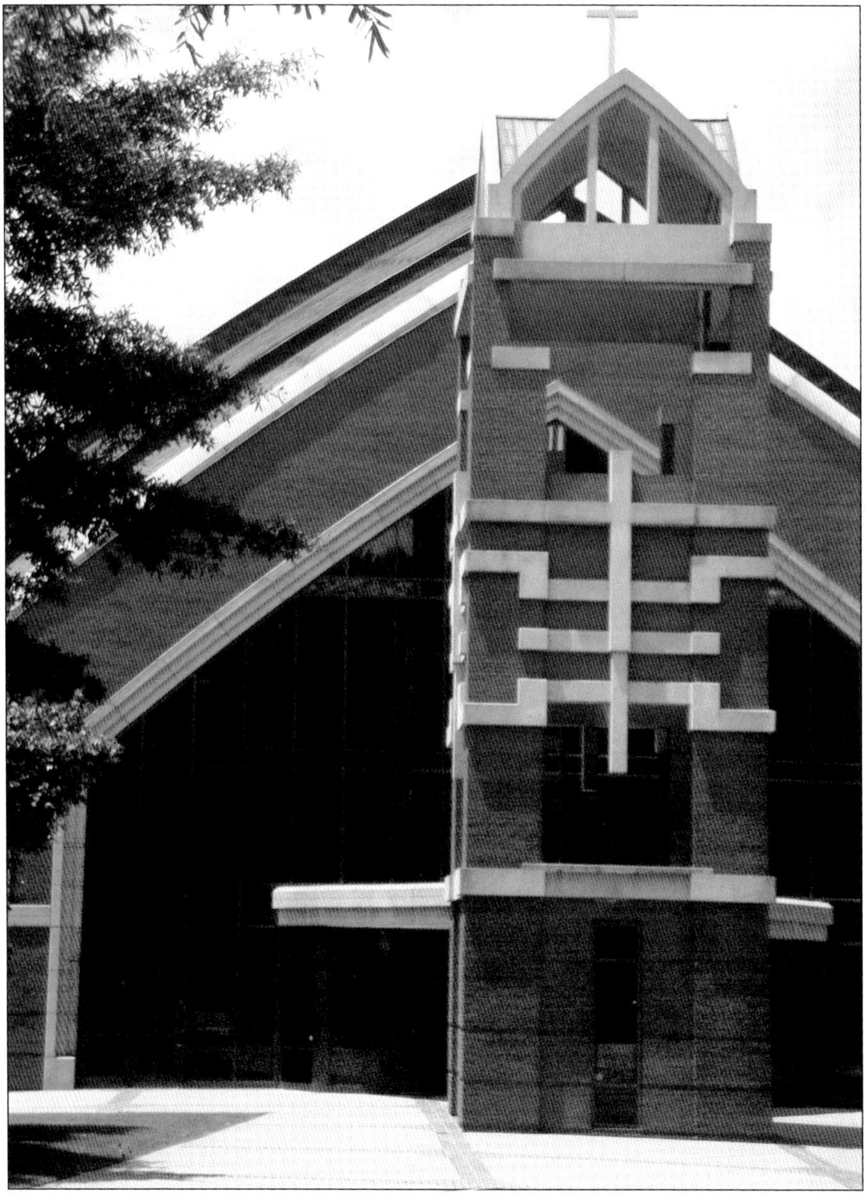

References to African forms are in evidence at the Horizon Sanctuary (1999), Stanley Love Stanley's new worship place for the congregation of historic Ebenezer Baptist Church. The building itself is modeled after an African tribal meeting hut, and the patina of the copper roof has mellowed to a grey reminiscent of African vernacular long grass thatch roofing, particularly the layered thatch in Mali, West Africa. In front of the sanctuary entry is a 55-foot-high monolithic precast concrete bell tower symbolizing the great city of Axum (the place where the Queen of Sheba set out to visit King Solomon in Jerusalem). The New Horizon tower, referencing a stele she erected to honor Solomon, is enriched by brickwork conceived as a weave-and-glyph-patterned obelisk. The sanctuary's apsidal end is shaped like a drum symbolizing the heartbeat and communication method of ancient Africa. Although the side of the sanctuary parallels Jackson Street, the axis of the sanctuary is not perpendicular to Auburn Avenue but oriented to align with the crypt of Martin Luther King Jr. (RMC.)

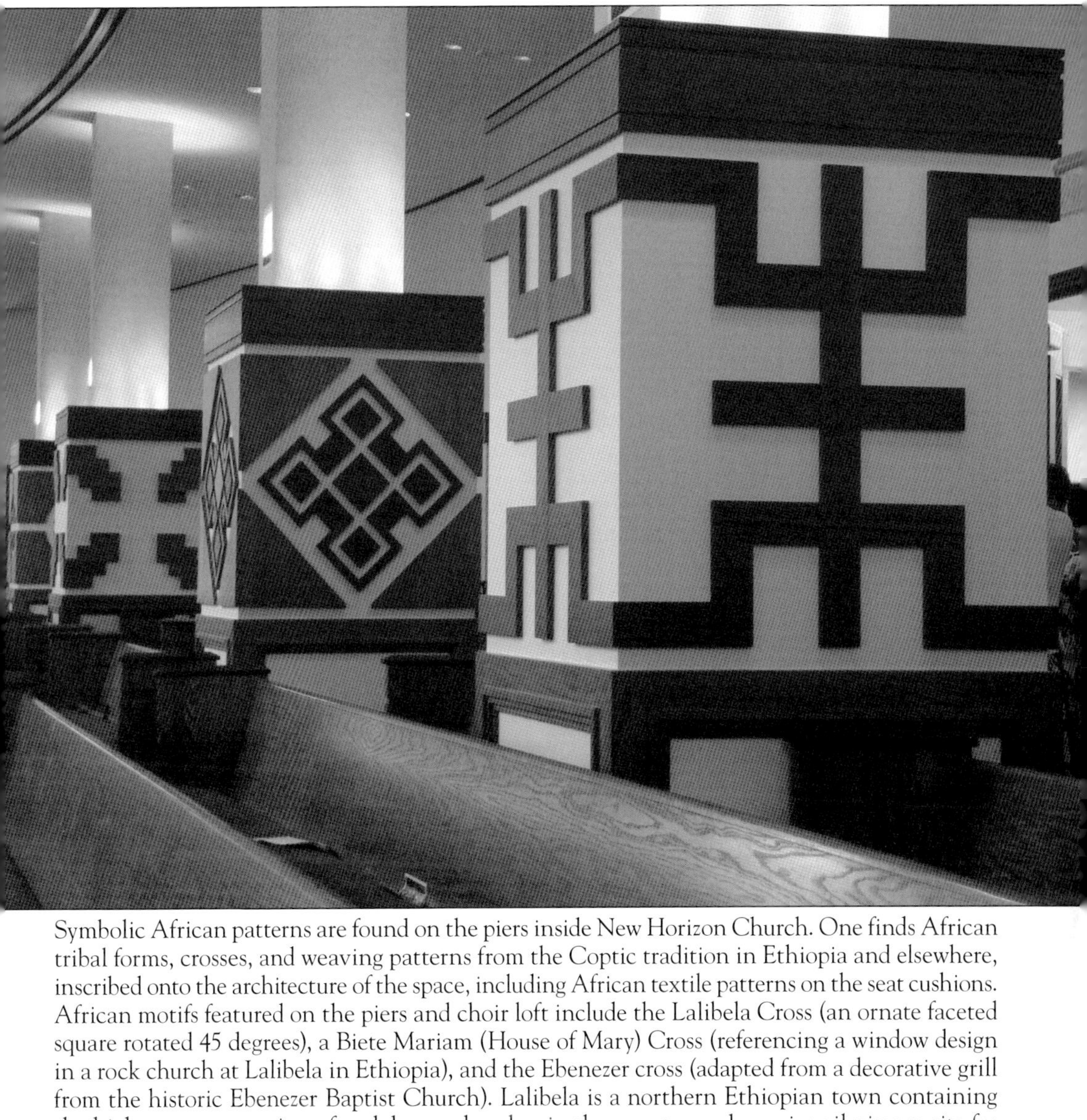

Symbolic African patterns are found on the piers inside New Horizon Church. One finds African tribal forms, crosses, and weaving patterns from the Coptic tradition in Ethiopia and elsewhere, inscribed onto the architecture of the space, including African textile patterns on the seat cushions. African motifs featured on the piers and choir loft include the Lalibela Cross (an ornate faceted square rotated 45 degrees), a Biete Mariam (House of Mary) Cross (referencing a window design in a rock church at Lalibela in Ethiopia), and the Ebenezer cross (adapted from a decorative grill from the historic Ebenezer Baptist Church). Lalibela is a northern Ethiopian town containing the highest concentration of rock-hewn churches in the country and a major pilgrimage site for followers of the Ethiopian Orthodox Church. These rock-hewn churches inspired architects Stanley Love-Stanley in its heavily sand-blasted, poured-in-place concrete Lyke House (2000), the Catholic center serving students of Clark Atlanta University, Spelman College, Morehouse College, and Georgia State University. (RMC.)

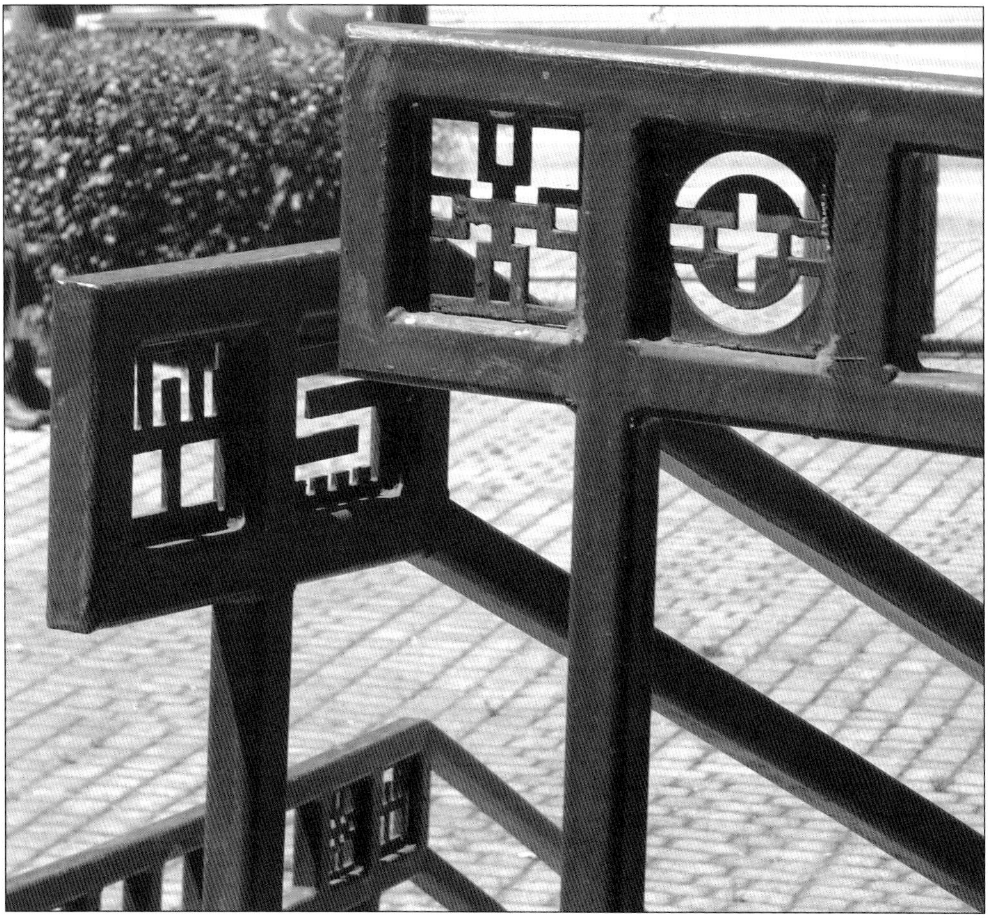

African geometric patterns provide the decorative infill in the openings on the stone wall and on the stairs and handrail at Dobbs Plaza, where they serve as a backdrop to Ralph Helmick's *Through His Eyes* (see page 76). The stone wall combines ancient and modern ideals: tapered front and rear to form a truncated pyramidal end, the wall conveys a rusticated primitivism resulting from the employment of archaic cobblestone work that avoids the precision and refinement of finished ashlar. Woven brick patterns recall the brickwork at the Great Zimbabwe. The perforations are less windows as vertical slits and square punctures, apertures filled with decorative iron motifs of African origin. While the asymmetrical and non-static arrangement of openings puncture the wall as Le Corbusier advocated in order to convey a modern *brut* aesthetic, the tectonic crudeness here finds its source in Africa. (RMC.)

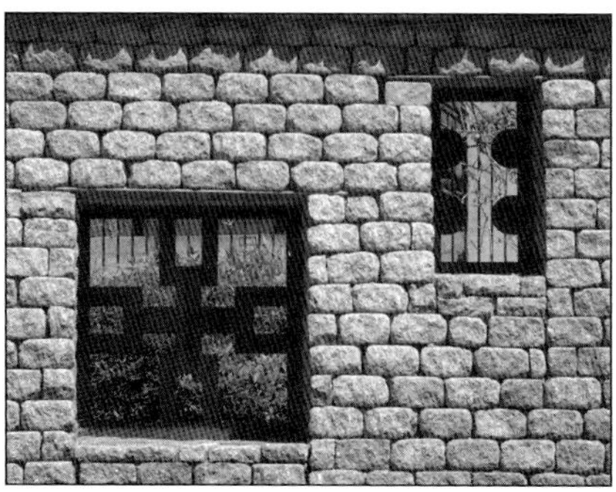

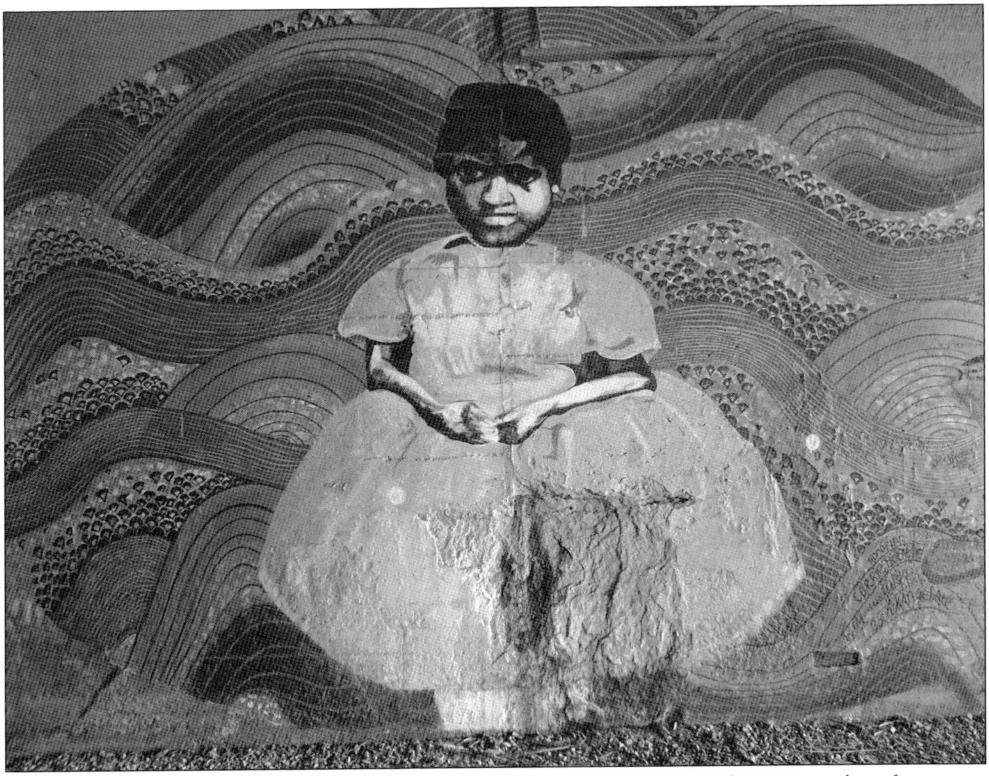

At the time of this writing, Charmaine Minniefield (1973–) was engaged in a virtual performance online of the Ring Shout titled "Let Us Come Together." Minniefield states, "I focus on the idea of protecting black narratives through my work." Originating in West African ritual and ceremony, the Ring Shout is a traditional African American worship/gathering practice reborn during enslavement in the American South in resistance to laws that prohibited those enslaved from gathering, except for worship, and forbad any form of cultural expression, including drumming. These laws were imposed in an effort to systematically dismantle communication, and ultimately, community. Art is communication, and "remembrance as resistance" is a theme in Minniefield's art, including her mural tributes to Ella Baker (below) and to Carrie (Steele) Logan (above), the latter a Georgia-born former slave and founder of the oldest black orphanage in the United States. (RMC.)

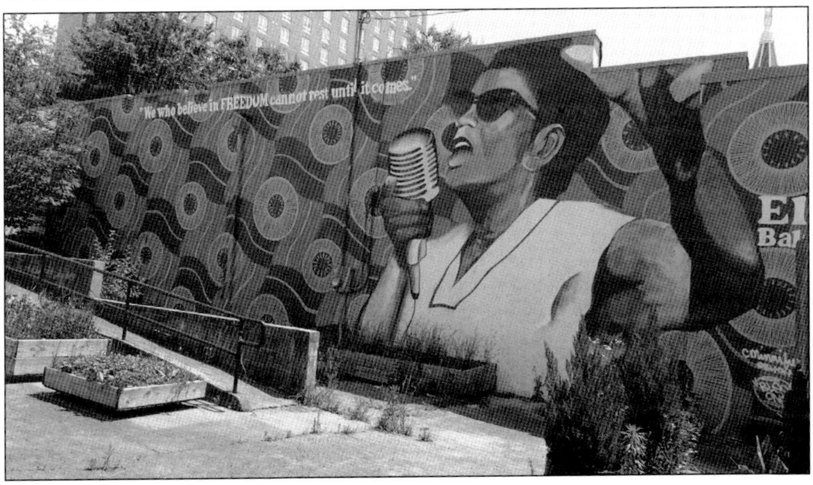

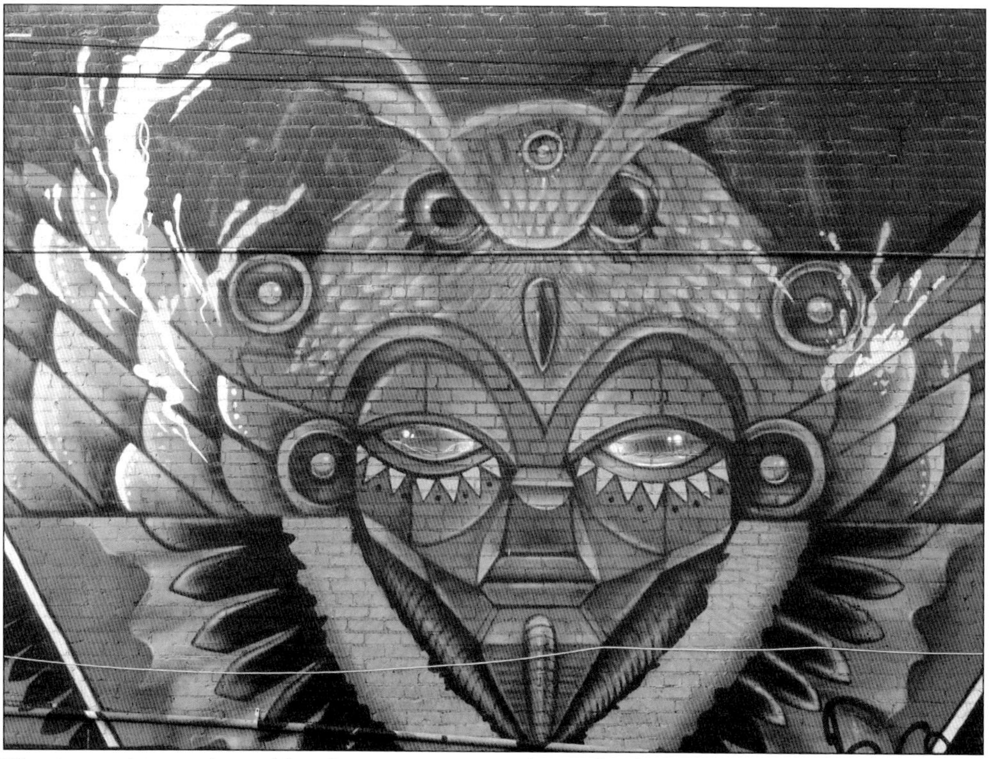

Theriomorphic masks and headgear appear in traditional cultures around the world including African, Eskimo, Native American, and Pre-Columbian societies of Mexico and Central America. Worn in village ceremonies and tribal dances, masks and headgear with animal features often represent departed ancestors, spirit beings, and invisible powers, transferred to the dancer or ceremonial participant. Theriocephaly has ancient roots as storytelling and artistic devices in the representation of deities. In ancient Egypt, for instance, Horus is represented with the head of a falcon, Anubis with the head of a jackal; in Greek mythology, the Minotaur has the head of a bull; and in Native American Abenaki mythology, the spirit Pamola has the head of a moose and wings and talons of an eagle. Whatever the source for the mural by Maria2 in Little Five Points illustrated here, the features reflect these ancient traditions. (RMC.)

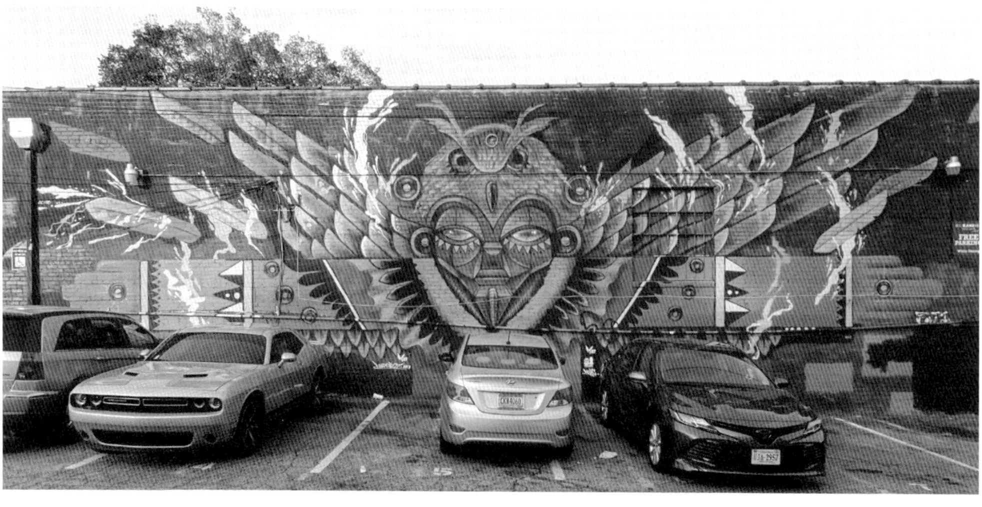

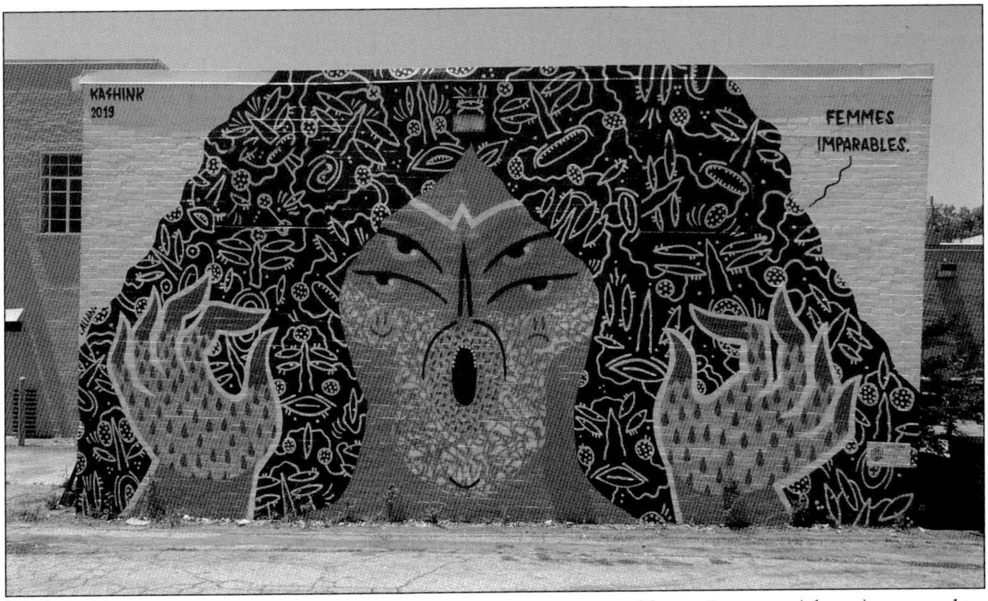

A frontal mask imagery also informs the mural *Femmes Imparables* in Decatur (above), painted in 2019 by KASHINK, who lives in Paris. The artist considers herself an activist celebrating diversity and confronting social norms, and much as Salvador Dali relied on a flamboyant mustache to draw attention to himself and his art, KASHINK wears a pencil-on mustache "as a sociological experiment encouraging random conversations with strangers about beauty, gender, norms, and freedom." She says her paintings are a form of self-portraiture. (RMC.)

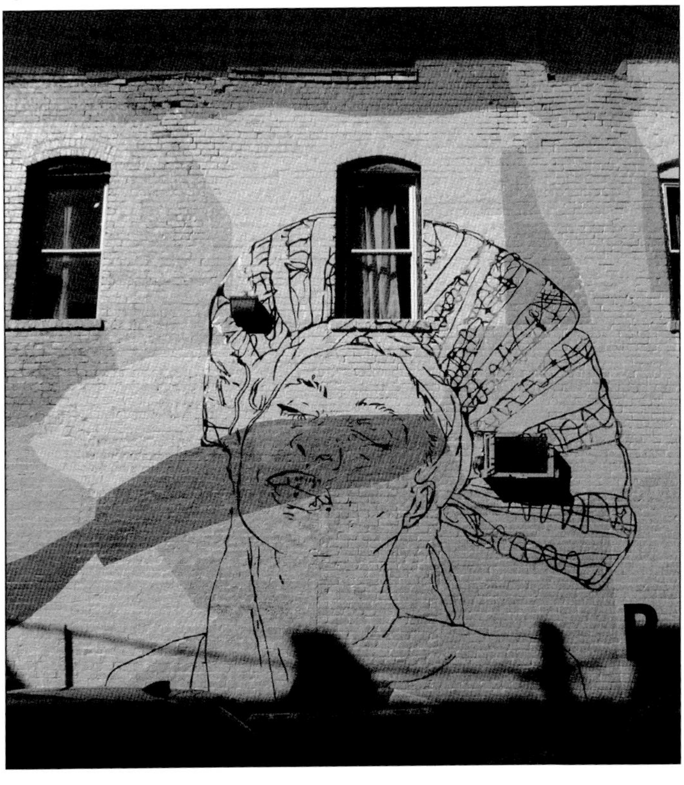

Black pride and women's empowerment motivated Nikia Phoenix of the Black Girl Beautiful organization and muralist Faatimah Stevens in their *Hey Brown Girl, You're Beautiful* mural. The mural on Peters Street SW in Castleberry features a friend of Phoenix wearing fashionable headgear and has become a favorite backdrop for fashion photos and selfies of women of color, an all too rare space in the city honoring black women. (RMC.)

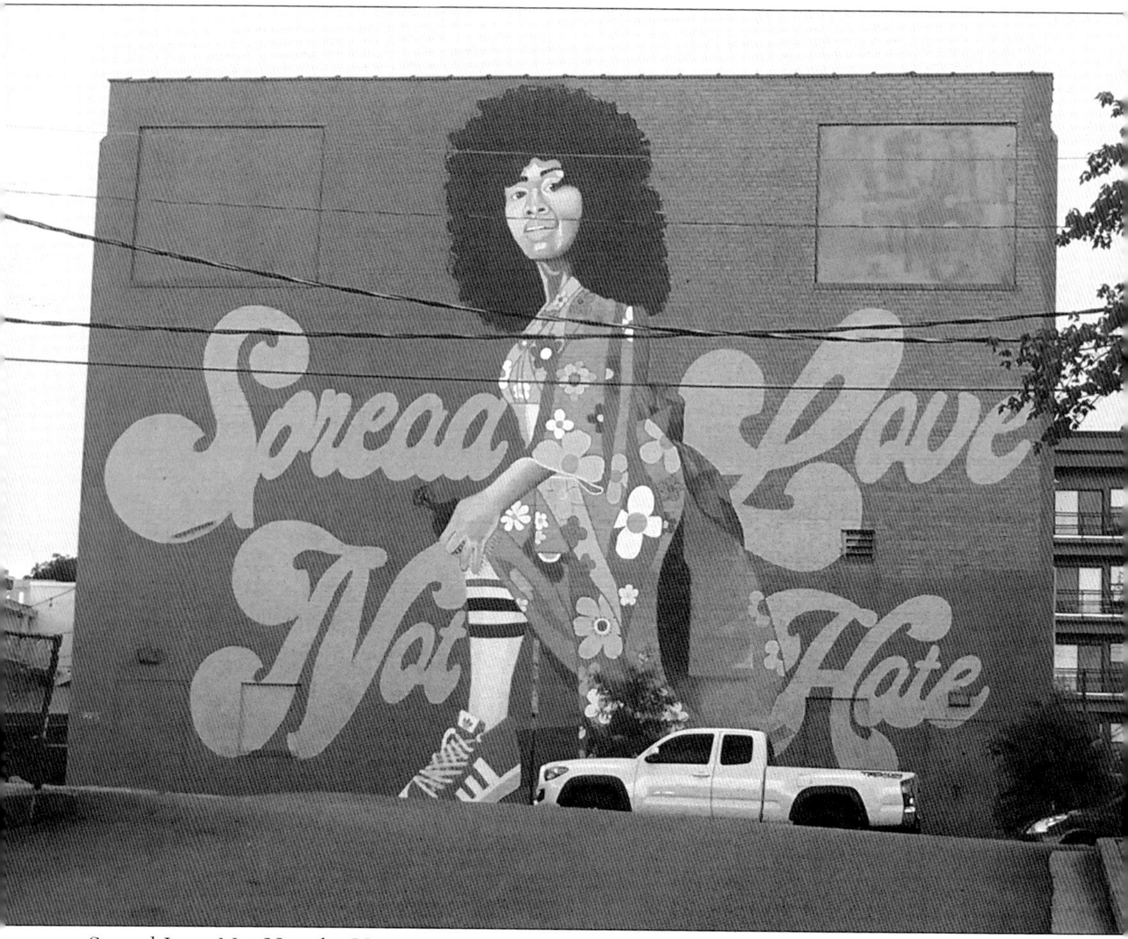

Spread Love Not Hate by Haitian American artist Yuzly Mathurin (1984–) is a recent mural at Briarcliff Plaza. It depicts a black woman in a floral kimono intended to celebrate black and Asian culture. "The piece speaks to the importance of honoring people of color regardless of their country," Mathurin has said. Ailene Farhshi in *ArtsATL* (published on June 24, 2021) described it as "bold portraiture that honors diversity and uplifts the marginalized." Citing influences from the Harlem Renaissance to hip-hop, Mathurin observes, "The rich patterns and colors in my work come from explorations of my obscured African heritage." Of Haitian background, Mathurin was born in Nyack, New York, raised in Orange Park, Florida, and moved to Atlanta in 2018. This mural, her largest in the city, "aspires to unveil the beauty of people of color." (RMC.)

Six

Immigrant and International Art

Atlanta's self-proclaimed declaration that it is an international city is no better validated than in its street art, both executed by artists from around the world, but also presenting the art of immigrants now living in Atlanta. The imported cultural expressions, both exotic and embedded with social and political meaning, enrich the streetscapes of our commercial strips and neighborhoods and renew the aesthetic of building elevations transformed from the abandoned and bland to the cosmopolitan, multi-racial, and universal. The work of immigrants illustrates that humans of all backgrounds and colors are fundamentally the same and hold similar values. Through immigrant art, Atlantans can experience a beauty, grace, expression of hope, societal harmony, and "pursuit of happiness" that is international.

The artist Yoyo Ferro was born in Piracicaba in the state of São Paulo, Brazil; Angie Jerez is from Bogotá, Columbia. Jurell Cayetano was born in Brooklyn, New York, to parents of Honduran and West Indian descent. Killimari's mother was a refugee from Vietnam, and his father was a soldier from Cambodia. Sanithna Phansavanh grew up in a refugee program in Kansas City after his mother escaped the communist regime in Laos during the 1970s. Cinta Vidal i Agulló, whose huge, Escher-inspired mural titled *Merge* is at Coda Tech Square, is from Barcelona. Agostino Iacurci is Italian born and Berlin based. Italian artists Sten (born in Rome) and Lex (born in Taranto) created a supergraphic stencil poster in the Sweet Auburn district comparable to stencil graffiti and stencil art they have executed in London, Paris, Barcelona, or their home base of Rome. Alexandre Monteiro, also known as Andrey V. Hopare, is based in Paris but has painted murals in Portugal, Cameroon, South Korea, India, and on the sidewall of the Little's Food Store on Carroll Street in Cabbagetown, Atlanta. He considers his street art to be "a weapon to release the walls from their gray straightjacket." Illustrated on page 117 is his city-block-long *Symphony* mural.

The huge mural titled *The Keep* for the 2019 Outerspace Project and located on the side of a housing tower at 563 Memorial Drive is by Sabek from Madrid. Also originally from Madrid is artist Chris Alvarez, also known as Pitoto. Janice Rago was born in Hawaii, and among the influences on her work is the imagery of the South Pacific. Aleksei Bordusov, also known as AEC, and Vladimir Manzhos, also known as Waone, are Ukrainian artists who worked together as Interesni Kazki and are primarily known for their colorful surrealistic artwork; such a mural is on the sidewall of Argosy gastropub in East Atlanta Village. Franco Fasoli, also known as Jaz, hails from Buenos Aires, Argentina, where he worked in theater scenography at the Teatro Colón; in Atlanta for the 2013 Living Walls Conference, he painted a ring of wild beasts around a campfire on a wall at 230 Flat Shoals Avenue at Memorial Drive SE regrettably now faded, but his horses mural rising over three stories on the north rear wall of 890 Memorial Drive at the Beltline remains splendidly legible. Alexi Torres was born in the village of Bermeja in Cuba, moved to Atlanta in 2003, and founded Buckhead Murals, establishing a second studio in Zacunda, Costa Rica. His brother Ernesto and Ernesto's wife, Lenia Castro (graduates of the University of Arts of Cuba), took the helm of the business when Alexi elected to concentrate on oils on canvas, and Buckhead Murals art is found across the city on warehouses, franchises, and large-scale office buildings both as public murals and commercial advertising.

Yehimi Cambrón was born in Michoacán, Mexico, and describes herself as a dreamer who, at eight years old, crossed the southern border with her family from Mexico; thus, she is "undocumented" and "illegal," but able to stay in Atlanta, teach art, and paint because of DACA (Deferred Action for Childhood Arrivals). Cambrón has said that her art is a statement of activism in that it "focuses on celebrating the humanity, resilience, and contributions of immigrants." Cambrón painted three murals for the public art project leading up to Super Bowl LIII titled "Off the Wall: Atlanta's Civil Rights and Social Justice Journey," and soon thereafter, she executed a mural in Decatur titled *Monuments: Our Immigrant Mother.* A "visual affirmation that celebrates immigrant mothers and the intersectionality of the immigrant community," the mural was selected by *Creative Loafing* magazine as 2019's Best Mural in Atlanta.

Buford Highway, including Cheshire Bridge Road to the south, has evolved to become a commercial strip with Chinese, Thai, Vietnamese, Mexican, and Caribbean restaurants, with neighborhoods in the Chamblee area of Buford Highway developing as characteristically populated by Hispanic and South Asian immigrants. The concentration has garnered the nickname "Chambodia" for the area, and it is here that the international flavor of Atlanta and notable immigrant art are especially evidenced in murals on shopping centers, liquor stores, car washes, and office buildings. The art tells of journeys taken and still underway, reflecting not only a geographic change for international families and the community's artists, but also a social change for the better life to which we all aspire.

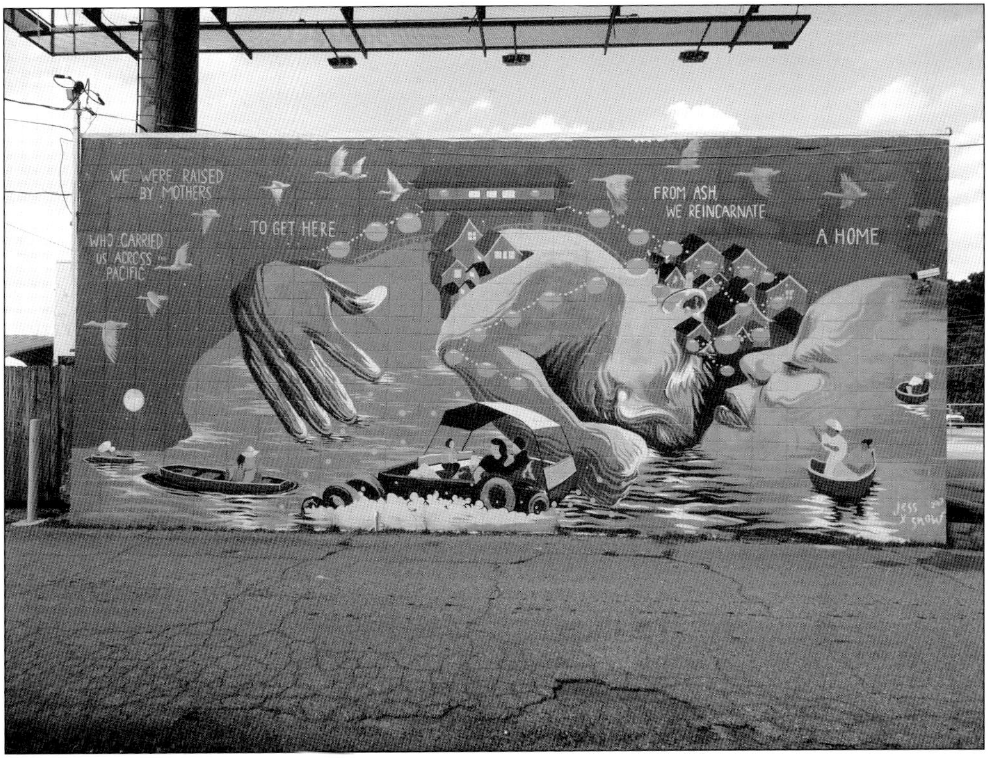

Jess X. Snow (1992–) is a Chinese Canadian muralist, filmmaker, and poet. Her parents emigrated from Nanchang after the Cultural Revolution in China and the muralist encapsulates the immigrant experience painted on different sidewalls of an auto repair shop at 4196 Buford Highway and sponsored by Living Walls and the 2017 BuHi Walk. "When we think of the immigrant narrative and journey, it is very different for different groups," Living Walls executive director Monica Campana told Lois Reitzes, host of radio's *City Lights*. Nonetheless, Asian, Hispanic, and other immigrant groups share the sentiment of the mother cradling a child and an understanding of the excerpt from a poem inscribed on the murals: "We were raised by mothers who flew across the Pacific to get here, from ash we reincarnate a home," and "We are Here to Stay." (RMC.)

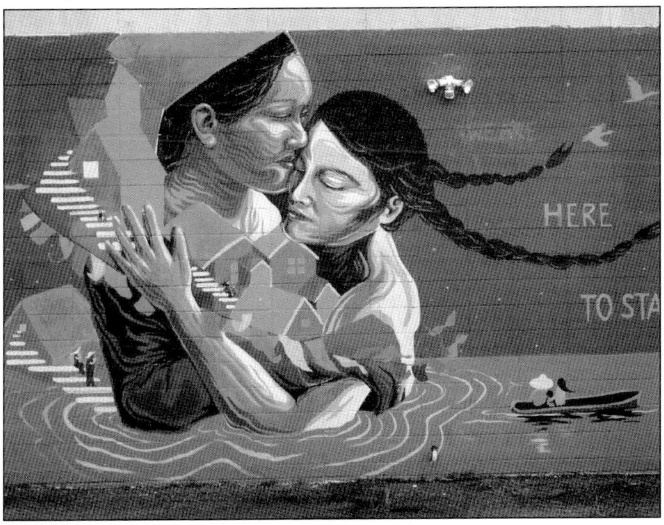

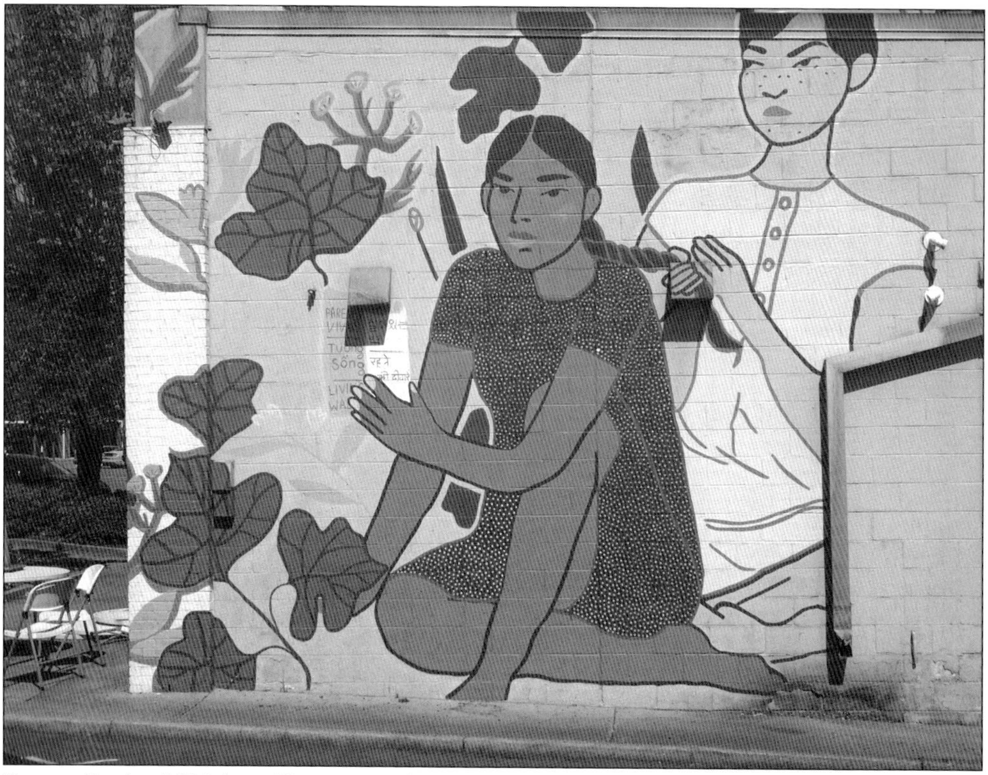

Dianna Settles (1989–) is a Vietnamese American artist in Atlanta whose work explores "moments of joyful stillness amidst the cascading series of crises called modern life." Deeply influenced by her 2014 trip to her father's home country of Vietnam, she found there "room after room of artwork featuring figures that I could, for the first time, relate to and see myself in. This began my skillful but indeterminate synthesis of traditional Vietnamese painting and the classical influences of European colonization." She found that this "in-between-ness" resonated with her as it does, she believes, with many non-white artists in the United States, and especially the South. "The presence of marginalized bodies in works of art is historically important," Settles believes. Like Jess X. Snow, Settles too painted a *Here to Stay* mural at 3375 Buford Highway in 2017. (RMC.)

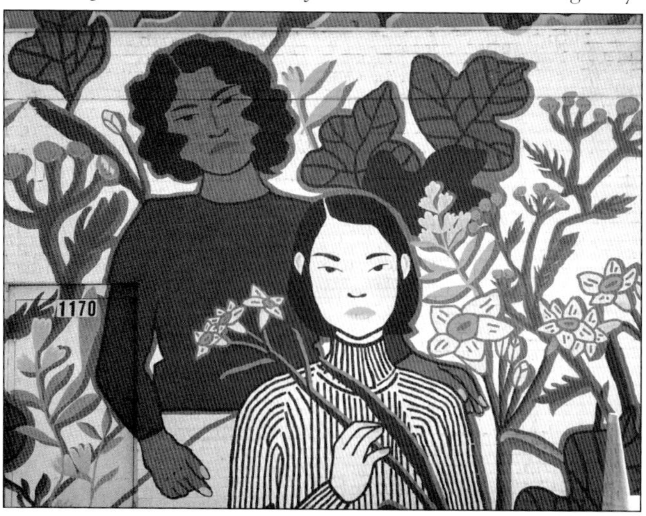

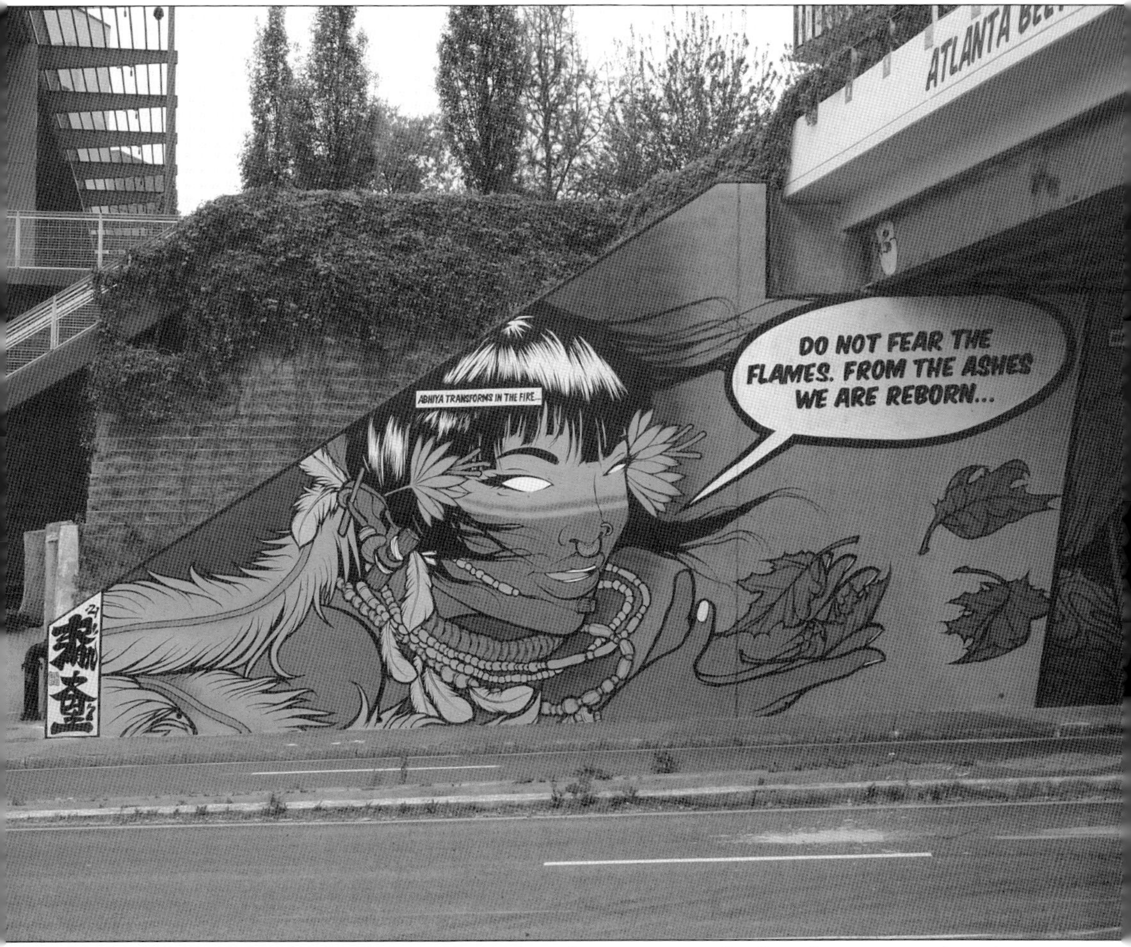

Brandon Sadler (1986–), also known as RisingRedLotus, is a multi-disciplinary artist based in Atlanta. He lived in Seoul, South Korea, for some time and "found deep parallels between my experience as a graffiti writer and the artistic principles of brush calligraphy based in the Chinese character system." His art "balances both ancient and modern techniques through the use of text, illustration, and painting." The result is a distinctive synthesis reflecting (according to Sadler's art statement) "influences from experience in American graffiti, studies in traditional Korean, Chinese, and Japanese calligraphy, ink painting, Ukiyo-e woodblock prints, comic books, and graphic design." His paintings of koi fish (symbols of prosperity and good fortune), lotus blossoms in water gardens, and Asian figures are signature works of RisingRedLotus, notably evident in his recent mural on the East Beltline/North Avenue underpass. The mural is a giant graphic novel titled *Gateway to Change: Abhiya's Way*, where a protagonist named Abhiya journeys through four seasons, learning a new life lesson in each. While the name "Abhiya" may have several interpretations, Sadler prefers the Sanskrit, which means "gift from God." (RMC.)

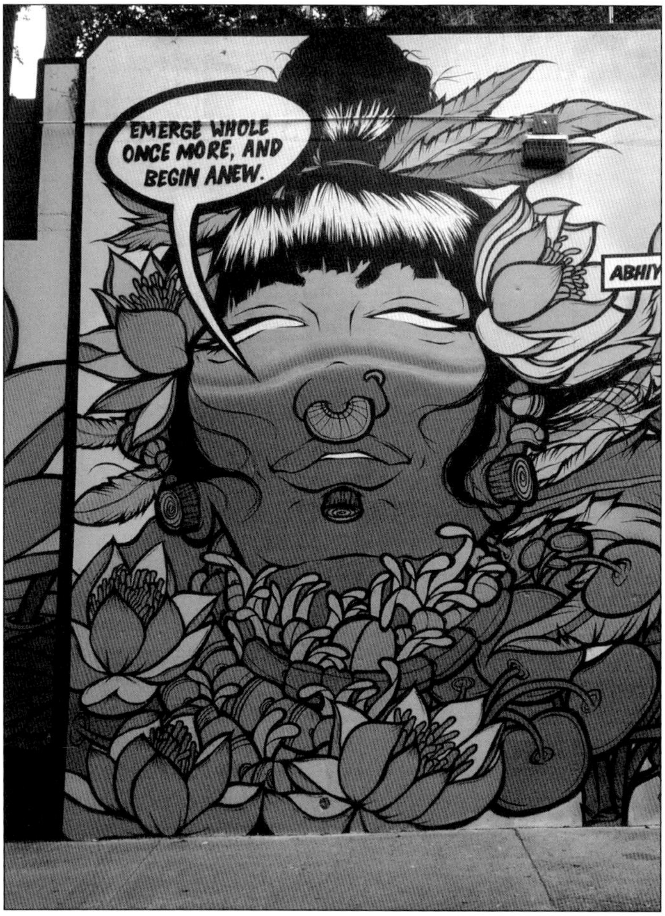

Sadler created Abhiya to act as a motivational spirit guide to remind us how to approach challenges. In one panel, Abhiya "is patient in the flood" reminding us that "the rain quenches the blaze, making the soil fertile once more," and another panel is inscribed with "Emerge whole once more and begin anew." In the mural's final panel, "Abhiya is whole once more," and emerges from her odyssey, saying, "Enjoy your life," flanked by three enormous koi. Throughout the cartoon mural, the colors are strong, reflecting both Asian and comic strip customary palettes. His studio art and murals, like traditional Asian scroll painting, combine calligraphic and scenic content. (RMC.)

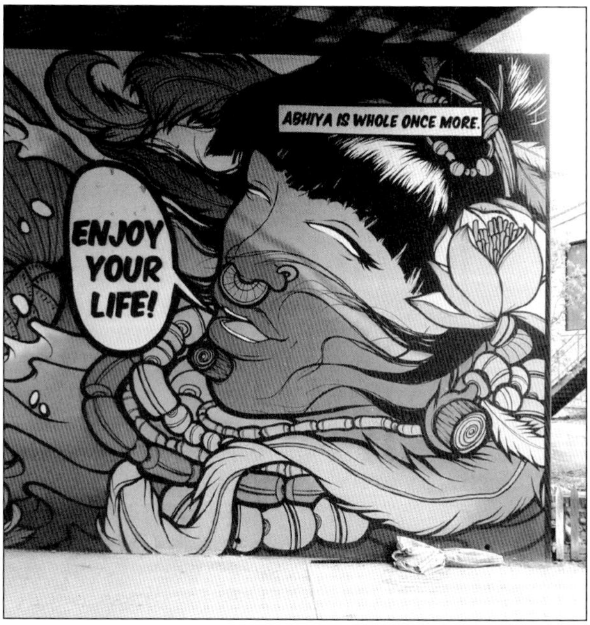

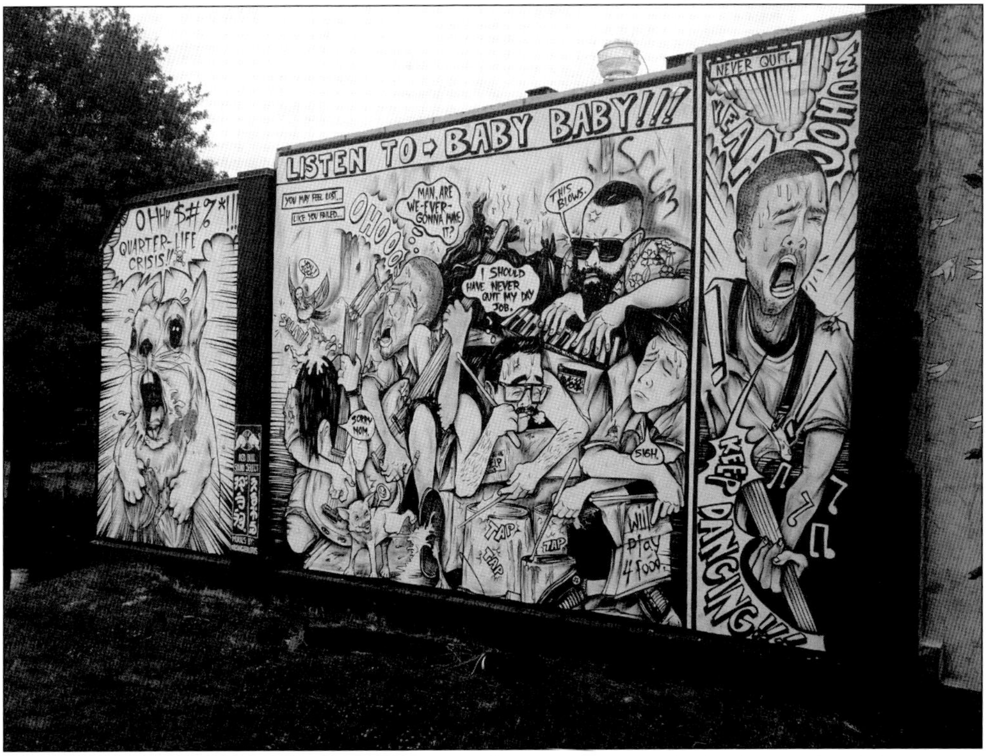

Two motivational murals in a monochromatic linear cartoon-style display a related dimension of Sadler's graphic styling. Neighborhood youth are offered encouragement in black-and-white imagery that is distinctive and striking. At the 597 Cascade Road *Innerspace* mural, an explosion of splashing and swirling white lines against an empty, black, cosmic background includes a title box, "The power of the cosmos rests within," and a phantom figurehead declares, "You have ALL you need INSIDE of you." Similarly, at 451 Edgewood Avenue, a rabbit declares, "Ohh $#%*!!! Quarter Life Crisis." Then, depression-inflicted figures are intermixed with messages "You may feel lost, like you failed," "Man, Are we ever gonna make it?" "I should have never quit my day job," and "Will Play for Food," but the final panel includes the title block "Never Quit." (RMC.)

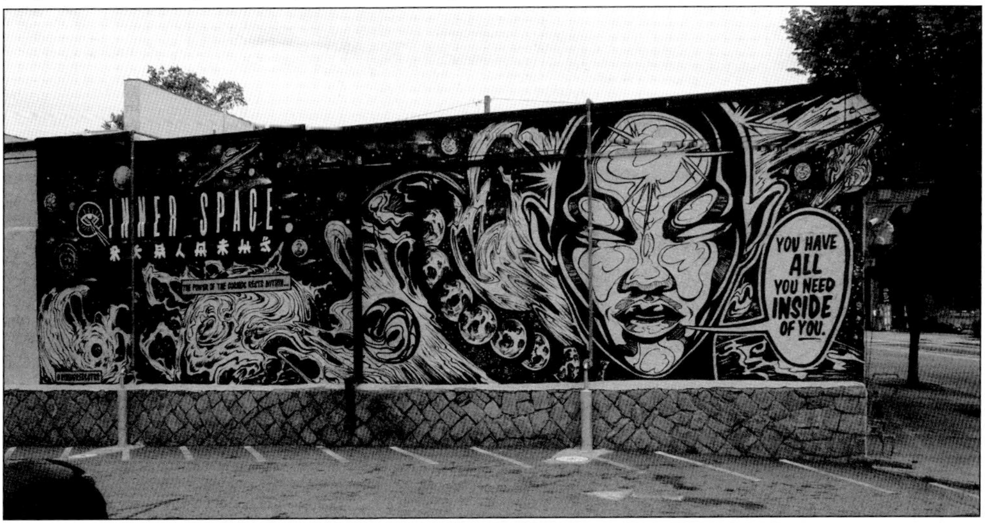

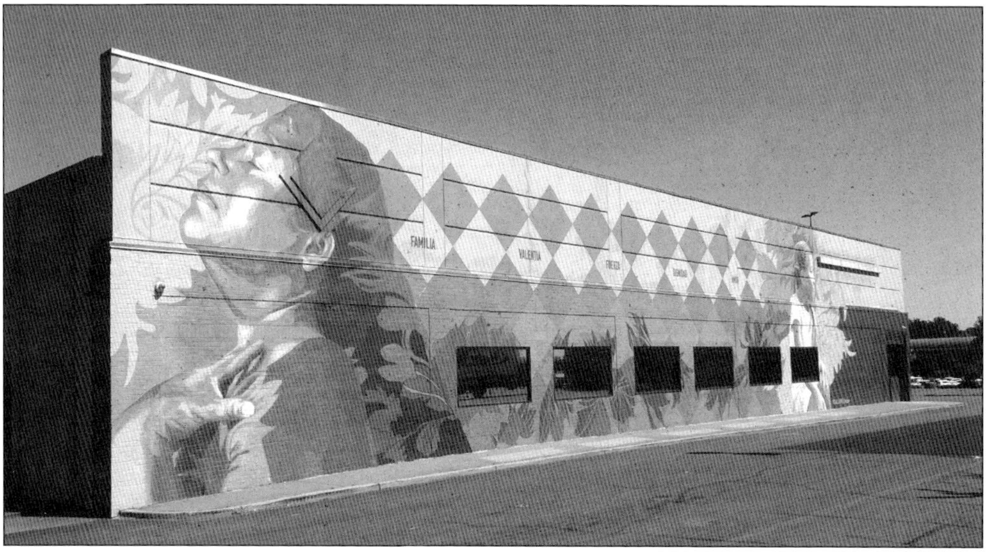

Michelle Angela Ortiz (1978–) was born in Philadelphia to Colombian and Puerto Rican parents. Her 2017 mural for Living Walls, The City Speaks was "based on the stories of families . . . fac[ing] the risk of deportation, displacement, and lack of educational resources for their children." A group of mothers, "Las Chicas del Clan," inspired the mural. One of them, Isaura, is shown with her eyes closed, imagining a life without fear. (RMC.)

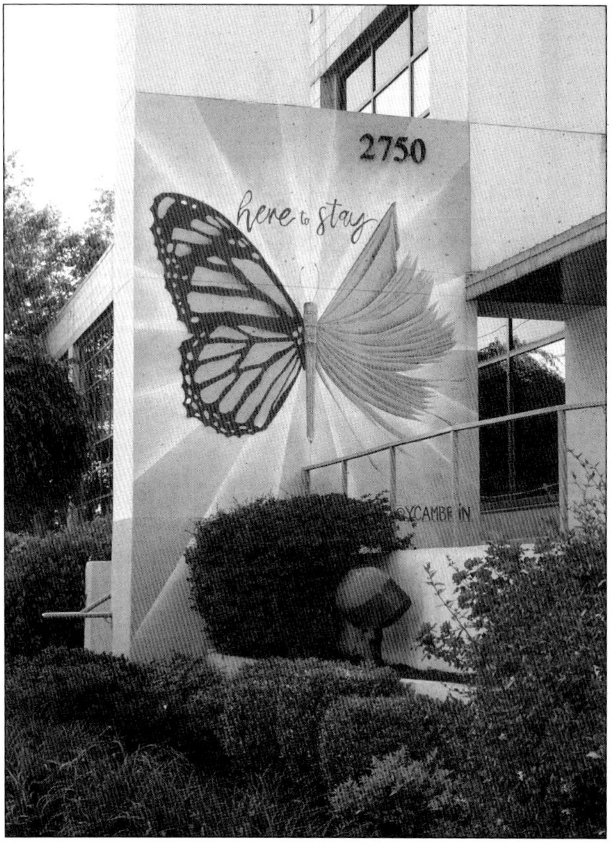

Yehimi Cambrón's first Atlanta mural, *Education is Liberation Monarch* (2017), depicted a monarch butterfly, with a pencil as its body, and with one wing of fluttering open book pages. When the mural became "a platform to advocate for the protection of undocumented youth" and those present were asked to phone their congressmen to support the Dream Act, the building owner painted over the mural. The butterfly reappeared at 2750 Buford Highway. (RMC.)

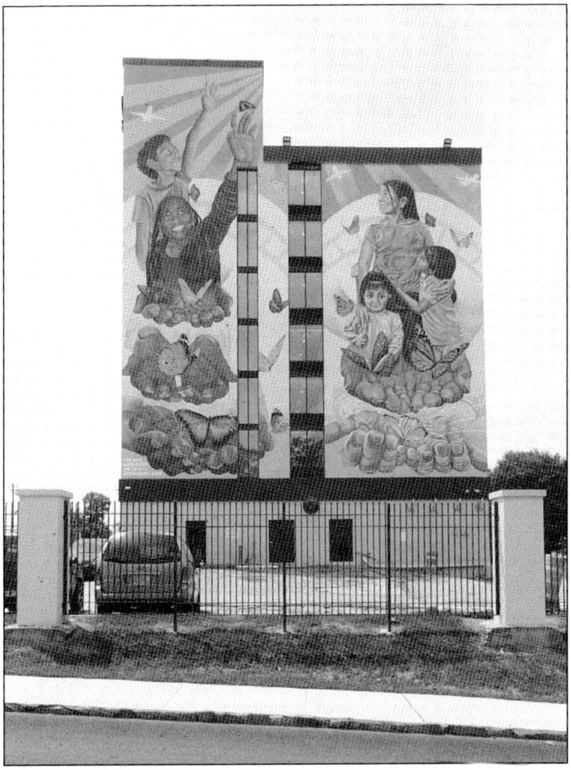

The mural *We Give Each Other the World* features children from the City of Hapeville who represent the diversity of the community, a work intended to encourage youngsters to be "limitless in their hopes and dreams for the future." The children reach hopefully skyward while they are elevated by the hands of adults from the community. Migrating butterflies, adopted by immigrant activists as symbols, are frequently and meaningfully evident in Cambrón's work. Millions of the butterflies migrate each winter from Canada to the warmer temperatures of the United States and Mexico, with the vast majority settling during the summer at the Monarch Butterfly Reserve in Michoacán, Mexico. Cambrón was born in Michoacán, and the symbolism for her of the monarch "is that migration [is] a natural process," and that here in Atlanta the immigrant children of the community are survivors. (RMC.)

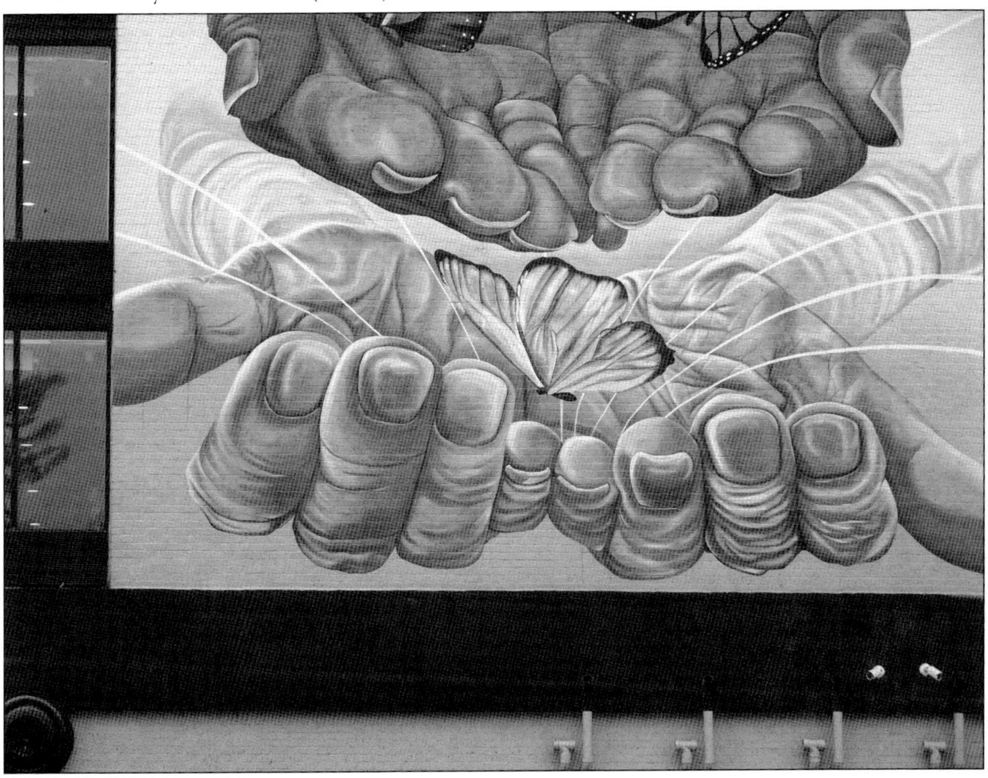

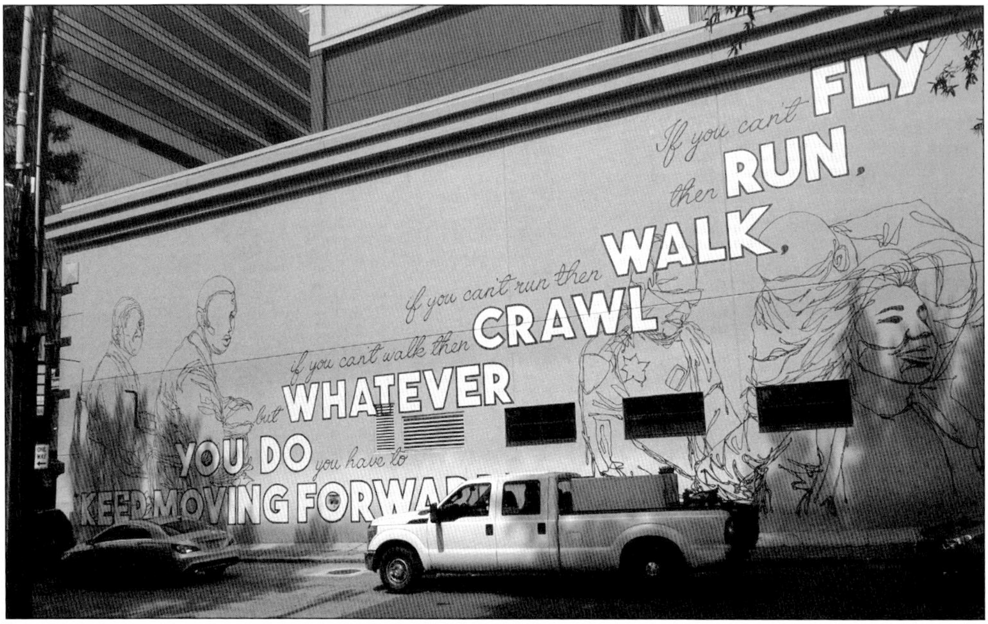

Freedom Fighters by Yehimi Cambrón is a large mural on the Williams Street rear wall of the American Hotel. In a stepped series of highlighted keywords, the quotation from Martin Luther King Jr. is referenced: "If you can't fly, then run; if you can't run, then walk; if you can't walk, then crawl; but whatever you do, you have to keep moving forward." (RMC.)

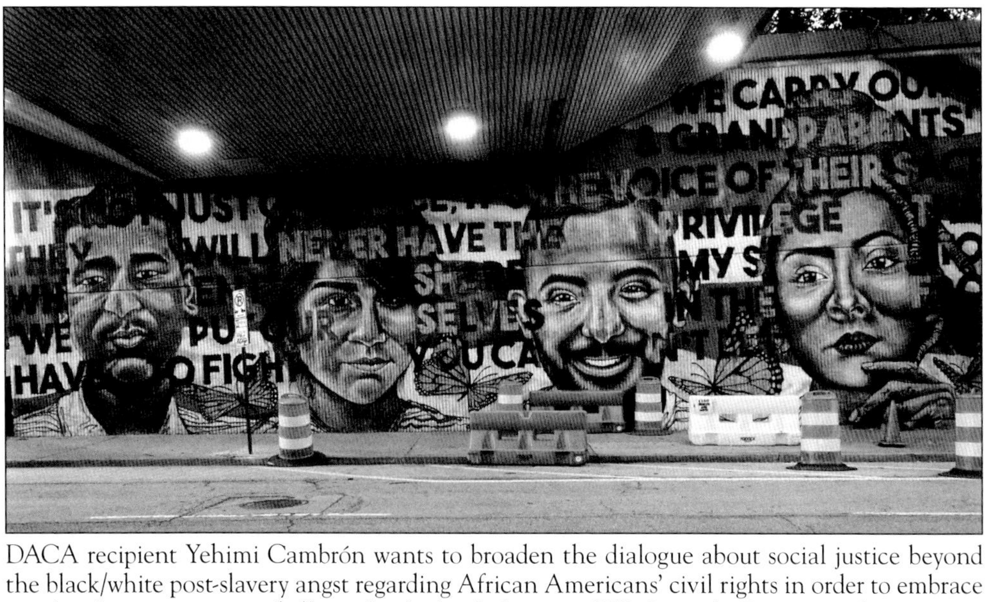

DACA recipient Yehimi Cambrón wants to broaden the dialogue about social justice beyond the black/white post-slavery angst regarding African Americans' civil rights in order to embrace equality for immigrants and all people of color. In her mural *We Carry the Dreams* are five portraits of "Dreamers," with the stripes of the American flag in the background. (RMC.)

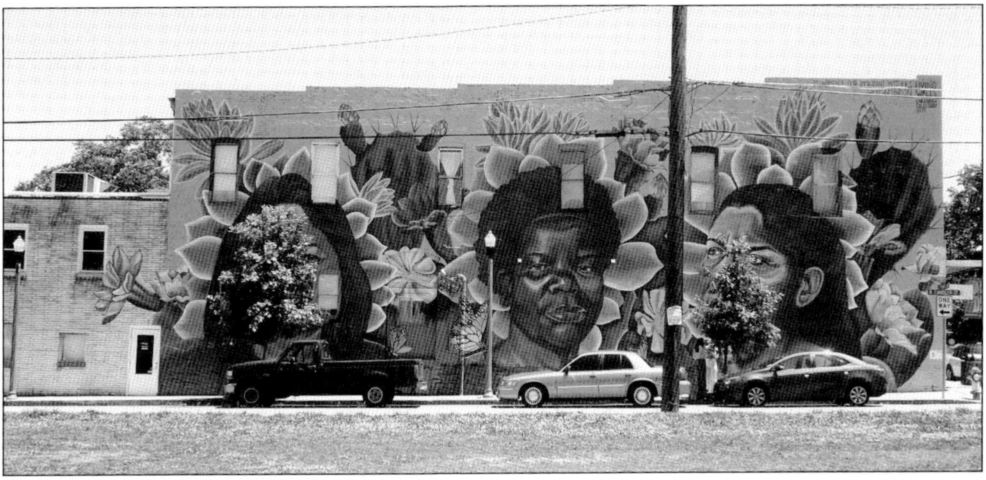

Yehimi Cambrón's mural at 302 W. Howard Avenue in Decatur titled *Monuments: Our Immigrant Mothers* illustrates three women, represented in head and shoulders portraiture and framed in decorative backgrounds of Cambrón's characteristic cactus flowers and butterflies. The mural fulfills the mission of sponsor Living Walls to create "intentional, thought-provoking public art to inspire social change and activate public spaces." (RMC.)

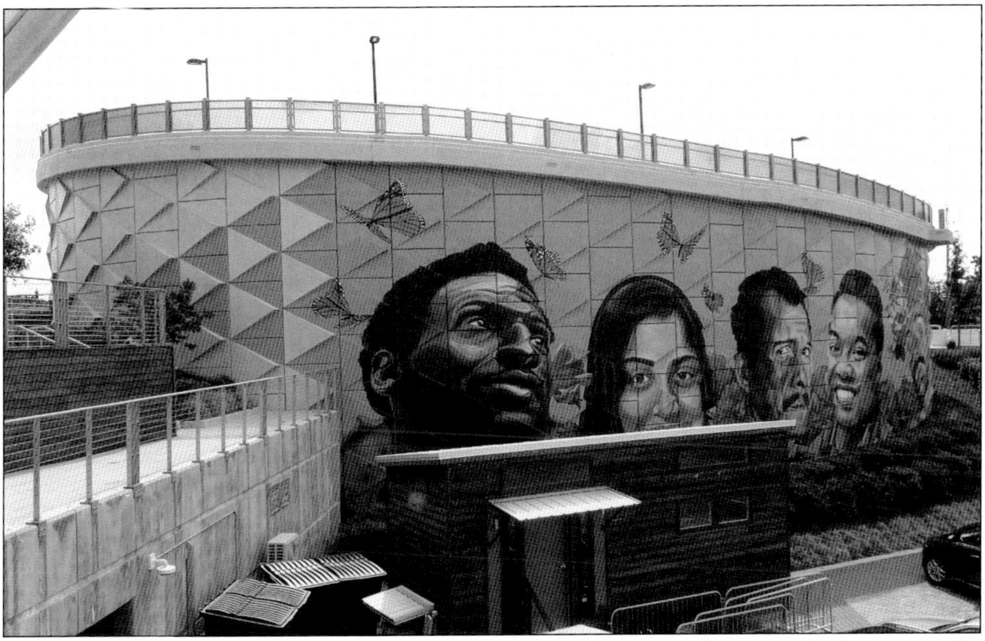

The curved wall overlooking the Home Depot Backyard at Mercedes-Benz Stadium provides the venue for Cambrón's *Faces of Atlanta's Immigrants: The Resilience of Our Community*. The DACAmented, or undocumented, people featured are, from left to right, Mamadou from Mali, Sumbul from Pakistan/Saudi Arabia, Candido from Mexico, Raymond from the Philippines, and Luis from Mexico. Each reflects "our community's grit and determination to thrive despite the limitations of their immigration status." (RMC.)

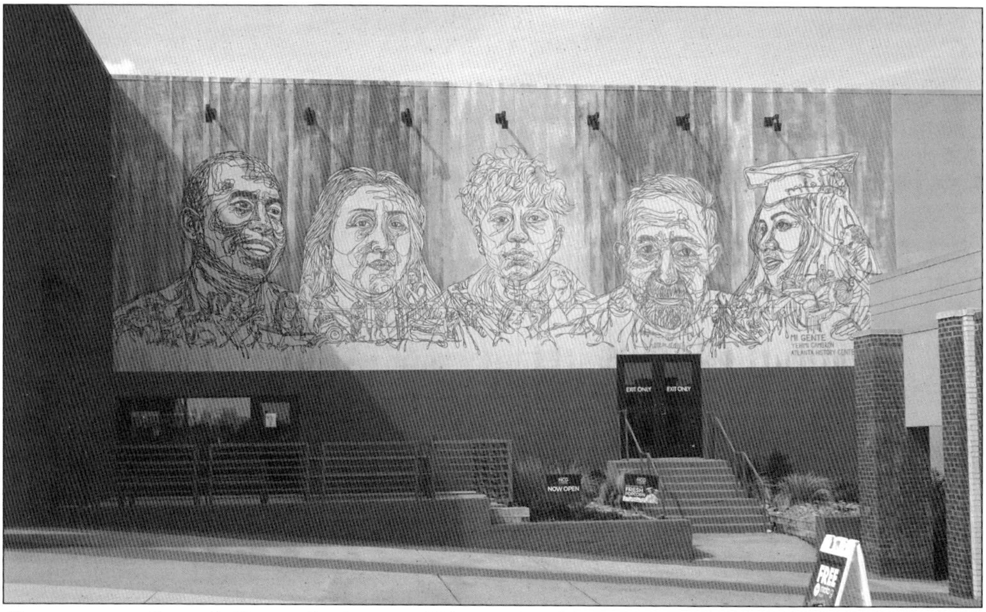

Showing excellent skill as a draftsman, Yehimi Cambrón sketched five portraits in energetic lines, with vignettes below, in a mural overlooking a major Buford Highway shopping center. The individuals, known to Cambrón and meaningful to her immigrant experience, are as diverse as the immigrant population itself. They are *Mi Gente* ("My People," as Cambrón entitles her mural) and seeks to capture "what we find beautiful and powerful about our community." (RMC.)

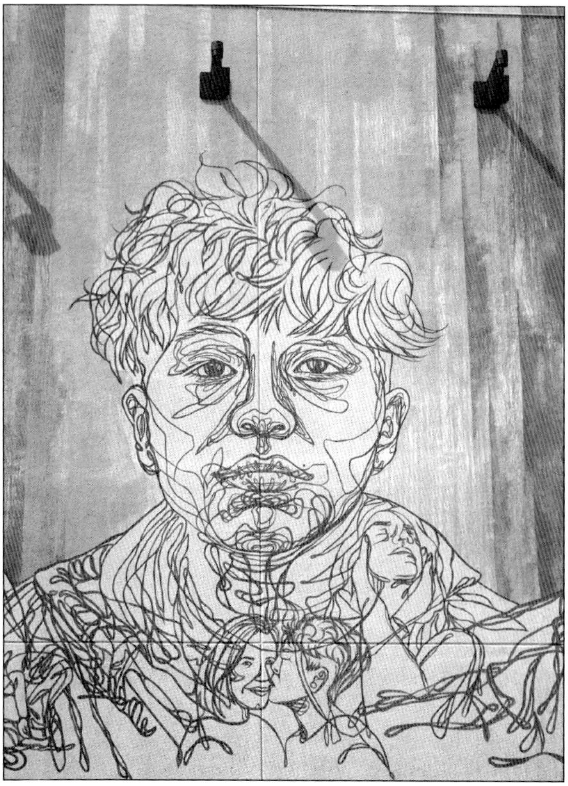

The center portrait in the Northeast Plaza mural is of Danny Cabrera (representing "Gender and Identity"), a former student of Cambrón from Cross Keys High School, where she teaches art. Both everyday people, as well as leaders, have contributed to the growth of the Atlanta community. "Painting *Mi Gente* felt like an act of gratitude to the community that welcomed me and contributed to my growth," the artist said in a press release. (RMC.)

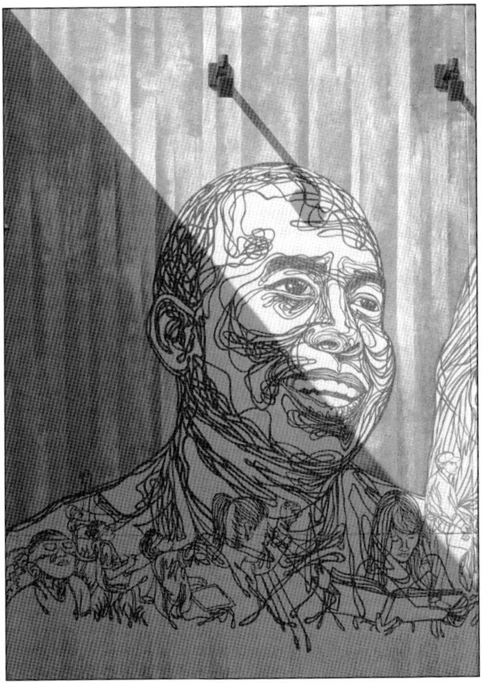

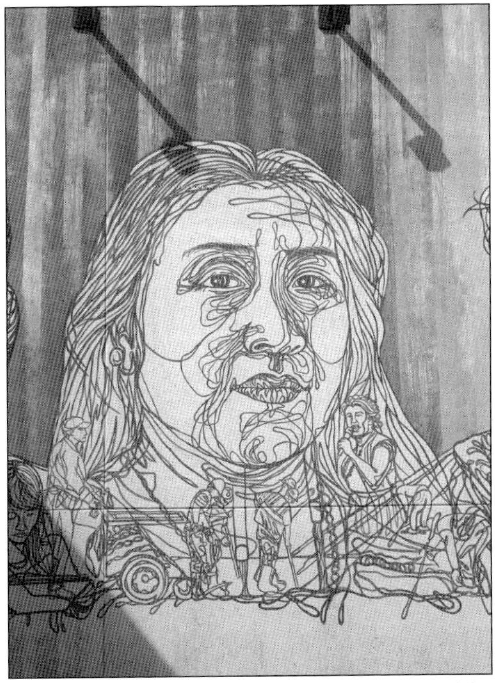

The four other likenesses in the *Mi Gente* mural are Jason Esteves, chair of the Atlanta Public Schools Board of Education (representing "Education," above left); Felipa Martinez, the mother of one of Cambrón's students at Cross Keys High School (representing "Labor," above right); Teodoro Maus, an activist and organizer who served as Mexican consul general in Georgia from 1995–2001 (representing "Political Advocacy," below left); and Arizbeth Sanchez, Freedom University's community engagement coordinator (representing "Dreamers," below right). (RMC.)

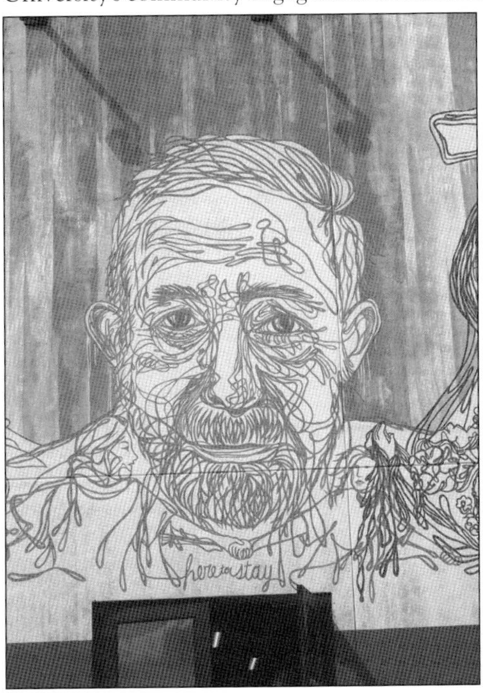

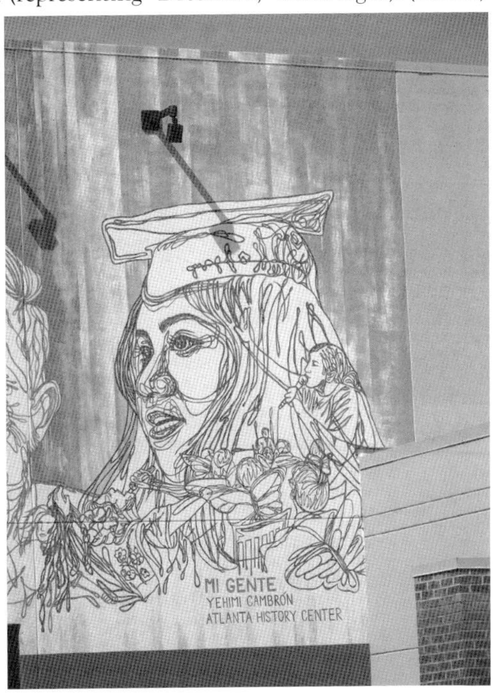

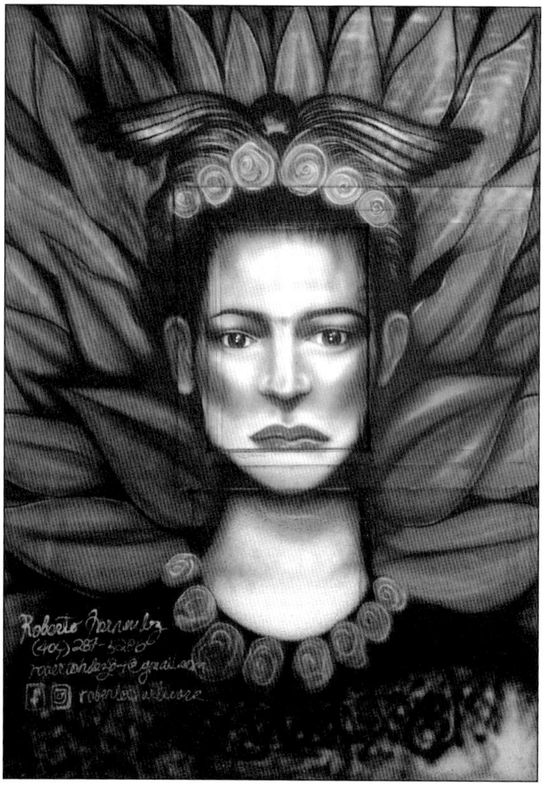

Mexican painter Frida Kahlo (1907–1954) was known for her portraits, self-portraits, and works inspired by Mexico and its pop culture. Employing a naïve folk art style, she explored questions of identity, gender, class, and race in Mexican society and thus has become an icon for Chicanos, the feminist movement, and the LGBTQ+ movement. Her work has been embraced internationally as especially representative of Mexican national and indigenous traditions. In Atlanta (and throughout the United States), the best-known Mexican holiday is Cinco de Mayo, which celebrates a key victory over France in 1862, during the Franco-Mexican War. The Atlanta restaurant Las Margaritas marks the day with a Frida Kahlo mural competition. The portrait of Kahlo (left) by Acapulco, Mexico–born Roberto Hernandez recalls the colors and frontal pose of many of Kahlo's portraits. *Dreaming of Frida* (below) was painted by @eyemassive. (RMC.)

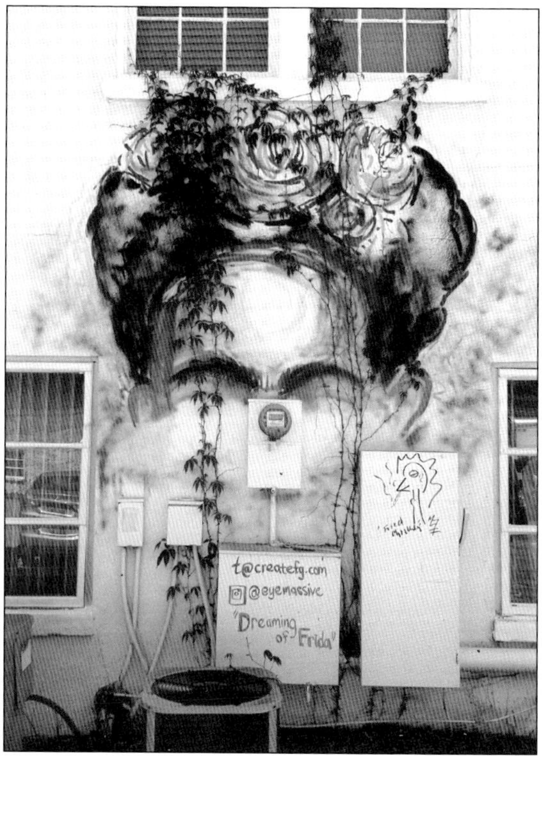

Roberto Hernandez also pursues a career as a body painter and face painter, appearing at local festivals and fashion venues, and it may be said that he has "face painted" the entry gate and walls of Fiesta Plaza with their own cosmetic and illusionist effects. Located opposite 4075 Buford Highway, the gates are accented by ram's horns, an elephant, heads of other animals, and sea creatures, some decorated as a mask and painted to simulate bas relief. An armadillo crawls across a shop façade, while an octopus, bunny, and other festively decorated animals accent the gate posts. Hernandez has indicated that the mural was inspired by brightly colored Mexican folk art sculptures of fantastical (fantasy/mythical) creatures called Alebrijes from the state of Oaxaca City. (RMC.)

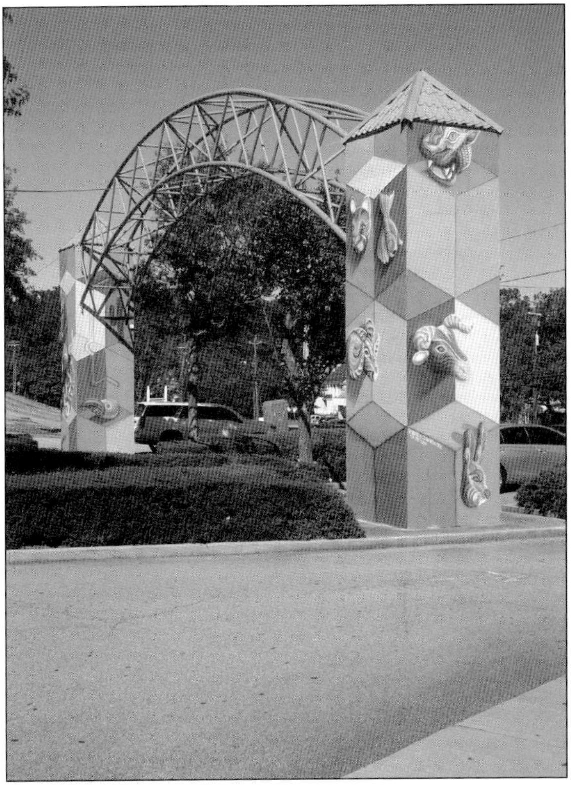

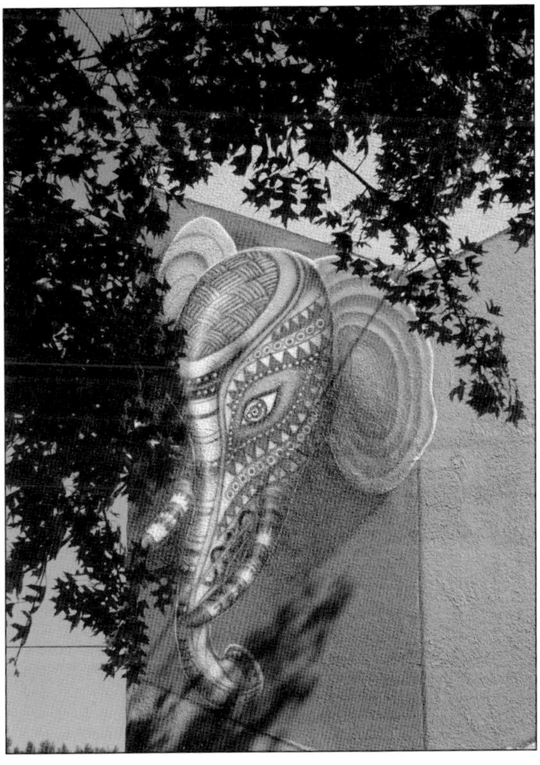

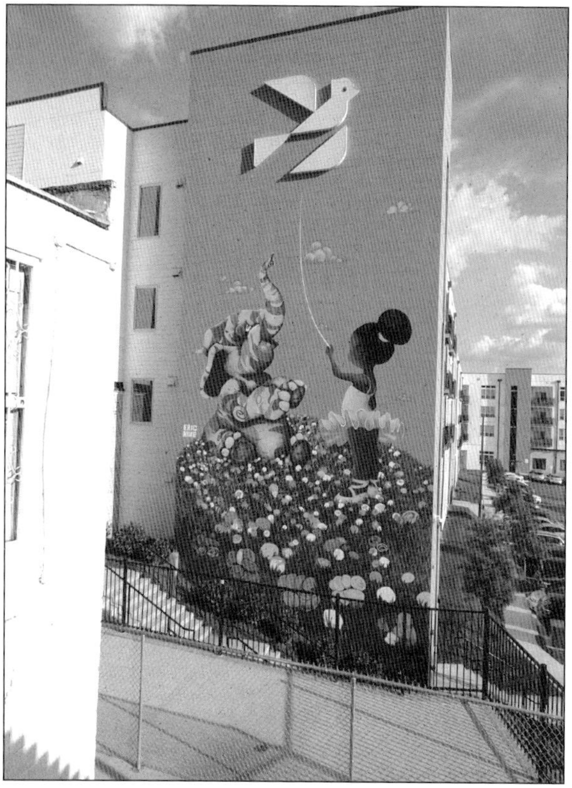

Two striking murals by Eric9 (also known as Eric Lopez, 1984–), a Puerto Rican American multimedia artist, are noted for their flowing floral displays, as foreground for a young African American girl at 1047 Boulevard SE (left), and a trail of transmogrified hair representing the human imagination and thoughts that transcend superficial differences in a 30-foot mural at 239 Peters Street SW in Castleberry (below). In the first mural, the young child flies a kite, formed as a white dove to symbolize peace and hope; she is imaginatively posed with one of Eric9's characteristically multicolored elephants, a signature motif that pops up in his other work around town. His murals celebrate the beauty of diversity and convey to neighborhoods throughout Atlanta messages of equality and inclusion presented with a charm and innocence uniquely his own. (RMC.)

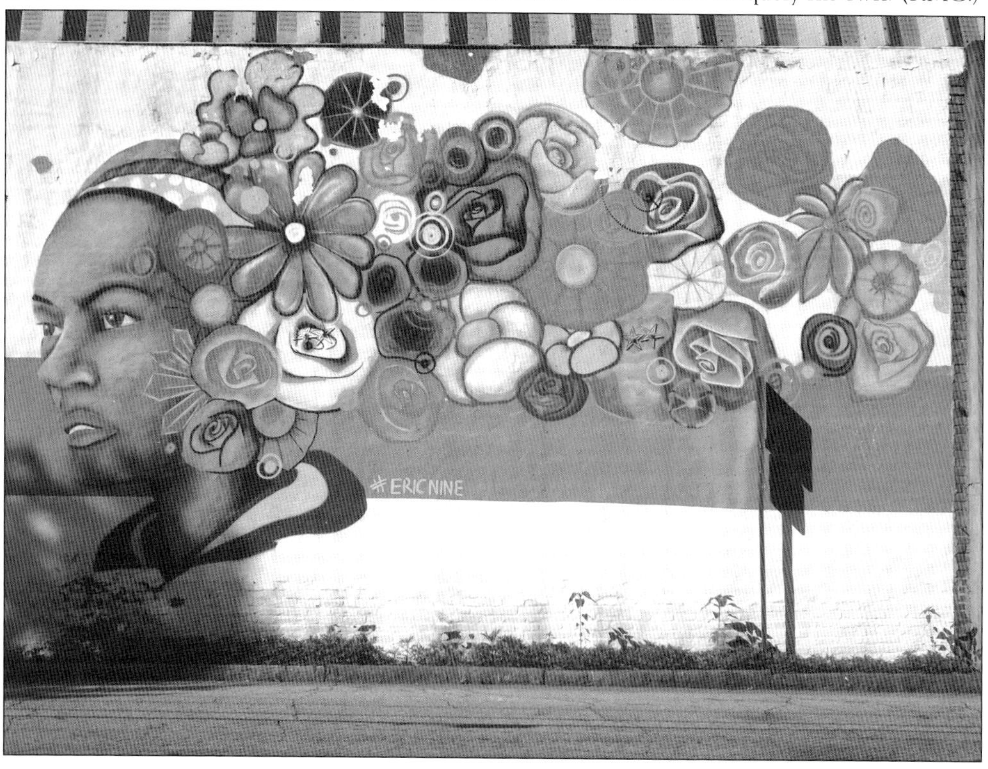

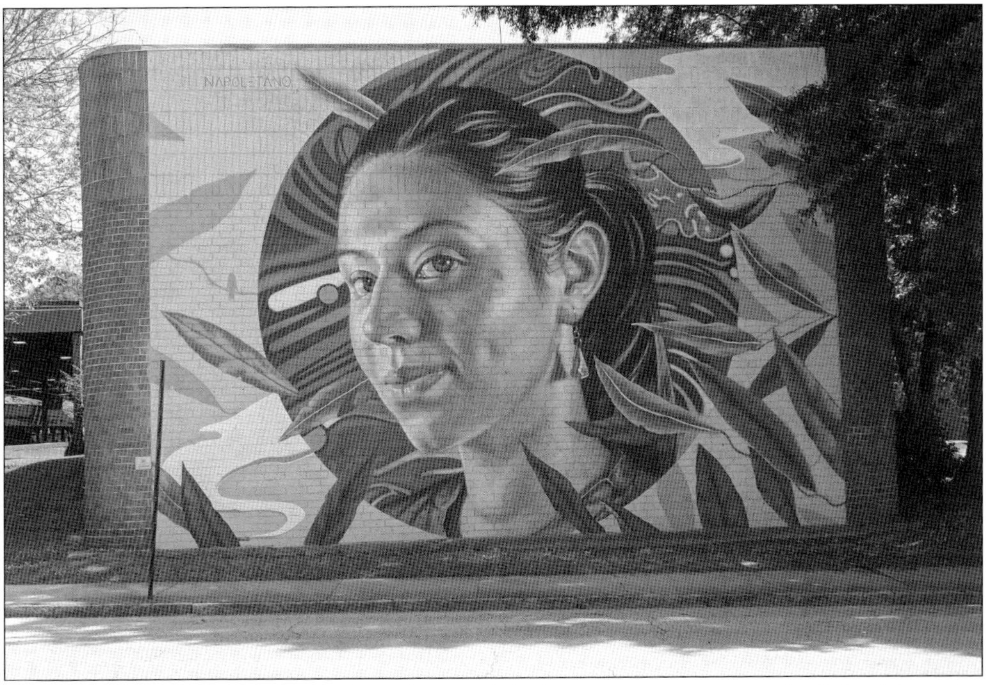

Charlotte artist Nick Napoletano (1990–) created this hyperrealistic portrait of a Columbian artist raised in Atlanta, enframed in a circle of blue swirling lines; the rondelle is set in a bubblegum pink background with floating green leaves. Her convincingly realistic pose captures attention and suggests a universality of the human condition. Napoletano's training in tempera and oil painting prompts his artistic styling that has been compared to Mannerism and the High Renaissance. (RMC.)

Cuban American artist Ernesto Torres (1987–) of Buckhead Murals and his wife, Lenia Castro (1990–) painted a photorealistic portrait of a woman titled *Hybrid*. She looks through a matrix of Spanish/Mexican tiles ornamenting a streetscape just south of the Five Points MARTA station. Ernesto's brother Alexi Torres (1976–) founded Buckhead Murals in 2003, but when his art turned to smaller-scaled, oil-on-canvas work, Ernesto and Lenia Castro took the reins and began to produce more commercial murals and hand-painted signs. (RMC.)

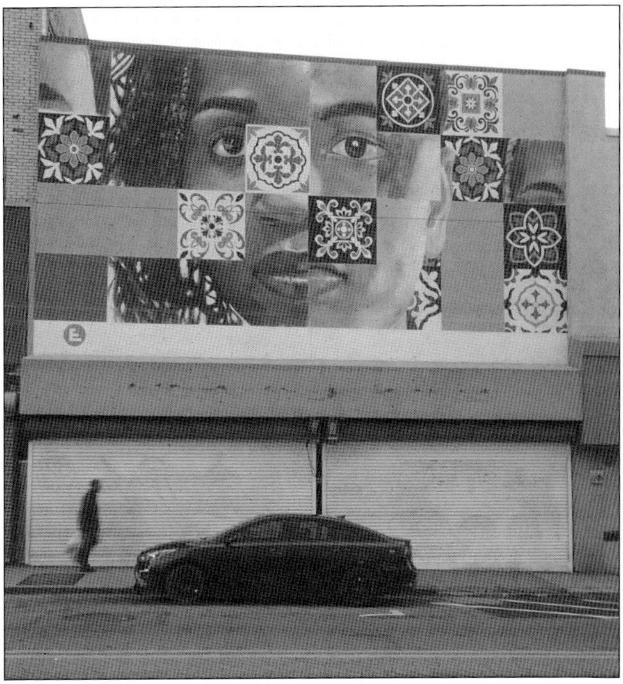

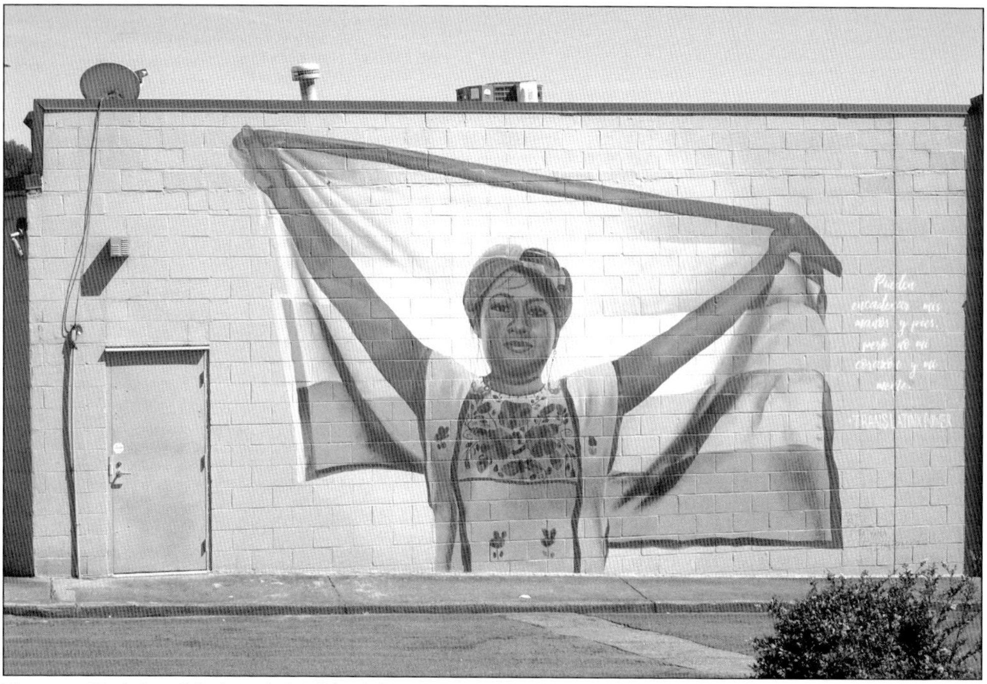

Tatyana Fazlalizadeh (1985–), a black/Iranian activist artist born in Oklahoma City, is best known for her global street art series *Stop Telling Women to Smile*, addressing sexual harassment in public spaces. Her art concerns itself with the daily oppressive experiences of marginalized people, as in her mural portrait (above) of Estrella, a Latinx trans woman activist in Atlanta. The mural, executed for the 2017 Living Walls, the City Speaks conference, is inscribed with (in Spanish and paraphrasing Kahlil Gibran) "They can chain my hands and feet but not my heart and my mind. TRANS LATINX POWER." In an underpass of the Beltline (below), Guatemalan-born LGBTQ activist artist Maite Nazario (2000–) depicts Kenie and Dionne in an embrace, part of her series of drawings/paintings of local queer couples of color. Nazario considers Atlanta a "refuge for all queer people in the South." (RMC.)

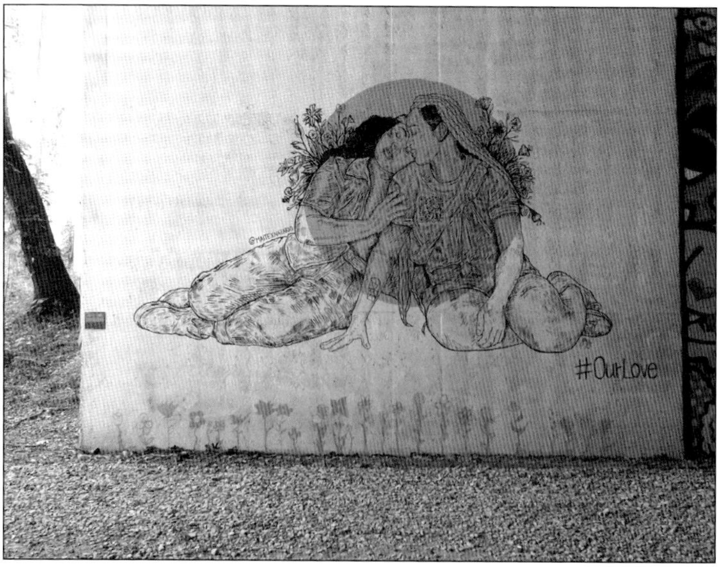

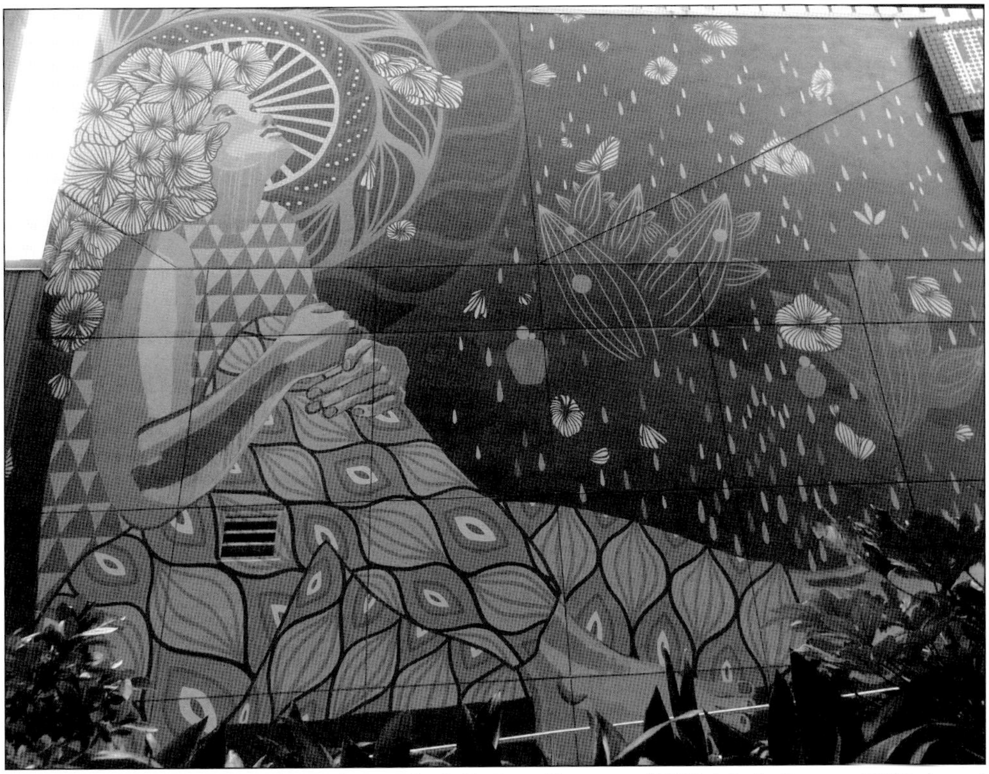

Chicana artist Laura Vela (1991–) joined Molly Rose Freeman (1987–), Lela Brunet (1985–), and Lauren Pallotta Stumberg (1981–) to create *Aurora* at Colony Square, a tribute to the Roman goddess of Dawn (above). The collaborating team fills most of the space with the colorful textile patterns of Aurora's flowing skirt washed in the light of daybreak, while the sister of Luna and Sol (moon and sun) awakens. This is the magical time between waking and dreaming, a symbol of hope, transcendence. In 2018, the same team created *Persephone Rising* (below) their largest mural to date painted on the wall of the Edge. Visible from the Edgewood Avenue overpass at the Beltline, the mural mixes pattern with realistic and abstract elements, depicting the goddess of spring rising from the underworld—everywoman, representing abundance and female strength. (RMC.)

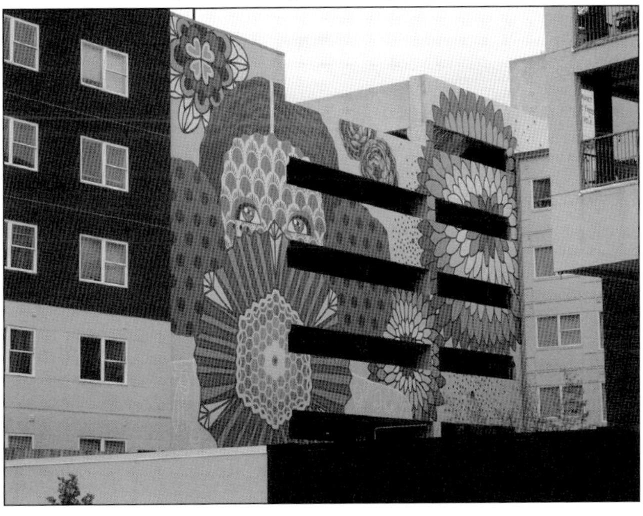

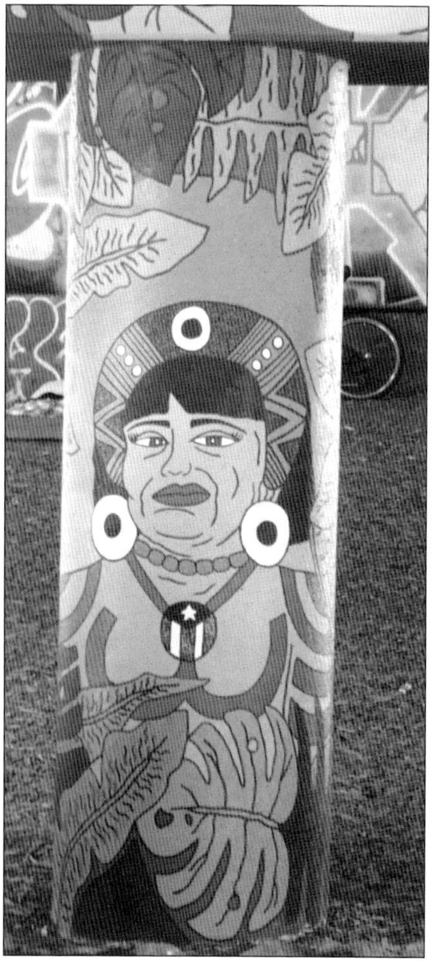

The art of the Caribbean inspires Lisette Correa (1984–), also known as Arrrtaddict, who celebrates the Taino people in her 2021 *Somos Borincanos* mural on the Beltline at Edgewood Avenue. While a concrete underpass may appear an inauspicious venue for art, Miranda Kyle of the Beltline views bridges as connections, points, and spaces for wayfinding and destinations. Moreover, the challenge for artists is to "push the boundaries of mural art and . . . flex their creative muscles and rise to the challenge of painting on complex architectural forms." Correa paints the overpass walls, underpass retaining walls, and concrete support piers; on a structural beam, she writes, "To be grounded in who we are today, we must first remember our roots." Somos Borincanos is dedicated to the artist's grandmother, whose portrait is seen in the center of three bridge support pillars (left). (RMC.)

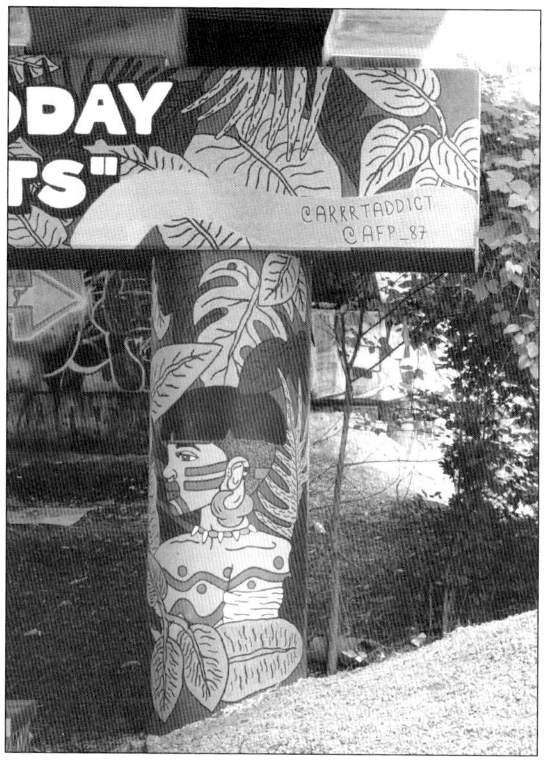

Somos Borincanos documents the all-female Taino tribe on La Isla de Borikén, a people indigenous to Puerto Rico and other Caribbean islands. Not only is the Pre-Columbian tribe not extinct, but the artist herself (she learned from a DNA test) is 12.7 percent Taino. She has painted the entire bridge to honor her ancestors. The strong tropical colors of the figures on the piers and overhead contrast with the black and white linear figures and symbols on a lower sidewalk retaining wall. The whole is a remarkable tribute to the Taino. Correa wants people in every city "to know the history of my people"; in New York, for instance, she recently painted a mural of Anacaona, the Taino Cacique who led her tribe and protected her child from the Spanish colonizers and would-be abductors by strapping the child to her leg. (RMC.)

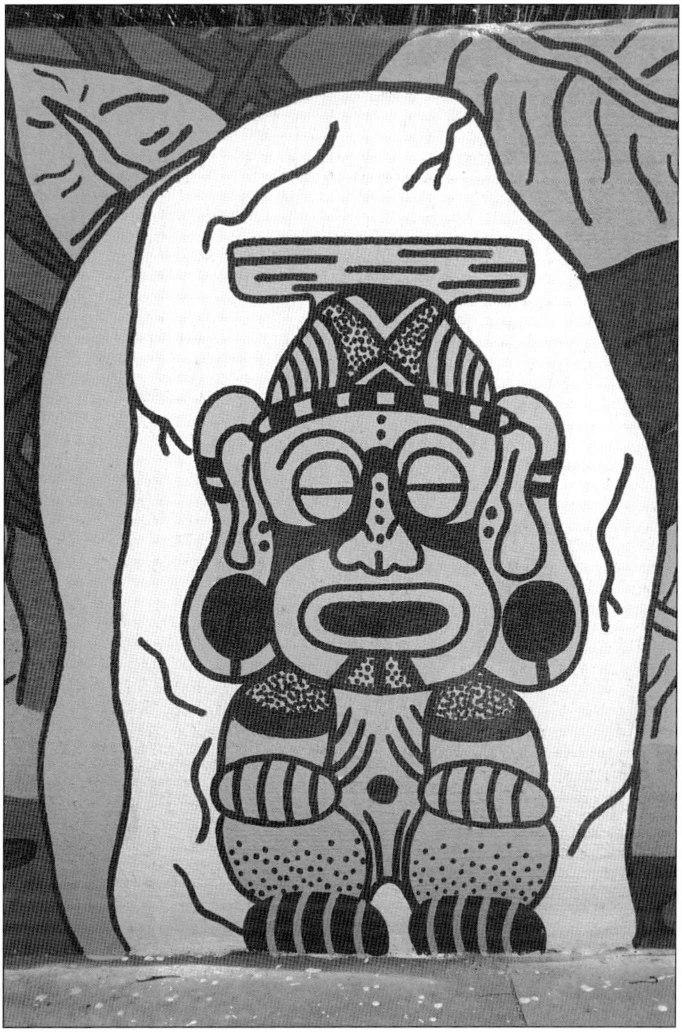

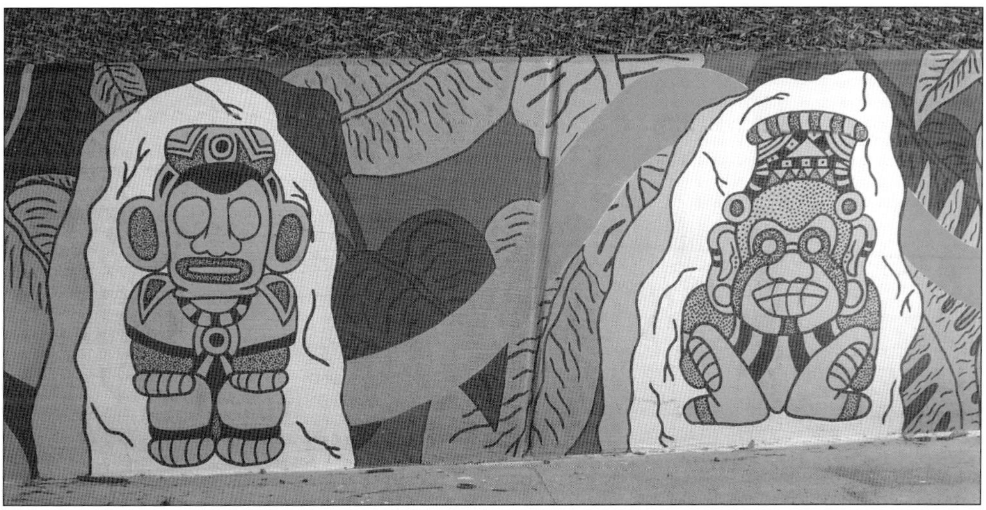

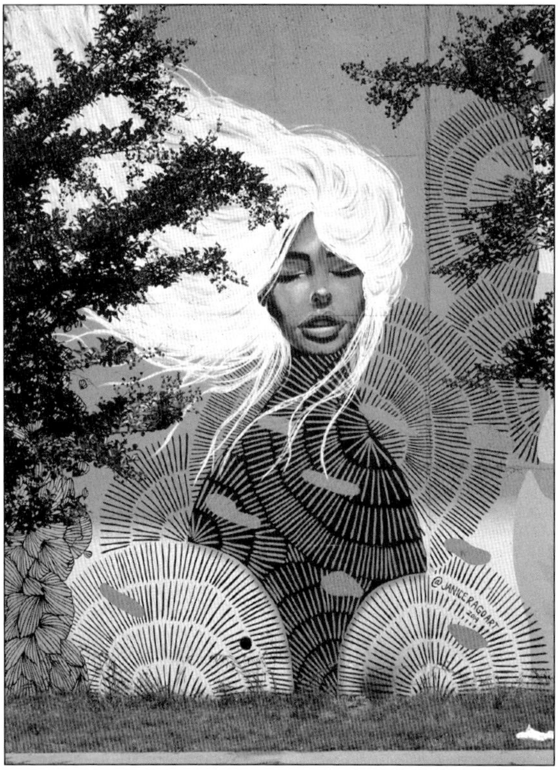

Janice Rago (1987–) was born in Hawaii and, as a youth, moved frequently. Her art reflects this mobility in its interest in Pacific cultures, Europe, and South Georgia. Her interest in feminine beauty is reflected in this striking mural on Wylie Street. She also recently completed a large floral mural on the south wall of Midtown Cleaners opposite Manual's Tavern, a charming bouquet to welcome the arrival of spring. (RMC.)

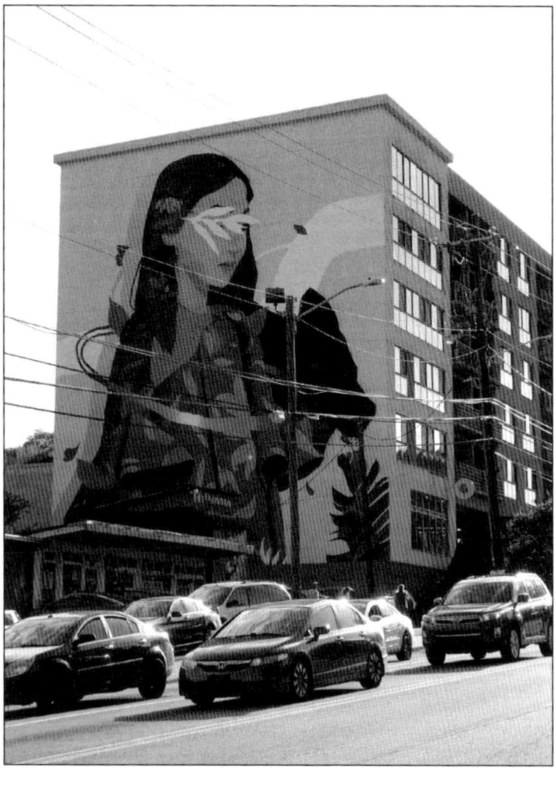

Over a seven-day period of sometimes inclement weather, the Madrid-born artist Sabek (1985–) painted the large mural titled *The Keep* on the side of the seven-story Oakland Park Condos building on Memorial Drive. Completed for the Outerspace Festival (curated by ABV Gallery), the mural represents the symbiotic relationship between nature and humans. (RMC.)

Native Americans are occasionally represented in Atlanta street art, at locations that used to be part of the Creek and Cherokee Nations. In 2018, several artists of Atlanta's Pillars Project painted murals on exhaust pipes (boxes) at Underground Atlanta, intended to showcase culture, diversity, and togetherness. The boisterous *Native Tongues* (right) by C. Flux Sing (also known as Craig Singleton, 1976–) was one of these. A rendition of Indian history of a different character is visible in the Lawton/White Streets underpass mural painted in 2009 by Louisiana artist Malaika Favorite (1949–). The vibrantly colored mural presents a landscape of West End's history from the land's occupation by Native Americans to the coming of the railroad and white settlement to Uncle Remus stories, each vignette overlaid with juxtapositions of scale, animal and bird profiles, and even a hint of influence from Marc Chagall's or Ben Shahn's dream imagery. (RMC.)

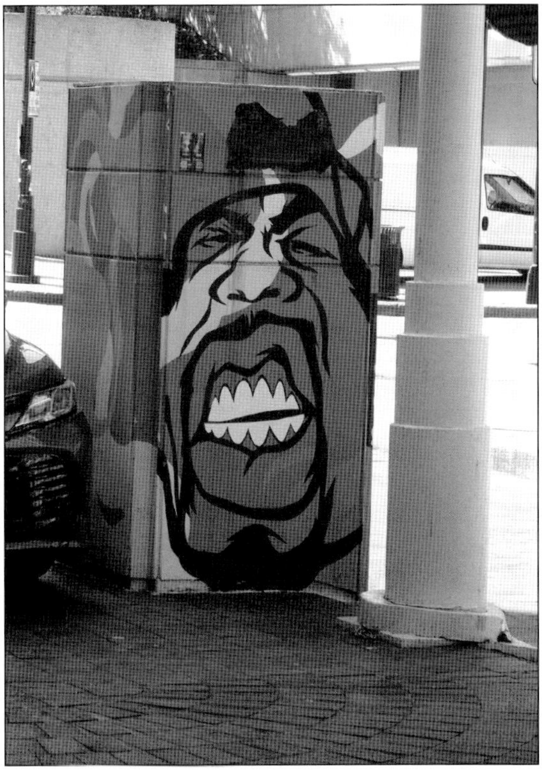

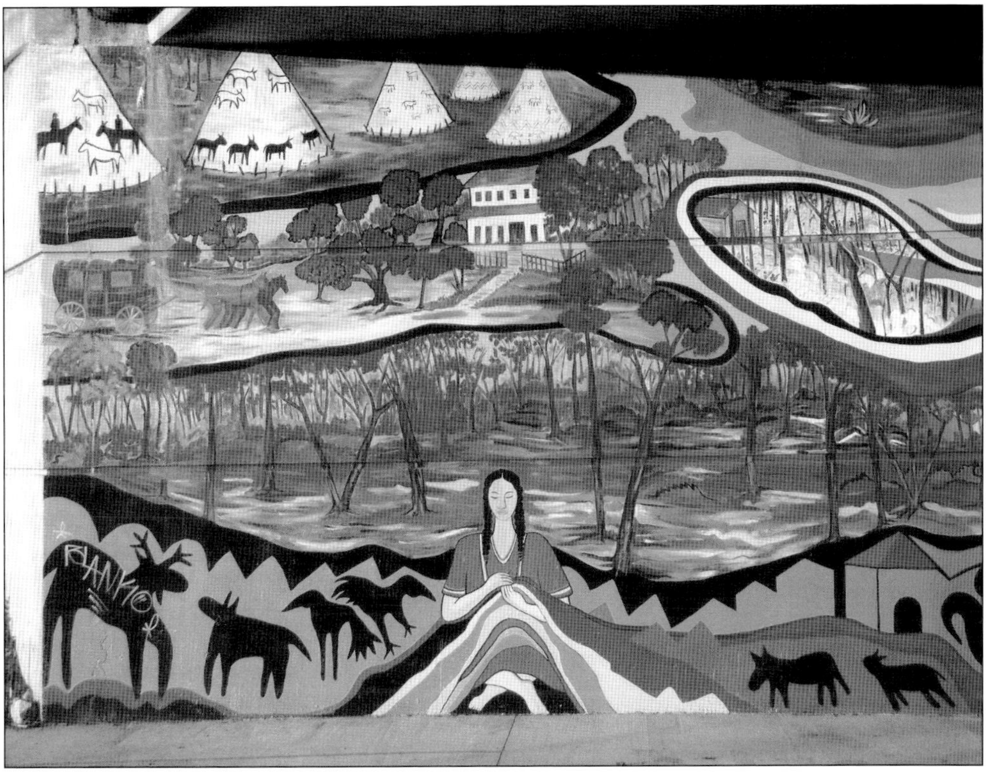

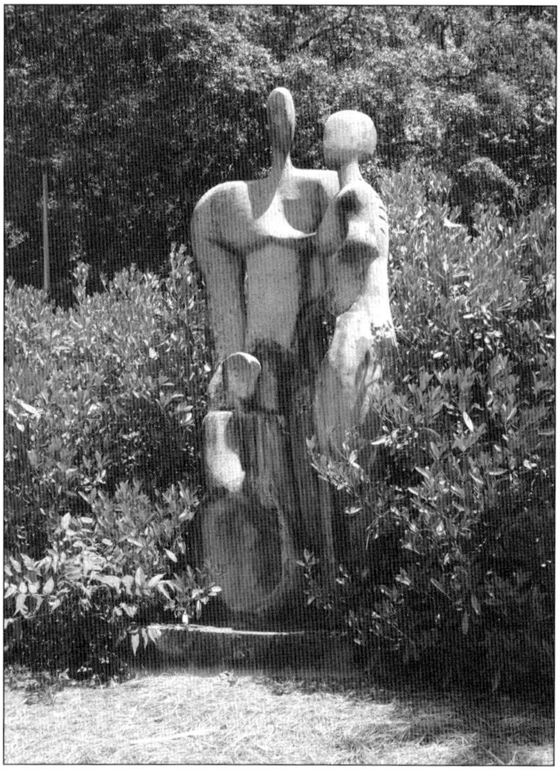

La Familia De Pie, or Standing Family, is a 1969 sculpture by English sculptor Elena Laverón (1938–). Nobel Prize laureate Mario Vargas Llosa (Literature in 2010) suggests "that the implacable dichotomy that separates matter from spirit is reconciled in Laverón's sculpture, with clear reminiscences of Picasso and [Henry] Moore (and primitive art)." Located on Piedmont Avenue at Renaissance Parkway, the sculpture is made of fiberglass, granite aggregate, and synthetic concrete surfacing. (RMC.)

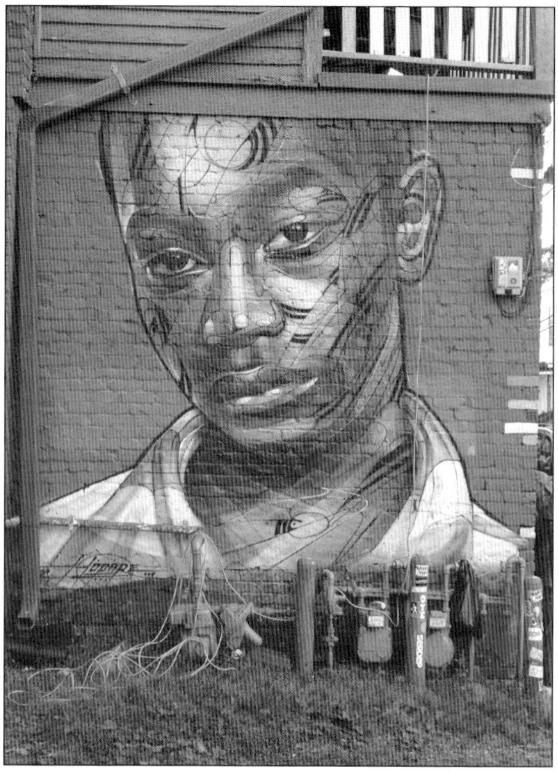

The work of other international artists is also represented in Atlanta's recent public art. Alexandre Monteiro (1989–), also known as Hopare, is a former graffitist and now enjoys a global reputation as a talented and sought-after Parisian street artist. Tucked away almost without notice on the side of Little's Food Store in Cabbagetown is one of Hopare's characteristic portraits of a young man. (RMC.)

Hopare's mural *Symphony* appears the work of a master modernist and certainly is one of the most distinctive murals in Atlanta. His blend of figural art and abstraction is here given monumental scale. It immeasurably enlivens the streetscape and east building elevations of Peachtree Center, displaying sweeping and freehand black lines in a powerful expression of abstract art. The whole mural is black and white with yellow highlights, and the kinetic energy is exhilarating. Large charcoal delineated faces peer through street trees at the north end of the avenue before the modernist scratchpad tapers off at the corner intersection. The art is both monumental canvas and somehow very much "of" the architecture; certainly, its movement responds to the passing traffic of vehicles, demanding of pedestrians, by contrast, to stop and experience street artistry at its very best. (RMC.)

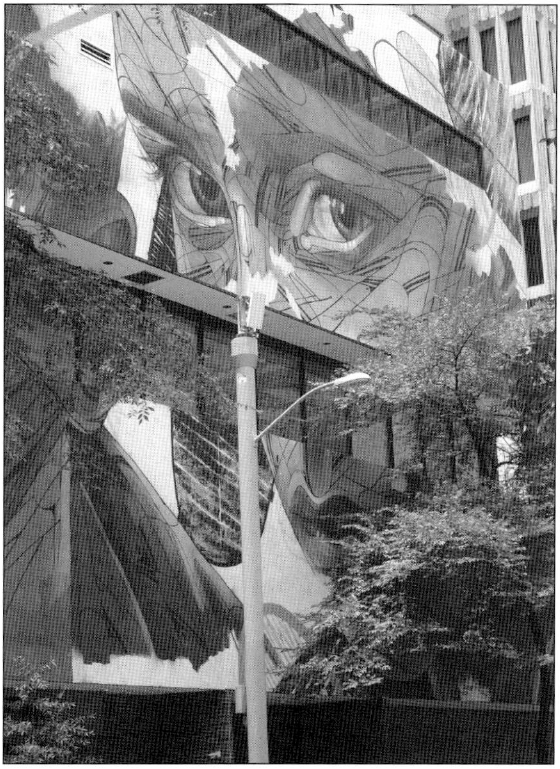

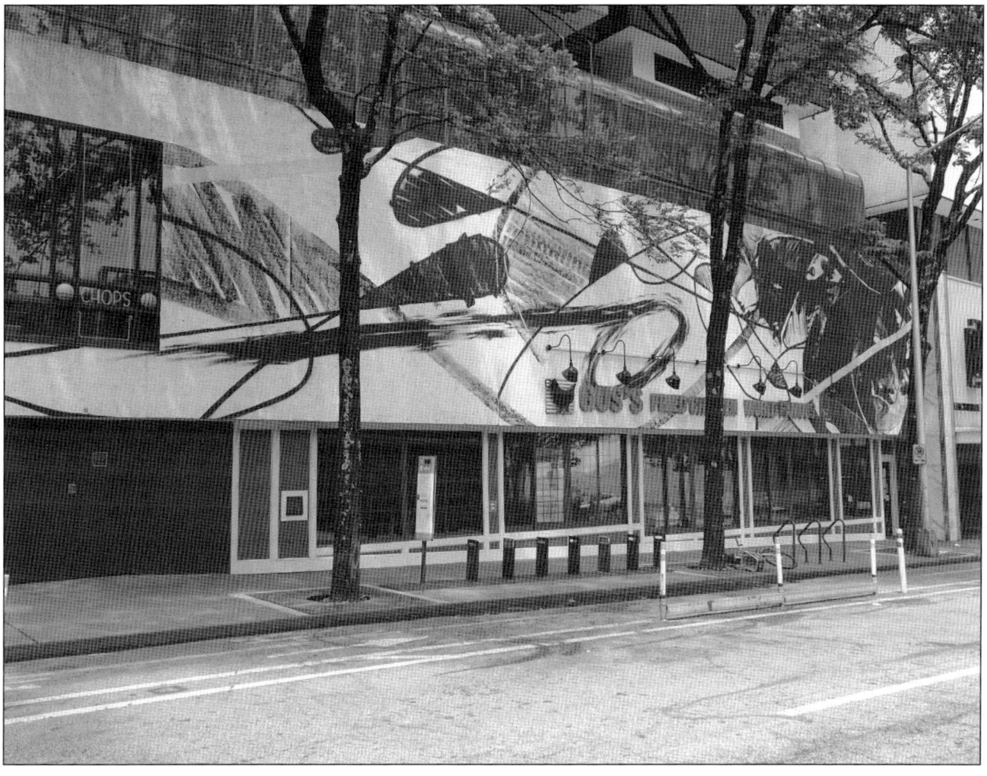

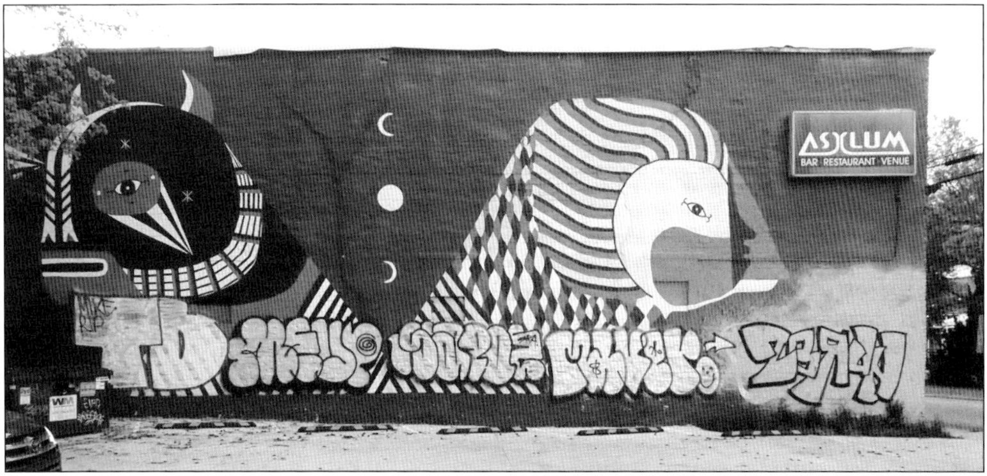

The work of Brazilian artist Fefe Talavera (1979–) is featured at the Asylum Bar Building in East Atlanta Village. Talavera was born and still lives in São Paulo, raised as a half-Mexican, half-Brazilian native. Her work (frequently collages) is inspired by Mayan or Aztec mythology and its Mexican heritage and is best known for its monsters made from letters cut from posters/advertisements found in the streets. (RMC.)

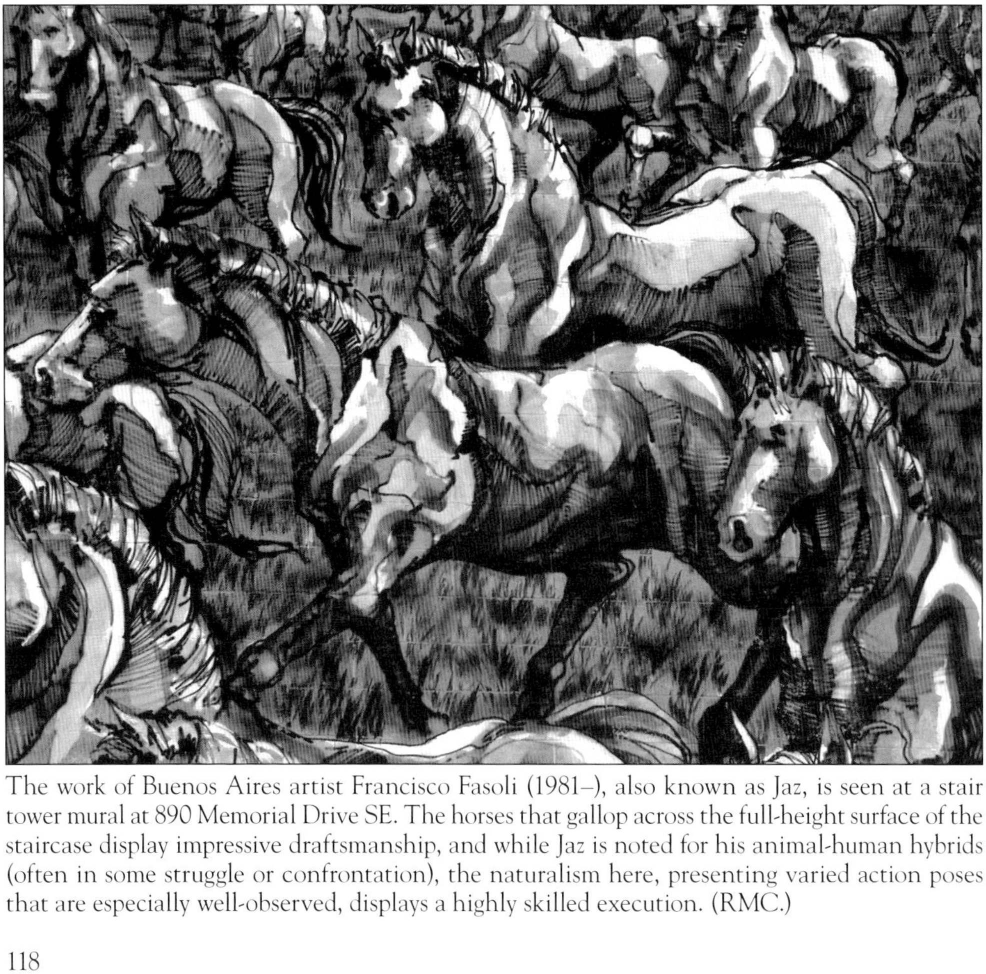

The work of Buenos Aires artist Francisco Fasoli (1981–), also known as Jaz, is seen at a stair tower mural at 890 Memorial Drive SE. The horses that gallop across the full-height surface of the staircase display impressive draftsmanship, and while Jaz is noted for his animal-human hybrids (often in some struggle or confrontation), the naturalism here, presenting varied action poses that are especially well-observed, displays a highly skilled execution. (RMC.)

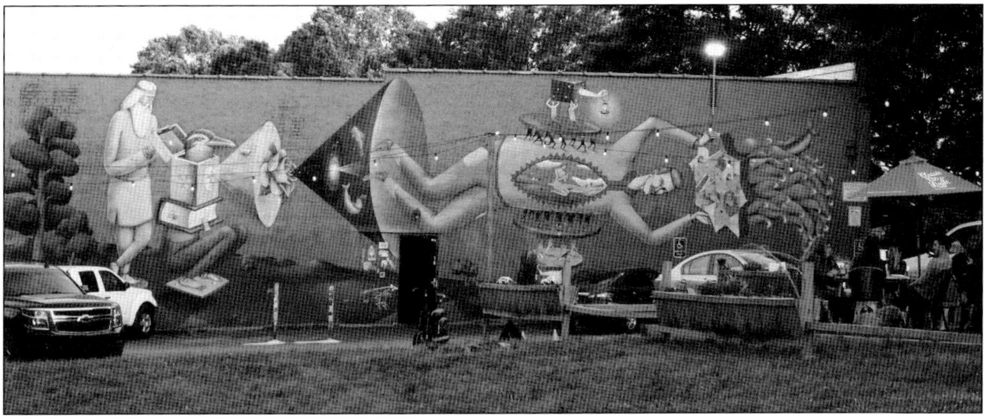

The north wall mural at Argosy in East Atlanta is by Ukrainian duo Interesni Kazki, two artists who collaborated between 2005 and 2016, although today work independently. Aleksei Bordusov, also known as AEC, and Vladimir Manzhos, also known as Waone, are from Kyiv and have painted here what is certainly Atlanta's most surrealistic mural. Inspired by science, religion, mythology, cosmology, and myth, Interesni Kazki's murals (as the name translates) suggest "interesting fairytales." (RMC.)

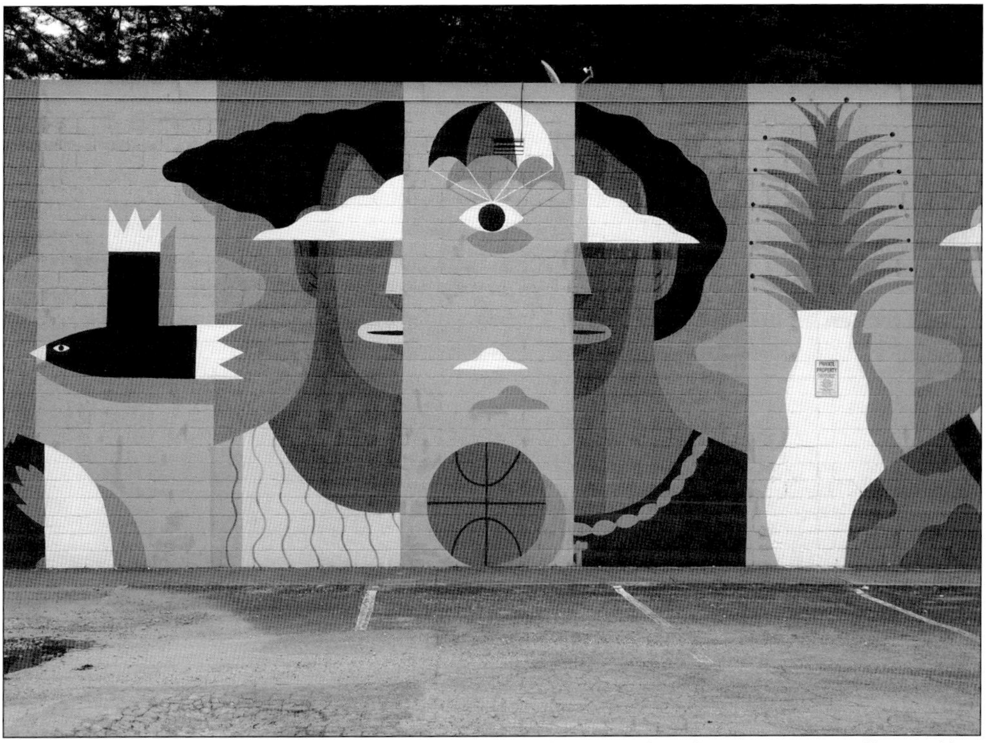

Agostino Iacurci (1986–) was born in Foggia, Italy, and lives and works in Rome. His flat profiles, frontal half figures, and hard-edged compositions are recognizable and may be Atlanta's only example of a kind of deconstructionist art. The row of paired and decomposed figures, vases, birds, and other objects is both mysterious and poetic while the style is uniquely personal. The 150-foot mural on Campbellton Road is called *Walter.* (RMC.)

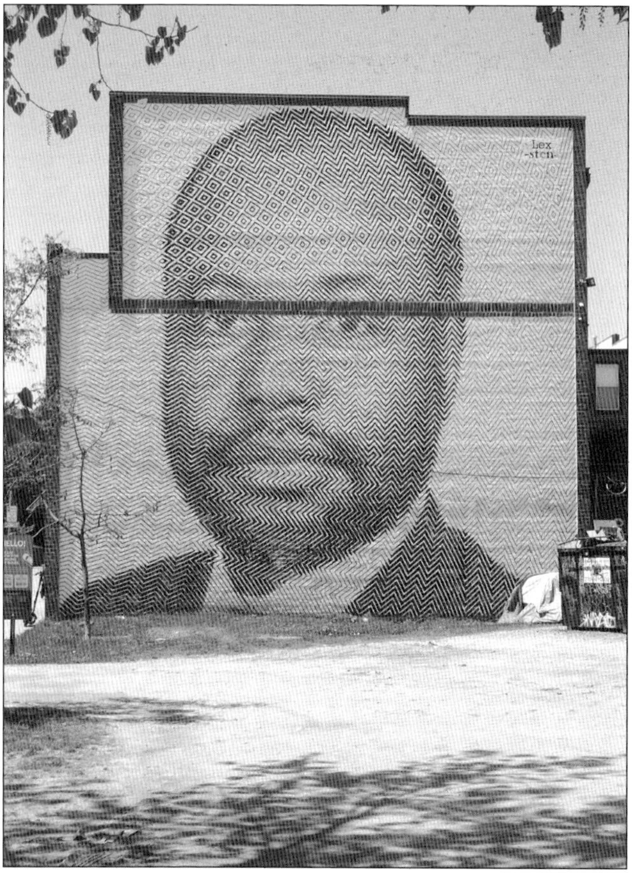

The "stencil poster technique" employed by Milan artists Sten and Lex for this 2012 mural creates a tight linear composition in black and white, which requires the eye to read the mural at a distant vantage point in order to see it as a portrait. The subject is unknown. Near view, like a microscopic view of the dots in a Lichtenstein or pointillist painting, reveal mere clusters of tight lines. (RMC.)

The Greek artist Stathus Sebalious (1992–), also known as Insane51, calls his unique form of street art "double exposure 3D." A pioneer of 3D mural art, he uses a palette of reds and blues so that an observer, wearing 3D glasses (one red glass and one blue), experiences a three-dimensional effect, and if the art is viewed through only one colored lens, some elements of the painting disappear. (RMC.)

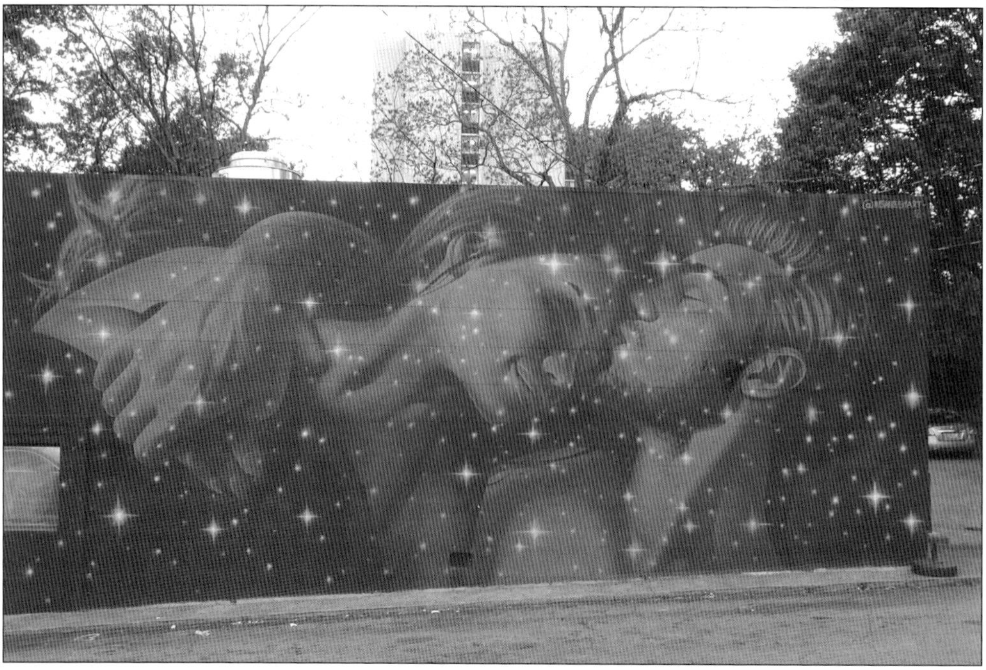

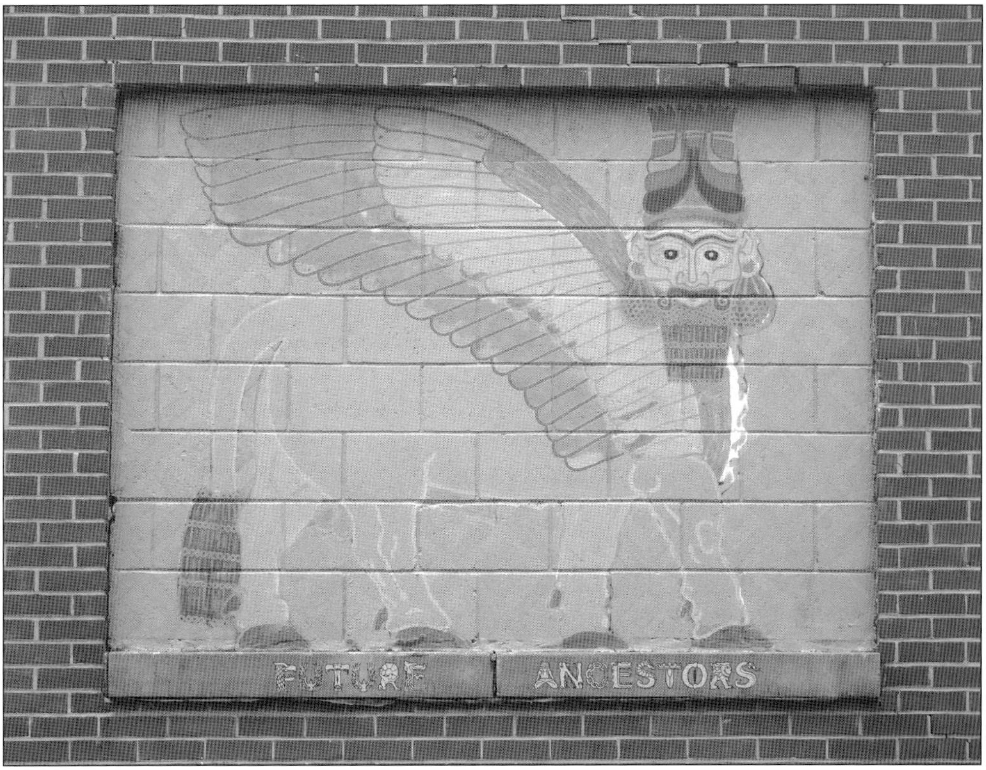

While Atlanta does not have a decorative neo-Assyrian monument as extravagant as Morgan Walls and Clements's 1929–1930 Samson Tyre and Rubber Company in Los Angeles, the 2015 mural at 55 Ormond Street is Assyrian-inspired. *The Guardian* is by Carl Janes (1973–), also known as Future Ancestors. The general term for winged guardian figures is geniuses; winged bulls with human heads are called lamassu. (RMC.)

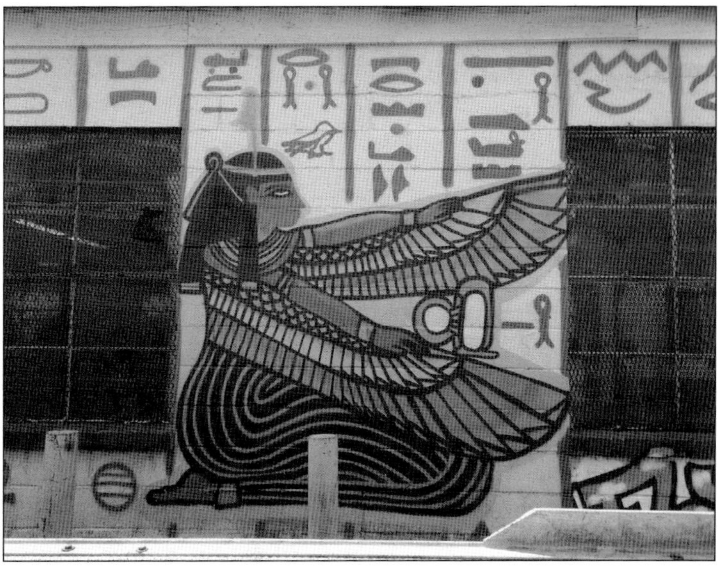

Mural art imagery inspired by wall paintings from ancient Egyptian tombs is in evidence at 226 Flat Shoals Avenue SE in a mural by Taji, an artist about whom virtually nothing is known. The presentation of figures with the body presented frontally and with head in profile, the winged goddess Isis (here), and background hieroglyphics define the borrowed style and content. (RMC.)

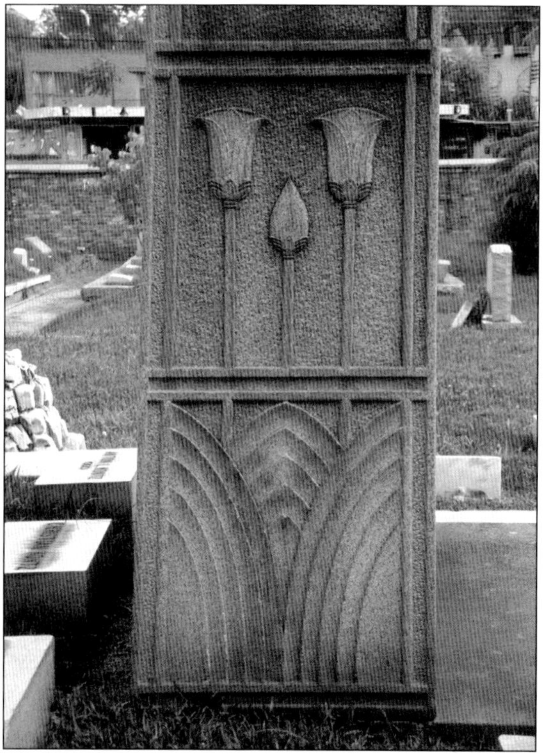

Nineteenth-century cemetery gates, such as that at the pioneer, picturesque movement's Mount Auburn Cemetery in Cambridge, Massachusetts, or the pylon at Grove Street Cemetery in New Haven, Connecticut, employed Egyptian architectural forms to symbolize death, immortality, and eternity associated with the ancient pharaohs and their mortuary tombs. At Oakland Cemetery in Atlanta, the Koontz tomb is unique in adopting the same formal and decorative language. (RMC.)

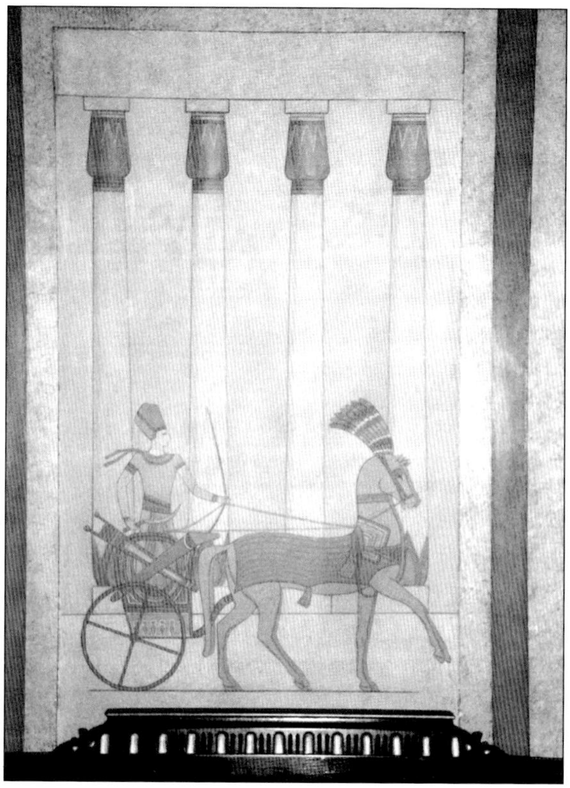

While Islamic or Moorish motives inform the architecture both inside and out at the Fox Theatre in Atlanta, Egyptian ornament on walls, furniture, and lighting fixtures serve as decoration in the Egyptian Ballroom, the men's lower lounge (seen here), and the ladies' upper/mezzanine lounge in the theater. This expression of Egyptomania in the 1929 theater responded to the discovery of King Tutankhamun's tomb and its art by Howard Carter in 1922. (RMC.)

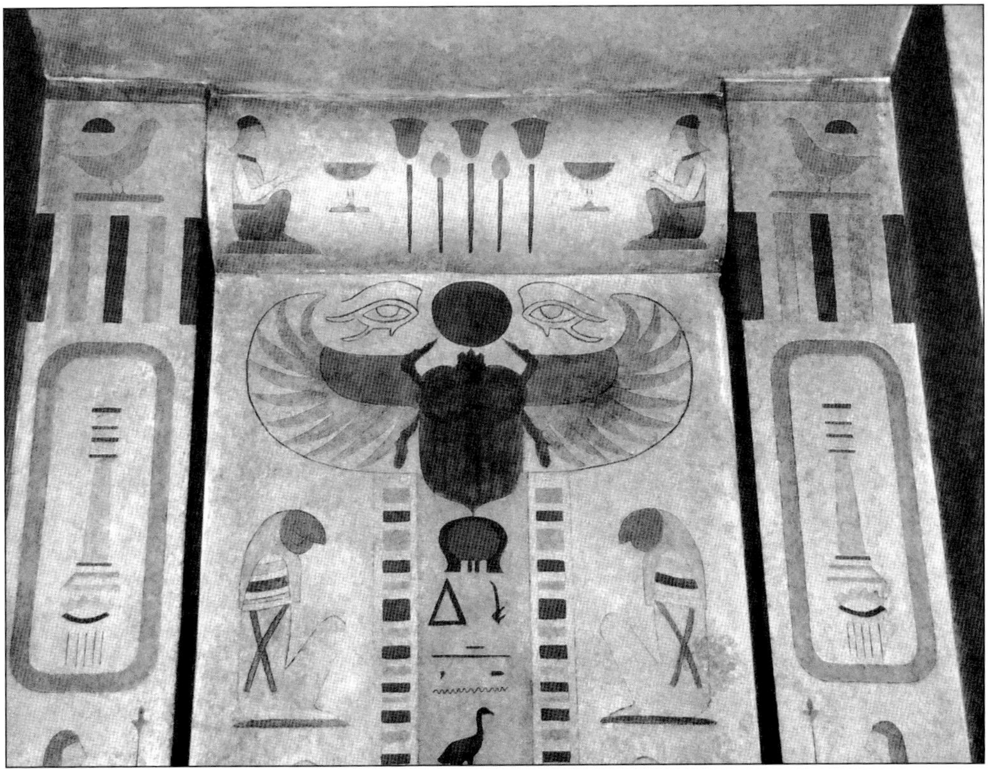

The ladies' upper lounge of the Fox Theatre is a masterpiece of period Egyptian Revival where ladies' cosmetic tables are adorned with flanking sphinxes, seating furniture and tall-back chairs are thrones in the adjacent mezzanine, and wall paintings appear expropriated from tombs in the Valley of the Kings. As was said at the time of the theater's opening, part of the show is the building itself. (RMC.)

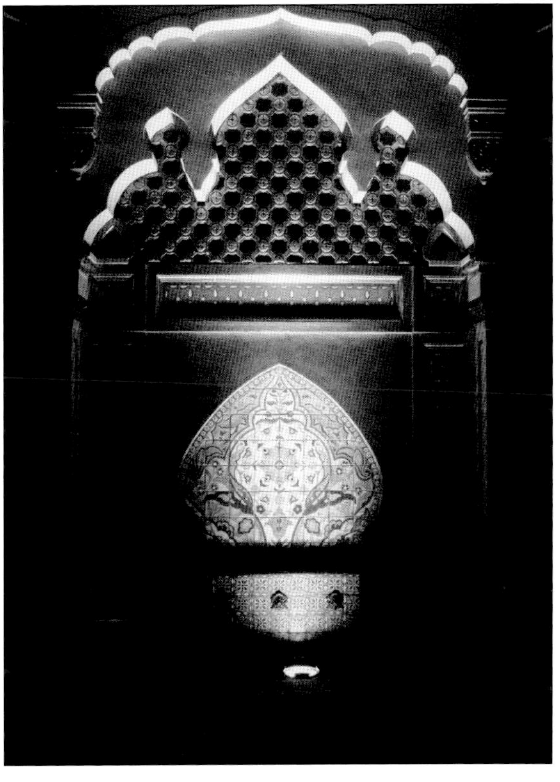

The Fox Theatre began as a project for the Shriners Yaarab Temple (Ancient Arabic Order of the Nobles of the Mystic Shrine). When the extravagant architecture and accompanying decorative art exceeded the Shriners' budget, movie mogul William Fox completed the building. Its stylistic cast was already set, however. The building is the most ornate work of Islamic (revival) public art in the city, notwithstanding the Al-Farooq Masjid on Fourteenth Street. (RMC.)

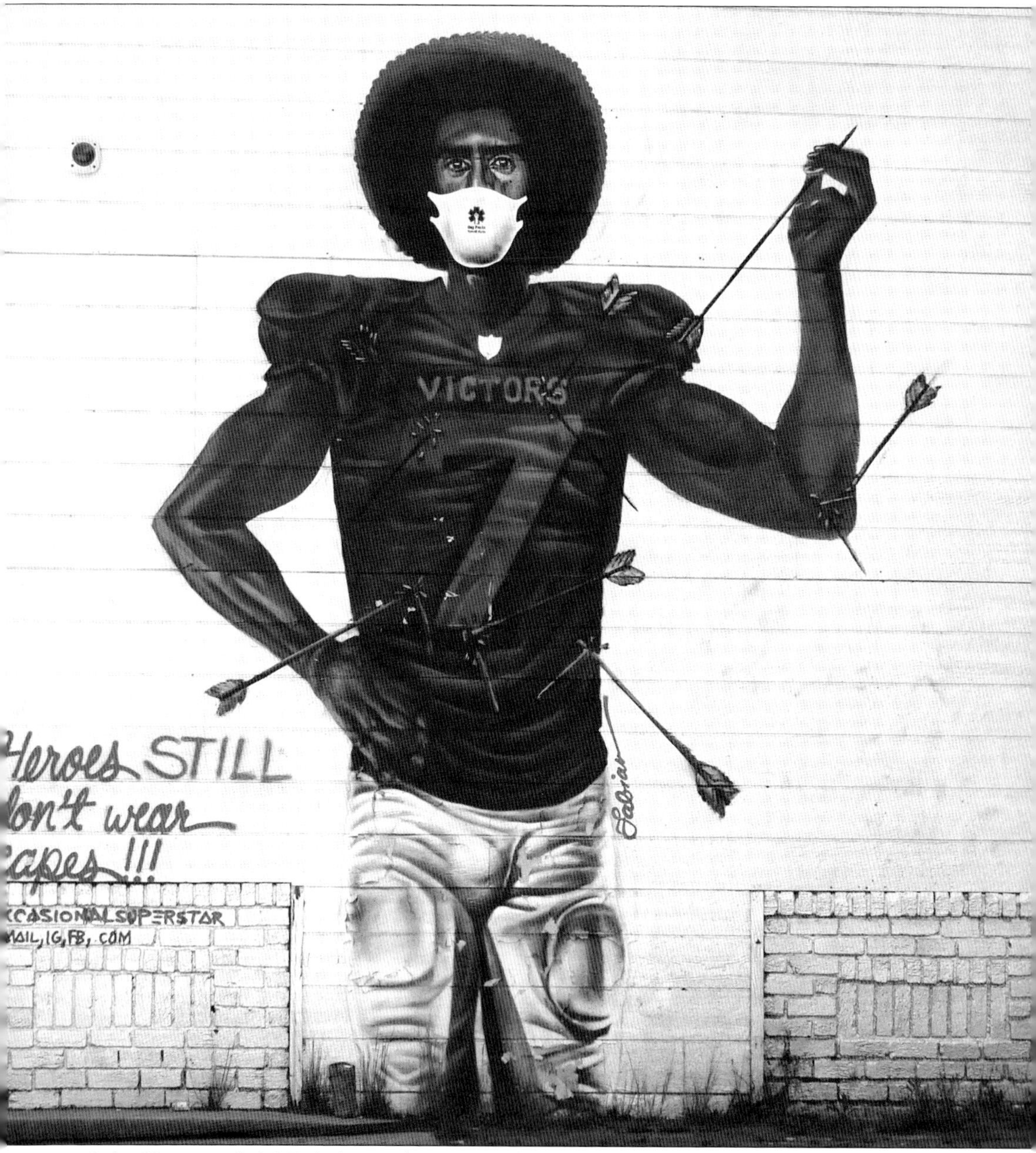

Colin Kaepernick (1987–), depicted as Saint Sebastian, is a mural by Fabian Williams, also known as occasionalsuperstar, one of several by him and others that have appeared since Kaepernick's notorious activist stance, beginning in 2013, of kneeling during the national anthem at the beginning of NFL games, protesting what he perceived to be police brutality and racial inequality in the United States. Quarterback Kaepernick played six seasons for the San Francisco 49ers in the NFL. However, his polarizing protests garnered highly visible responses, including from Pres. Donald Trump in 2017, who said that NFL owners should fire players who protest during the national anthem. Kaepernick became a free agent after the 2017 season but remained unsigned; he filed a grievance against the NFL but withdrew it after reaching an undisclosed settlement with the league. He remains unsigned. (RMC.)

Seven

Sports Art

Atlanta is a sports city, with national franchises in the major sports and with a secular order of athletes worshipped on weekly sports sabbaths by adoring fans whose church programs and guides to the order of service are scorecards and portable radios or iPhones for simultaneous sportscasting. Within the holy sanctuary of the gridiron, experiences of ecstasy and shouts of hallelujah result from the ascension of the kicked ball to the sacred space between the goalposts or from the entry of the puck or soccer ball into a netted cage, where the devil of the opposite team (as on a Last Judgment tympanum) seeks to block passage. The mysterious transcendence of a batted home run beyond the earthly limits of the outfield is, for the gathered congregation, transformational, as chants ensue. In order to witness such ecstasy-inducing miracles, "game day" becomes the day of Hajj. On game day, worshippers take pilgrimage to Mercedes-Benz Stadium, Truist Stadium, or State Farm Arena (all names bought by an act of secular indulgence that would make Martin Luther blush), and crowds en route rival devoted followers approaching Santiago da Compostello or even Mecca; it is saint's day for tailgating in the parvis. And lest the reader concludes that the metaphor is unduly stretched: who but a religious zealot would pay $1.5 billion dollars to construct a venue used on only a relatively few holy days a year?

Yet the public continues to accept the political or social babblings of a jock as all-wise, indeed as holy script. If they kneel or do not kneel, they have committed a mortal sin, and icons of kneeling "heroes" appear painted on urban walls to sanctify those national cathartic events and their apostles. In a mural painting by "occasionalsuperstar" artist Fabian Williams, for instance, Colin Kaepernick appears as a martyr shot full of arrows. The rendering references the martyrdom of St. Sebastian, who was killed during the Roman emperor Diocletian's persecution of Christians; at first, Sebastian was tied to a tree and shot full of arrows, the subject of 16th- and 17th-century paintings (by Il Sodoma in about 1525, for instance), and after he survived, he was clubbed to death.

Atlanta has enshrined its Sunday heroes all across town, albeit in less traditionally religious pose or character: in statues at ballparks and stadiums, as public sculpture in city parks, and on murals—one recording the famed 715th home run by a true and admirable great. (Another mural references his lifetime record of 755 homers). Soccer murals display an emblematic letter "A," or feature a golden phoenix, while other art depicts a falcon or a hawk. Included in the city's sports art are busts and life-size figural statues of sports figures just as nobly rendered as those historic bronze portraits of, and monuments to, military, political, and social justice leaders. If Ruskin was correct in suggesting that art is the most trustworthy indication of a society's values, then it may be no surprise to observe the extent of "sacred" sports art that is commissioned as well as the extent of destruction of past "secular art" at the hands of secular iconoclasts that is currently indulged in.

In balancing the urge for *xīnǎo* with society's need for memory, monuments fall in and out of favor, with the rationale for iconoclasm reflecting everything from current whim or fashion to the backlash culture of today's woke society. Citizens of Richmond, Virginia, for instance, have recently removed their historic equestrian statues and bronze sculptures dedicated to Robert E. Lee (1890), Stonewall Jackson (1919), Jefferson Davis (1907), J.E.B. Stuart (1907), and Matthew Fontaine Maury (1929)—all longstanding civic monuments of public art adorning the city's Beaux-Arts Monument Avenue. On the other hand, their sports art remains: preserved at the end of the same avenue is Paul DiPasquale's 1996 bronze statue of tennis player Arthur Ashe. The earliest and finest of the Monument Avenue landmarks, the now-removed Robert E. Lee equestrian monument, is listed in the National Register of Historic Places and Virginia's Landmarks Register; indeed, Monument Avenue itself is a National Historic Landmark District. The Lee monument was designed and fabricated in France by Prix-de Rome winner Antonin Mercié (1845–1916), a highly respected sculptor, member of the Institut des Beaux-Arts, president of the Société des Artistes Français, and Grand Officier de la Légion d'Honneur. It may say something about today's society that a Change.org petition was launched proposing to replace this Mercié masterpiece with a statue of Oderus Urungus (née David Brockie), the late lead singer of the heavy metal band Gwar.

In the meantime, statues of historic figures nationwide fall like guillotine victims during the Reign of Terror. Locally, Dekalb County has already removed Thomas Jefferson from its county courthouse grounds in Decatur, and in Atlanta, several of the statues and monuments documented herein are targets for hoped-for cleansing. We all need our heroes, however flawed they may appear to others, but erasing history is an act that history itself suggests is fraught with danger. Gislebertus's 12th-century sculpture at Autun has survived the iconoclasts for 900 years, despite its depiction of the devil and hell itself in the stone.

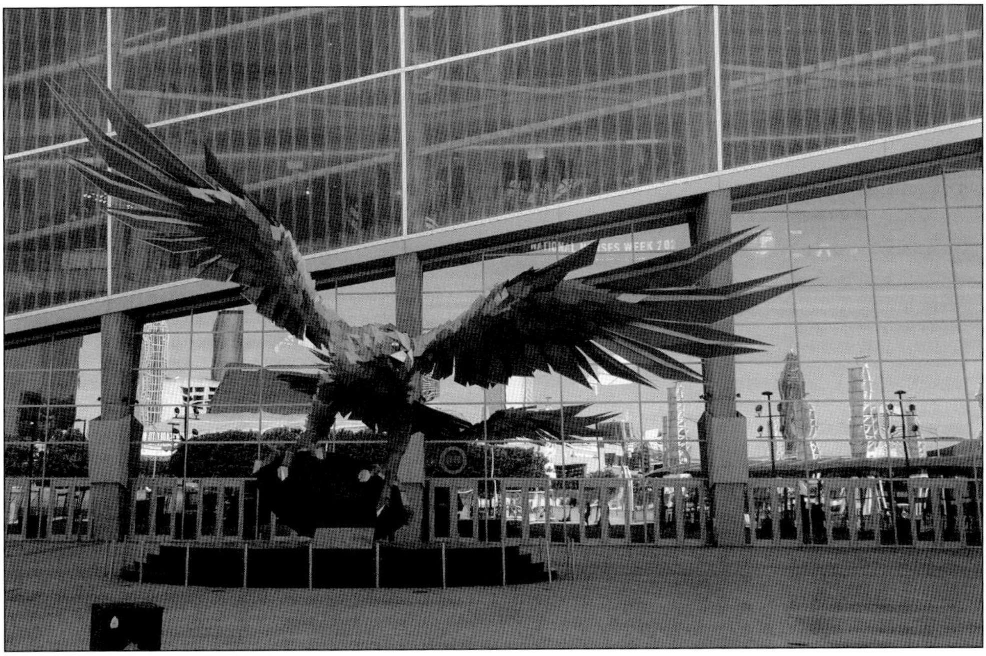

The *Atlanta Falcon* sculpture at Mercedes-Benz Stadium is the work of Gábor Miklós Szőke (1984–), a sculptor based in Budapest. Weighing 73,000 pounds and with a height of 41 feet and a wingspan of 68 feet, the falcon is the world's largest avian sculpture to date. Szőke had already designed the largest bird sculpture in Europe as well as his *Colossus* in Slovakia, the world's largest equine sculpture, the latter rivaling the 24-foot-high recreation (7.3 meters) of the Sforza horse by Leonardo da Vinci, displayed at the High Museum in 2009–2010. In 1482, Ludovico il Moro, the Duke of Milan, commissioned what was intended to be (but unbuilt in his day) the largest equestrian statue in the world, a monument to his father, Francesco Sforza, larger even than Donatello's 1453 *Gattamelata* or Verrocchio's 1480–1488 *Colleoni*. In modern times, it is Gábor Miklós Szőke, who is best known for gigantic animal sculptures, often, as here, fabricated of stainless steel. The *Atlanta Falcon* skeleton of massive stainless steel plates supports wings formed of several thousand laser-cut steel plates of different sizes. (RMC.)

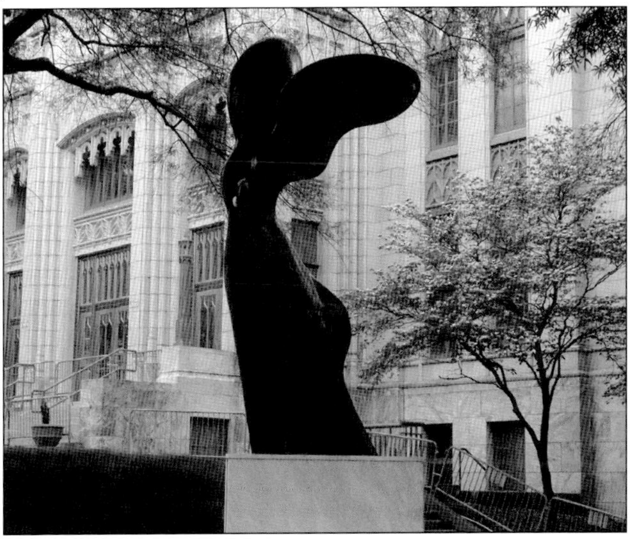

Nike is the Greek goddess of victory, and this abstracted *Nike* is the work of Greek sculptor Pavlos Angelos Kougioumtzis (1945–), gifted to the City of Atlanta to celebrate the Centennial Olympic Games in 1996. Versions of the statue have been donated to host Olympic cities since. Among Kougioumtzis's bronze sculptures in European cities are *Socrates* (1995), *Sibilla Deifica* (1996), *Aphrodite* (marble, 1999), and several versions of *Prometheus*. (RMC.)

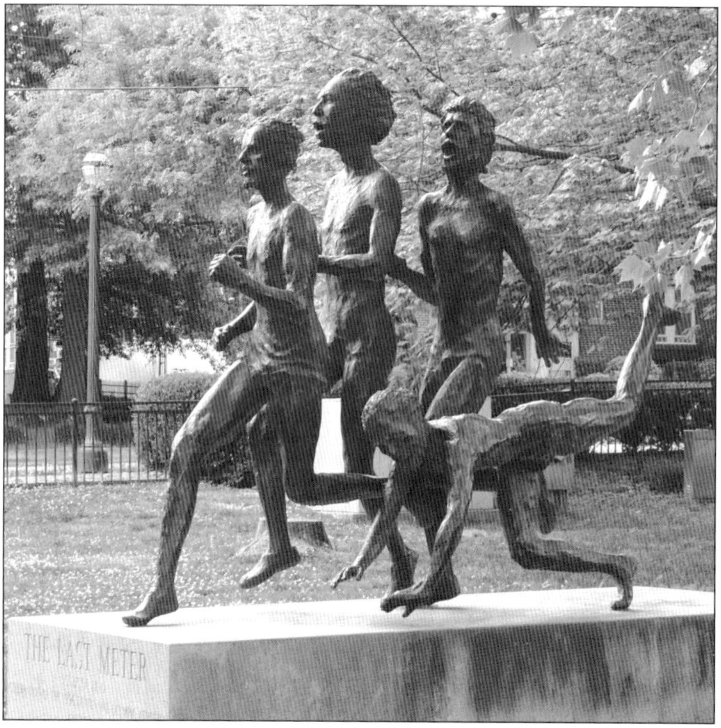

Last Meter depicts four runners at the finish line of the 5,000-meter final race at the Montreal Olympics (1976). Lasse Virén (Finland) won gold (his fourth), Dick Quax (New Zealand) silver, Klaus-Peter Hildebrand (Germany) bronze, and Rod Dixon (New Zealand) was in fourth place. The bronze monument by sculptor Eino Romppanen (1940–2018), initially on loan to Atlanta for the games, was replicated for permanent display in Piedmont Park. (RMC.)

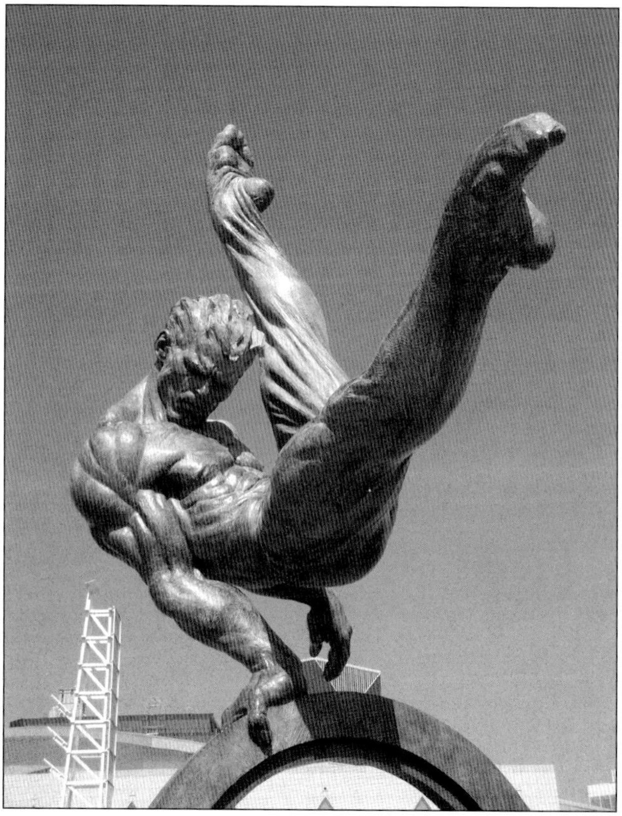

The Flair by Richard MacDonald (1946–) is a tour de force. With arms and legs dramatically flaring out, the gymnast's body is full of motion, balanced on a ring, and seems impossible physically to fabricate as a monumental bronze statue touching the earth at only one point. The artist donated the work to the State of Georgia and the City of Atlanta to commemorate the Olympics and dedicated it to Olympic athletes and to "all those who exemplify determination and dedication in the pursuit of excellence." Also on the inscription is a quote from Pierce Rice, "The great tradition of Western art has been, and should continue to be, not merely representational work, but the idealization of the human form, the glorification of both heroic individuals and the heroic possibilities of mankind." (RMC.)

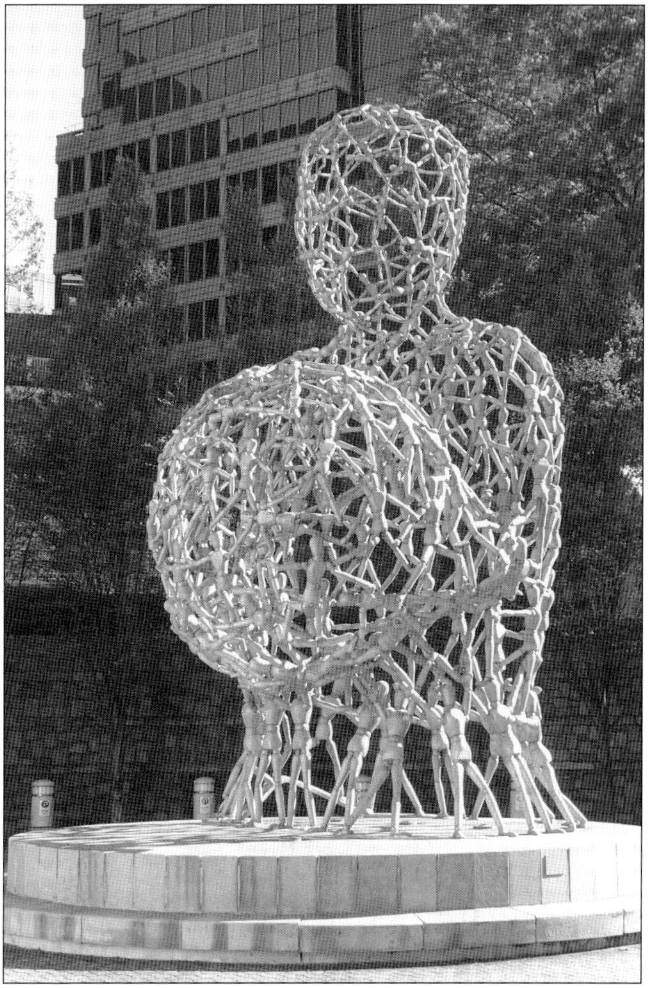

British sculptor Tony Cragg (1949–) fabricated this aluminum sculpture in 1996 to commemorate the Atlanta Olympic Games. It was created for display at Centennial Olympic Park but is today on a plaza outside the Atlanta Memorial Arts Center. Cragg's early works were site-specific installations of discarded "found objects." His subsequent (the 1970s–early 1980s) "assemblages," were systematic arrangements of fragments that formed larger images. In his *World Events*, individual figures, like gymnasts forming an acrobatic human pyramid, stand on shoulders, arms extended, hands touching shoulders or clasping hands of flanking figures, to create an open frame whose form suggests a larger figure, 26 feet high from waist to head, holding a large globe. Sir Tony Cragg was knighted in the 2016 Birthday Honours. (RMC.)

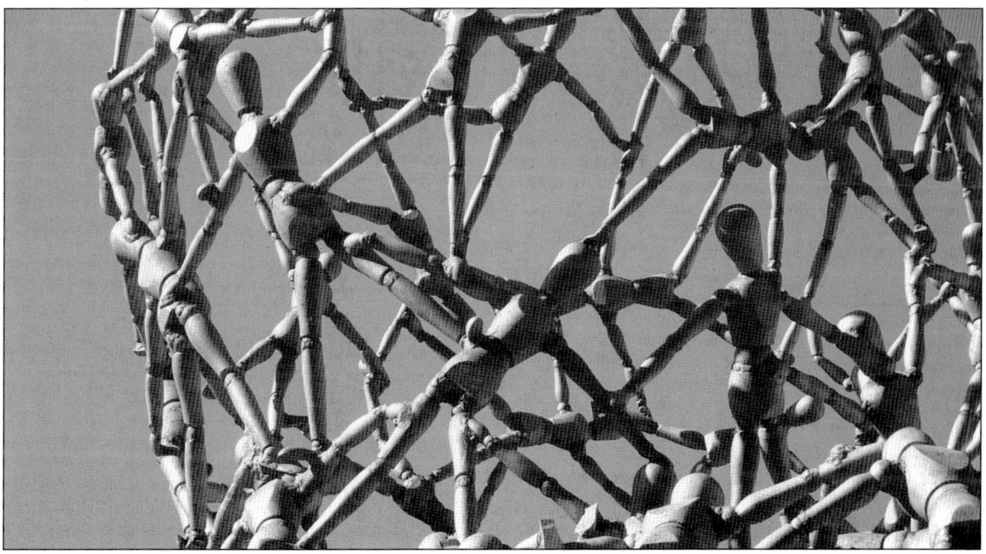

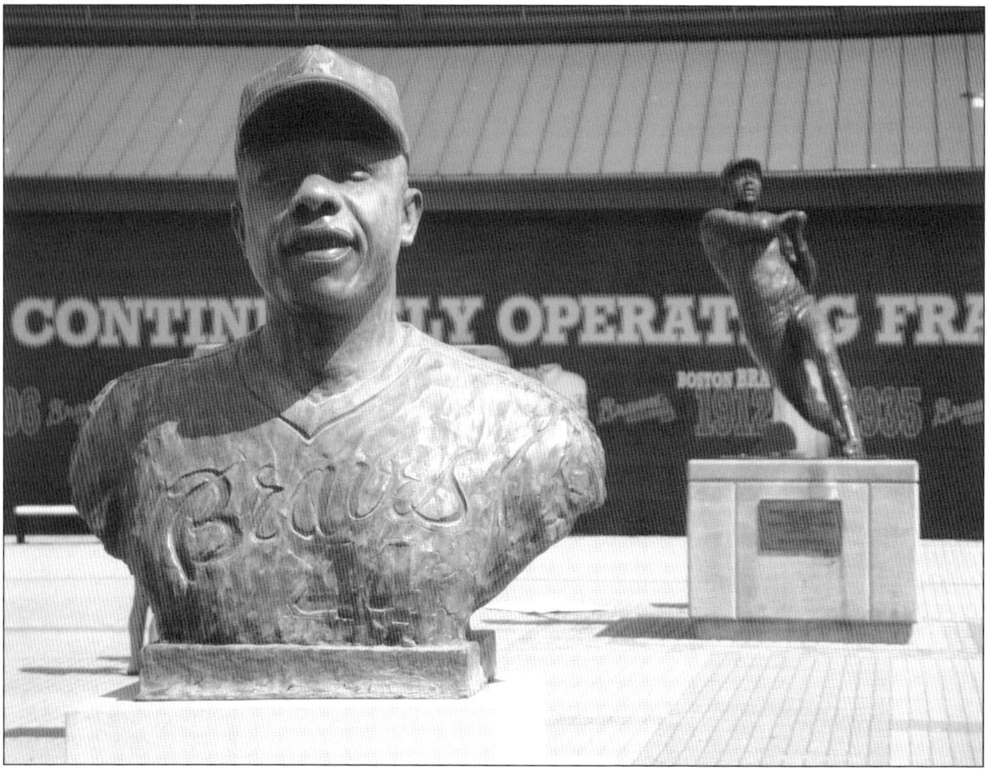

Henry Lewis "Hank" Aaron (1934–2021) was an outfielder with the Milwaukee Braves/Brewers (1956–1965) and Atlanta Braves (1966–1976) who broke baseball records including the most All-Star Games played (24, matching Willie Mays and Stan Musial) and 755 career home runs (now second to Barry Bonds's 762). "Hammerin' Hank" most famously broke the career home run record of Babe Ruth when he hit No. 715 on April 8, 1974, in Atlanta. The mural (below) is part of a larger urban wall painted by Sean Schwab, part of The Loss Prevention, celebrating Aaron's career record of 755. This early bust of Aaron (above) was donated to the city as a celebration of his No. 715 homer in 1974. The sculptor and present location are unknown to this writer. In 2002, Pres. George W. Bush conferred upon the popular athlete the Presidential Medal of Freedom. (RMC.)

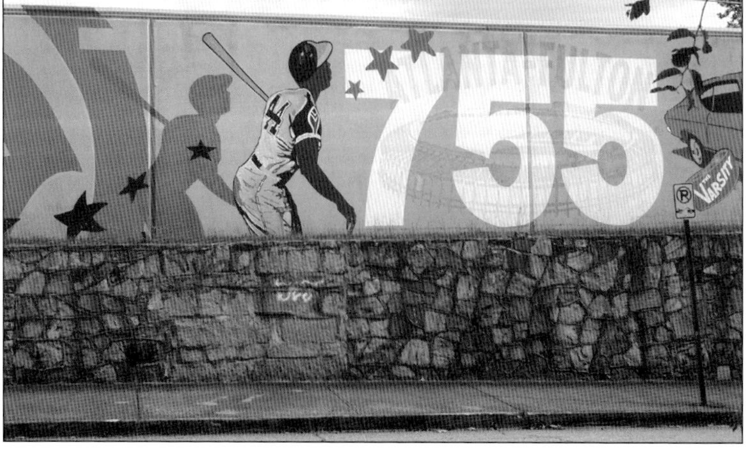

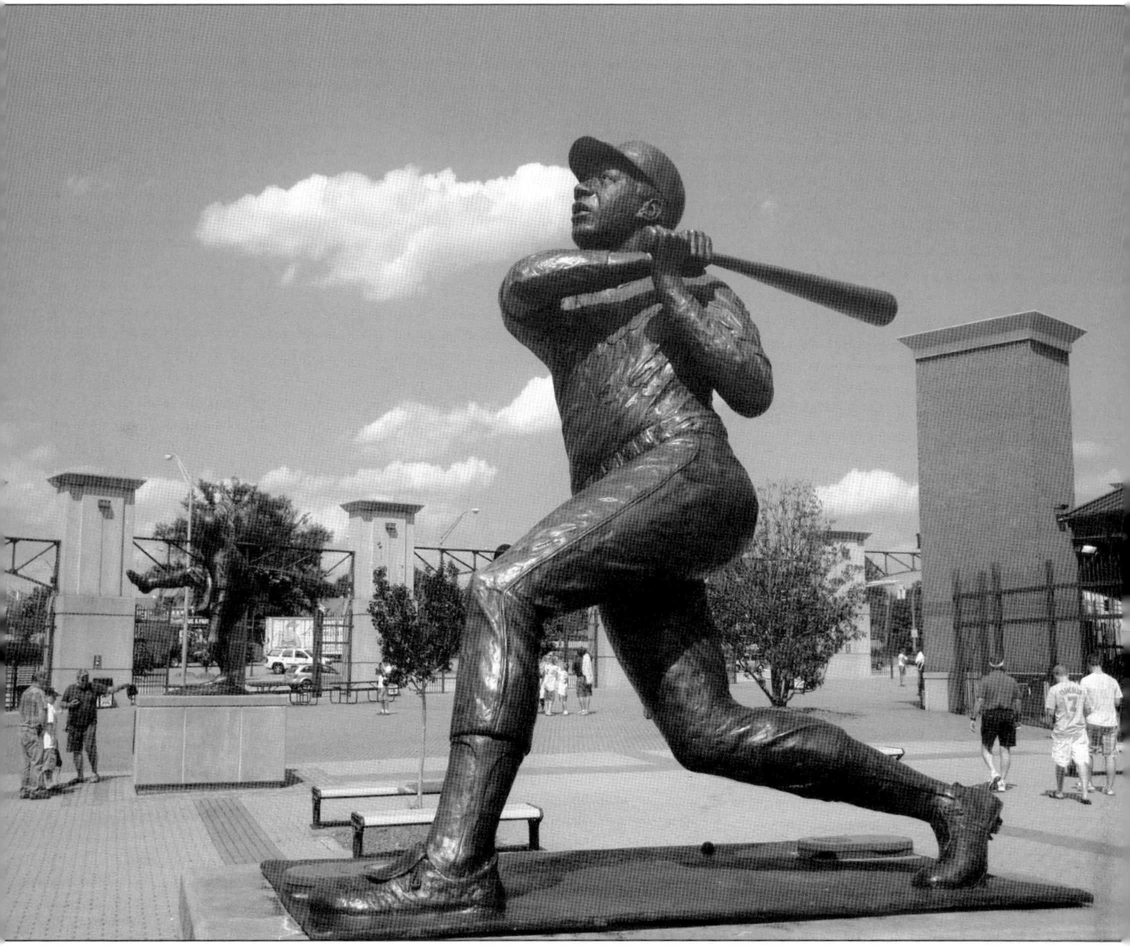

The 1982 statue of Hank Aaron is by Ed Dwight Jr. (1933–), who, before he transitioned mid-career to sculpture, was a test pilot and the first African American to enter the Air Force's astronaut training program but who was controversially not officially selected to join NASA. Following a controversy over ownership of the Dwight statue of Hank Aaron (the Braves or the people of Atlanta), the city prevented its transferal to Cobb County, and the statue is currently planned to be featured in a projected plaza at a new baseball stadium that Georgia State University (current owner of Turner Field) plans to erect on the footprint of the former Atlanta Fulton County Stadium, where Aaron hit his 715th home run. In the meantime, in 2017, a second Aaron sculpture by Bulgarian-born American Ross Rossin (1964–) was unveiled at Truist Stadium. A bronze by Brian Hanlon (1961–) of longtime Braves manager Bobby Cox is also at Truist. Meanwhile, images of Hank Aaron continued to spring up all over Atlanta. (RMC.)

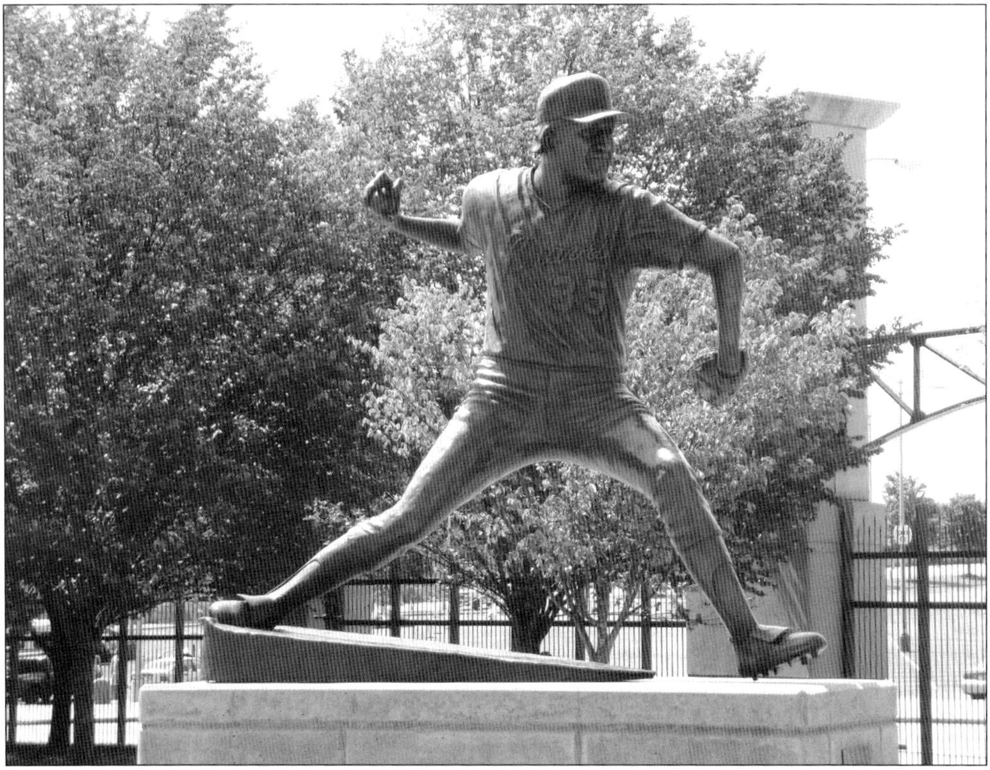

The 1977 bronze by Felix de Weldon (1907–2003) of Ty Cobb (1886–1961, below) is now at the library in Royston, Georgia, about 90 miles northeast of Atlanta. Like bronzes of other historic players, it was originally at Atlanta-Fulton County Stadium. The 1986 Phil Niekro bronze (above) was sculpted by Ed Dwight Jr. (see page 131) and followed the Braves' move to Truist Stadium in Cobb County. Ty Cobb is recognized as the "leading batsman of all major league history" with a career batting average of .367 and 4,191 hits. Niekro is remembered as the winningest knuckleball pitcher in baseball. Sculptor Dwight specializes in commemorating major figures in black history. His work includes 70 sculptures for the St. Louis Arch Museum in the series Jazz, an American Art Form featuring performers Louis Armstrong, Miles Davis, Duke Ellington, Ella Fitzgerald, and Charlie Parker. (RMC.)

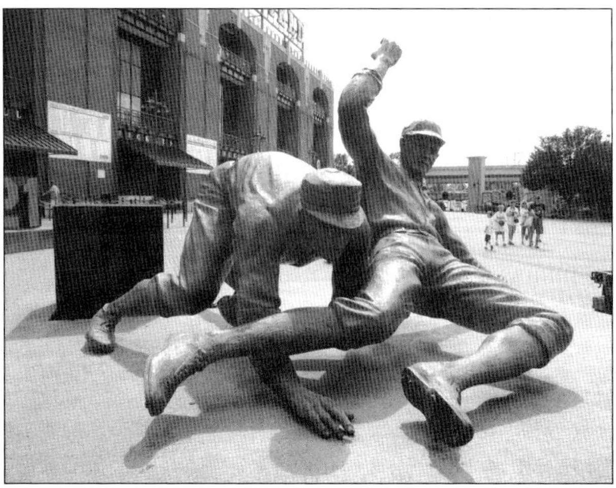

The 2003 bronze statue of Warren Spahn by Shan Gray (1956–) is one of three casts; the other two are in Oklahoma. Spahn's record of 363 career wins is tops among left-handed pitchers, a feat achieved despite missing almost four seasons during World War II military service when he won a Purple Heart. Originally with Aaron, Cobb, and Niekro at Turner Field, the Spahn sculpture is now at Truist Stadium. (RMC.)

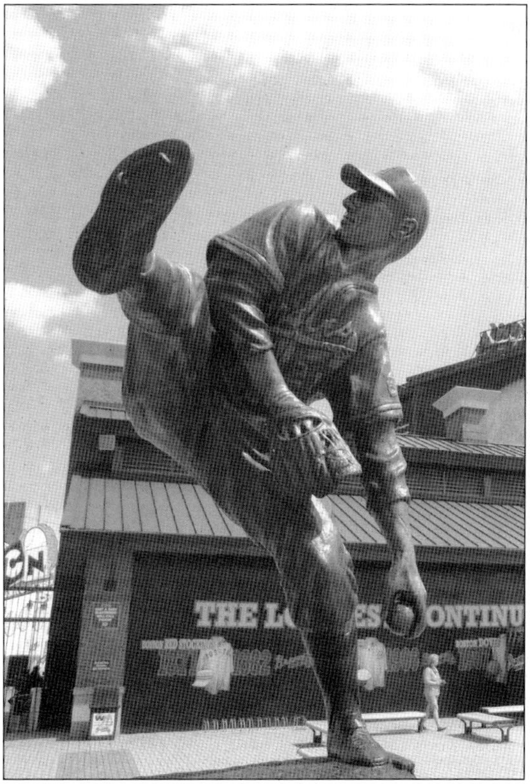

Like ghost signs of faded commercial advertisements on abandoned urban walls, the image of Hank Aaron's swing and glance out to the left-field ballpark wall almost half a century ago remains an indelible memory. The preservation of such a time-worn image is an indication of Atlanta's love for Aaron, whom Princeton University honored with a doctorate of humanities for his "imperishable example of grace under pressure." (RMC.)

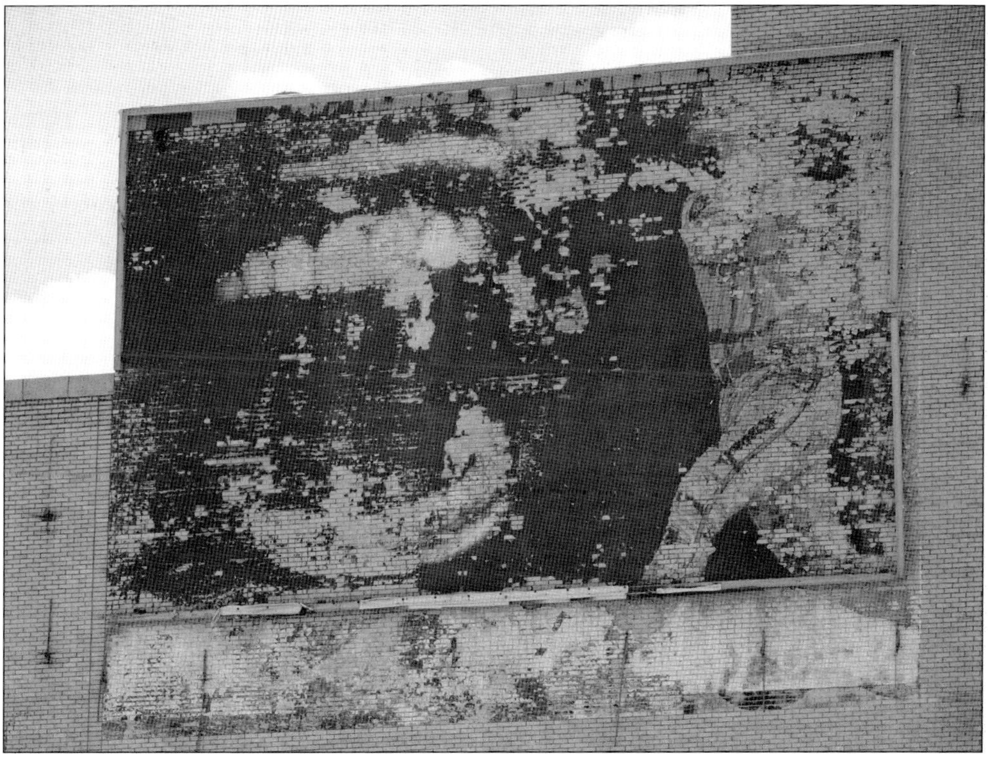

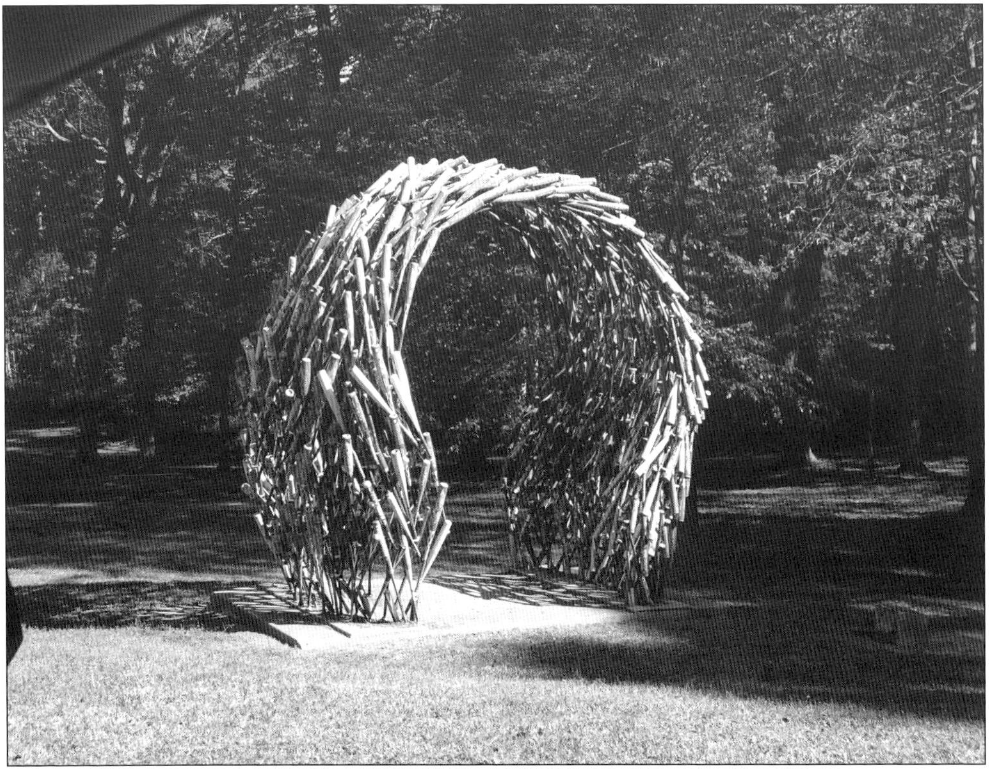

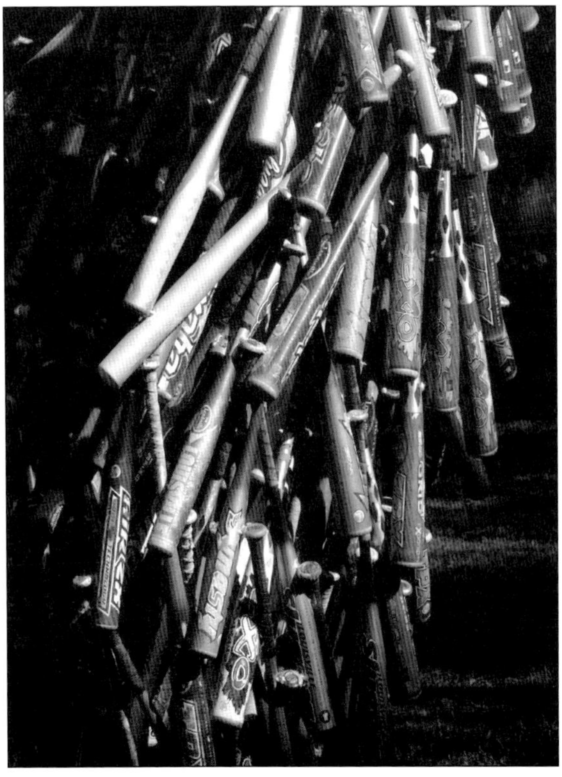

Created by sculptor Christopher Fennell (1983–), *Bats Baseball* (2009) is a 12-foot-high "found object" artwork, roughly the shape of a baseball, that forms an open spherical arch fabricated of 800 reclaimed aluminum baseball bats welded together. The work was commissioned by the City of Atlanta for Southside Park. Fennell believes that recycled materials offer an audience familiarity and connection with the art through the observers' familiarity with the materials. His background in engineering contributes to his understanding of "how the materials can be formed, shaped and connected into a structure" and the result can be provocative, dynamic, or (as here) witty. (RMC.)

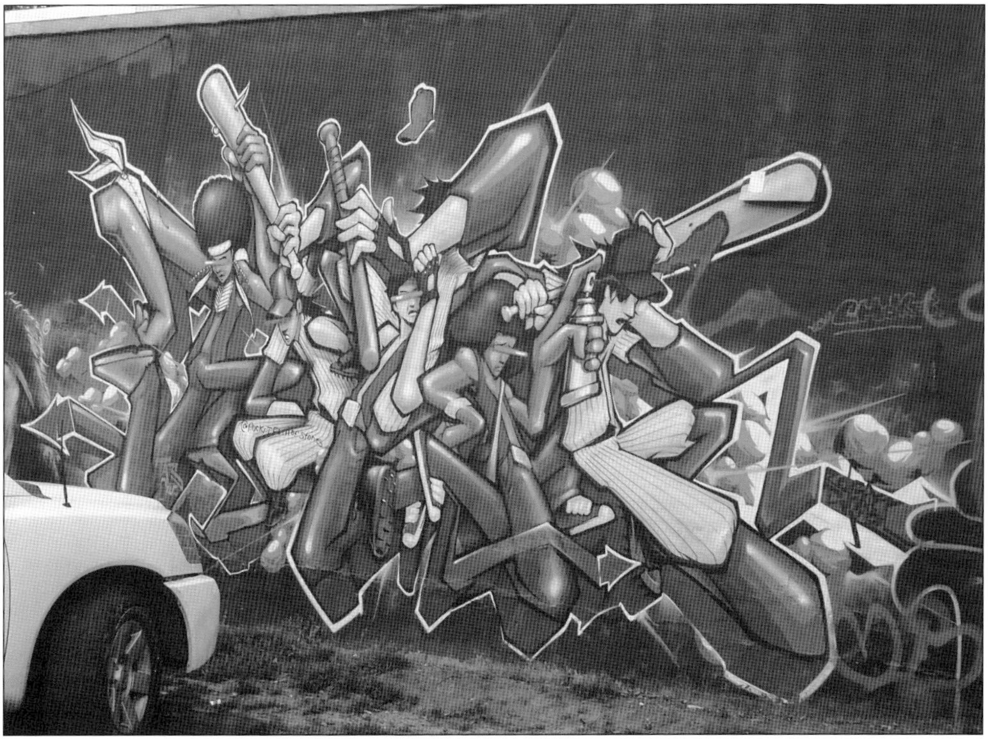

Mistertotem2 (Amir "Totem" Alighanbari) paints murals in a variety of styles, but perhaps the most exciting images present an explosion of forms and colors that is perceptually complex. The mural above spells "Totem" in graffiti script while a melee of angular arms, legs, and uniformed torsos suggest the theme of baseball: we observe baseball bats, jersey-clad figures in dugout poses, and a marching band drum major. The hashtag refers to the southern hip-hop rapper UGK's "Pocket Full of Stones" may be a reference to the early death of Pimp C (1973–2007, also known as Chad Butler) at 33. Quieter, traditional murals continue to be painted to honor others recently deceased. The 2021 mural on Hot Dog Pete's new store on Georgia Avenue in southeast Atlanta is the most recent tribute to baseball icon Hank Aaron, who died in 2021 two weeks before his 87th birthday. (RMC.)

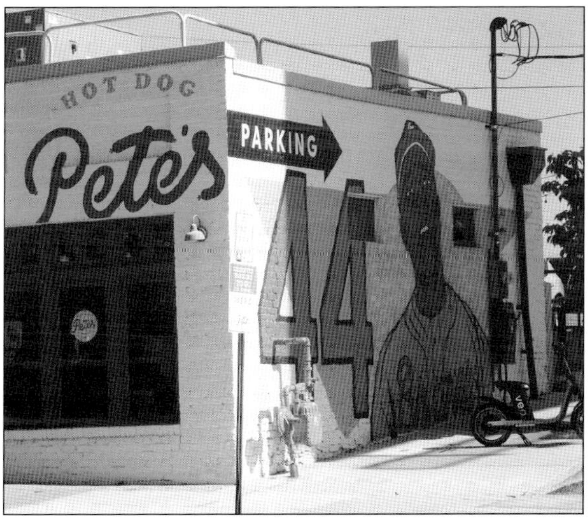

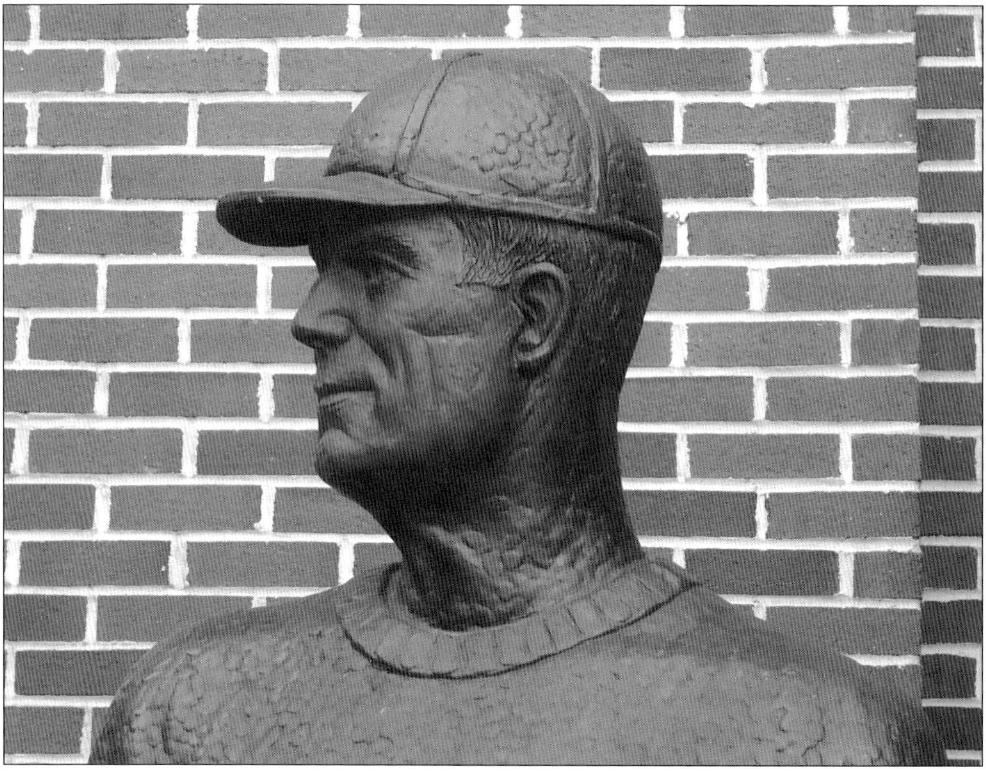

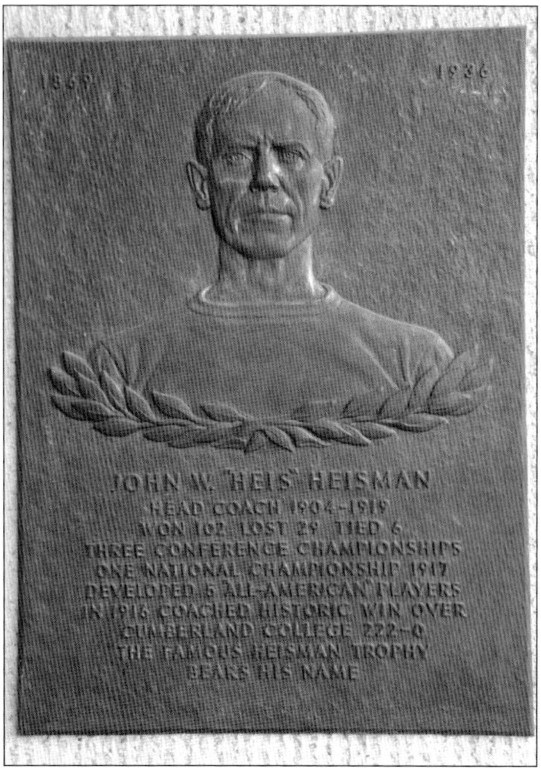

John Heisman (1869–1936) is best known as the namesake for the Heisman Trophy given annually to the most outstanding player in college football, usually a quarterback or running back. Heisman was Georgia Tech's first successful football coach (1904–1919) winning four consecutive SIAA [Southern Intercollegiate Athletic Association] championships, 1915–1918. He also coached Tech basketball (1908–1909, 1912–1914) and baseball (1904–1917) before moving on to Penn and ultimately to Rice. The 1988 figural sculpture seen above at Tech's Callaway Plaza is the work of one of his former players at Rice, sculptor William M. McVey (1905–1995). The Heisman dedicatory plaque (1983) on the wall of the nearby Edge Building is by Granville Wellington Carter (1920–1992). John Heisman's football record at Georgia Tech of 102 wins, 29 losses, and 6 ties is referenced on the plaque as is Tech's 1916 lopsided defeat of Cumberland College 222-0. (RMC.)

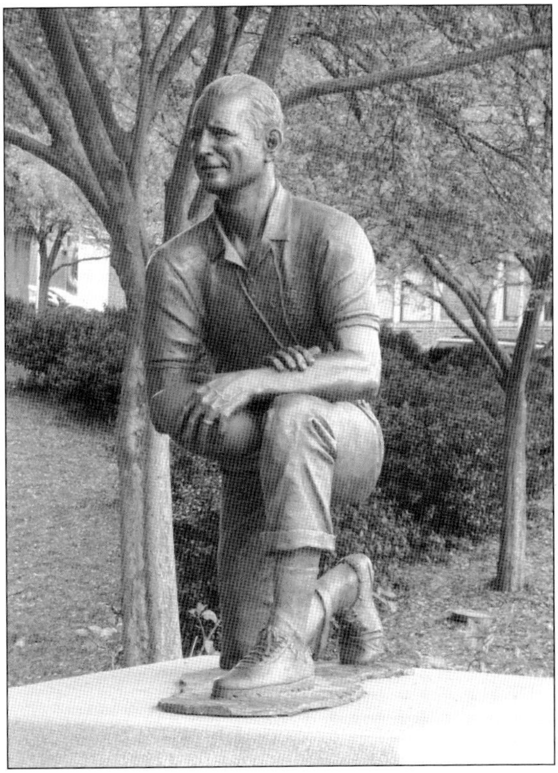

Robert Lee "Bobby" Dodd (1908–1988) followed in Heisman's footsteps as a highly successful assistant football coach (under William Alexander, 1931–1944) and coach (1945–1966). At retirement, his record was 165-64-8. Named athletic director in 1950, he continued in that capacity until 1976, completing 57 years of service to the school. Two months before his death, Georgia Tech named its football stadium after Dodd. At the edge of Callaway Plaza is a life-size bronze statue of Dodd kneeling that captures his most famous pose on the sidelines as coach; it is the work of Don Haugen and his wife, Teena Stern Watson, and was unveiled in 2012. The 1982 bas relief of Dodd on the nearby Edge Building is by Julian Hoke Harris (see chapter two). (RMC.)

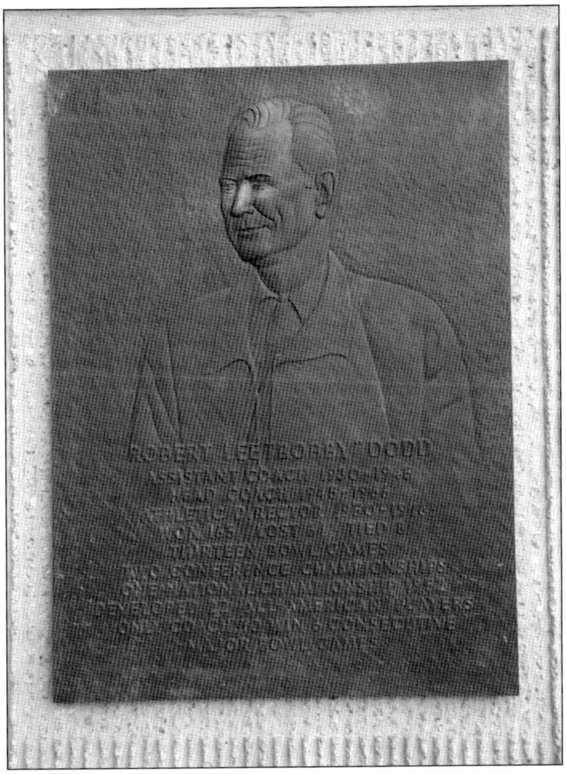

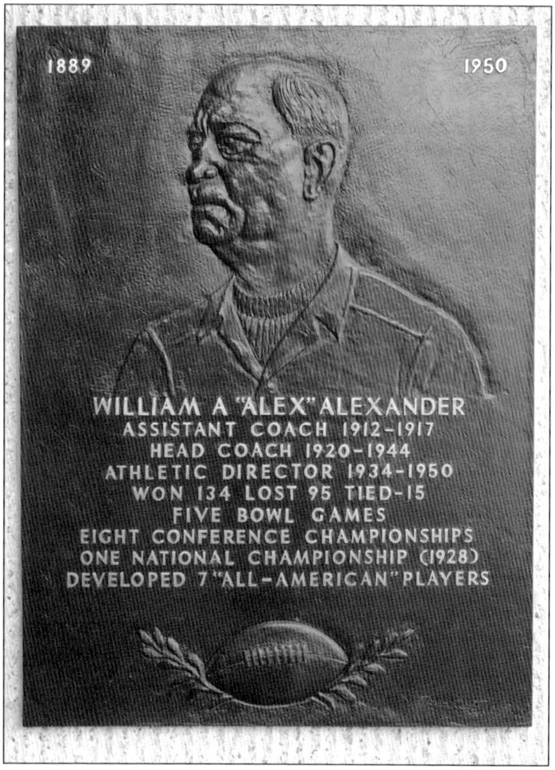

Two other bas reliefs on the Edge Building at Georgia Tech commemorate the careers of two other historic figures of significance to Georgia Tech sports, Coach William Alexander (1889–1950, left) and Homer Rice (1927–, below). Alexander succeeded John Heisman as head football coach, serving from 1920–1944 and achieving a record of 134-95-15. Although there is a bust of Alexander in the Tech archives, and a bas relief at Tech's Alexander Memorial Coliseum (now McCamish Pavilion) both by sculptor Julian Hoke Harris, the 1983 bas relief on the Edge Building is by Michael Lantz (1908–1988). Homer Rice served as director of athletics at Georgia Tech (1980–1997) and developed the Total Person Program, the model for the NCAA Life Skills Program in place at universities throughout the nation. His 1998 bas relief on the Edge Building is by Martin Dawe (1956–) of Cherrylion Studios. (RMC.)

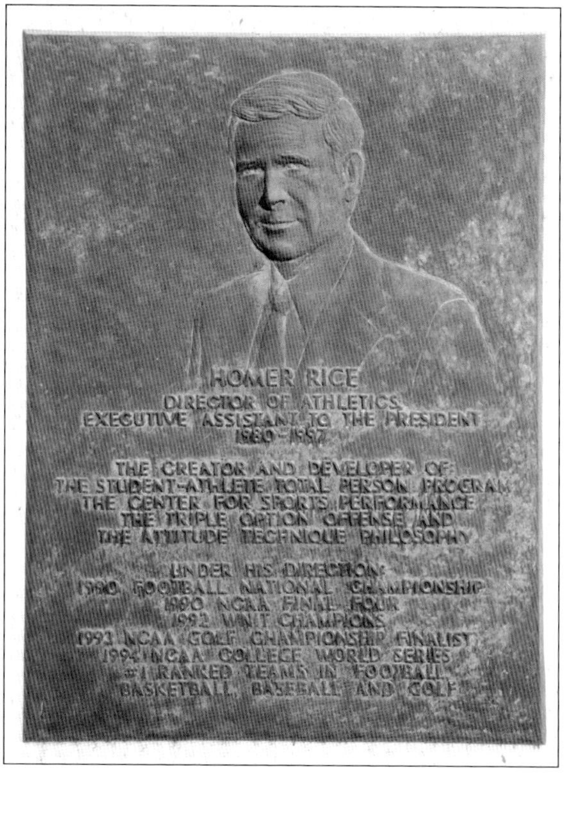

Golf is also represented in public art in Atlanta. The city's best-known golfer was Robert Tyre "Bobby" Jones Jr. (1902–1971) winner of the (pre-Masters) Grand Slam of Golf in 1930 (four major championships in Britain and the United States (amateur and open). Bobby Jones founded and helped design the Augusta National Golf Club in 1933 and cofounded the Masters Tournament first played there in March 1934. The bas relief seen right of Jones swinging a golf club is by Julian Hoke Harris, dates to 1973, and is displayed on the Edge Building on Georgia Tech's campus. The 18-hole Brown Mill Golf Club is the subject of print art work by photographer Hank Margeson (1948–) displayed at the Rosel Fann Recreation Center. Margeson's work there includes six silkscreen murals with images of the Atlanta community, including the diptych of golfers seen below. (RMC.)

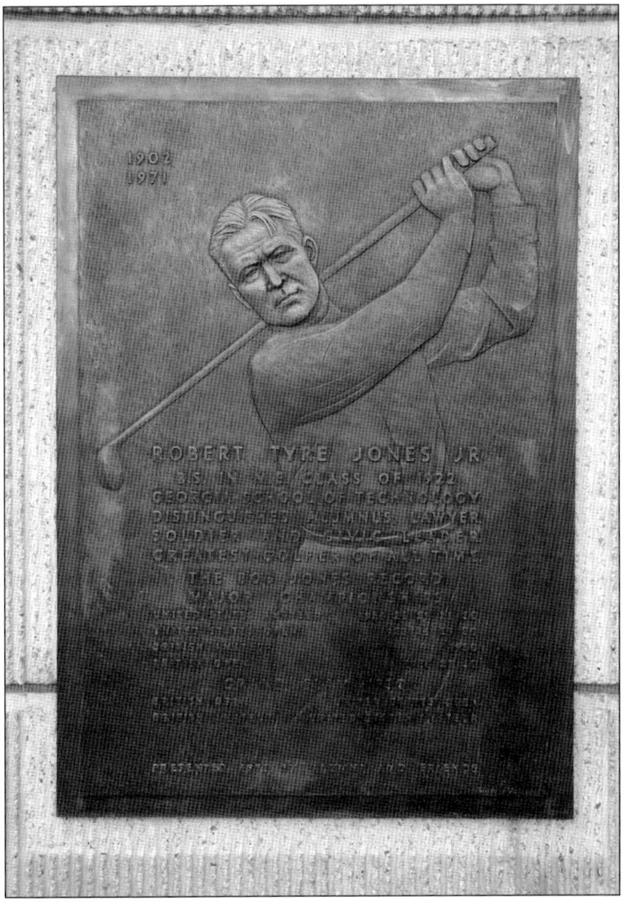

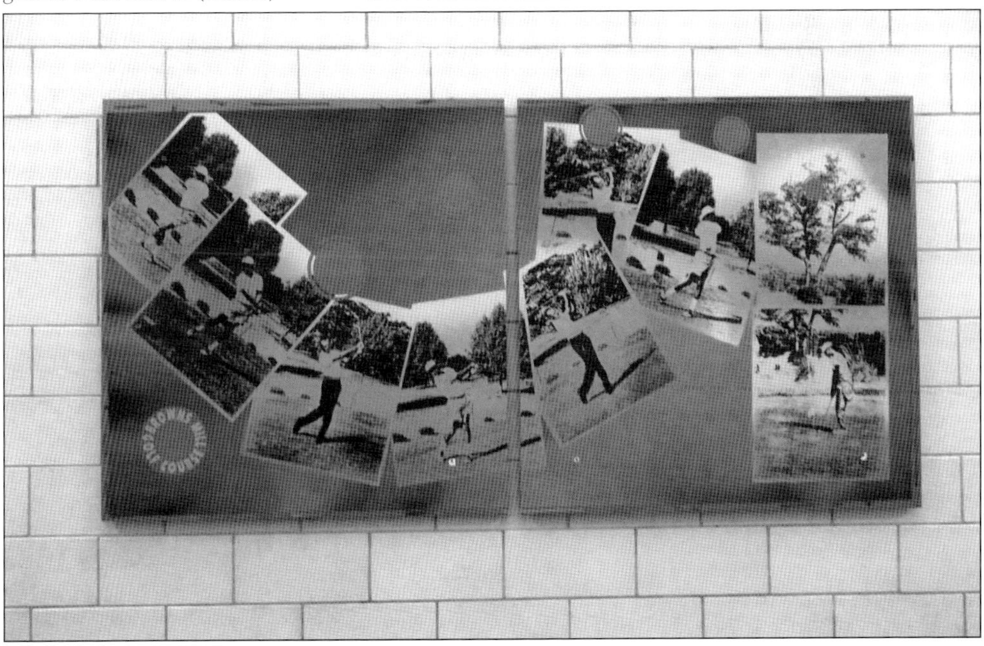

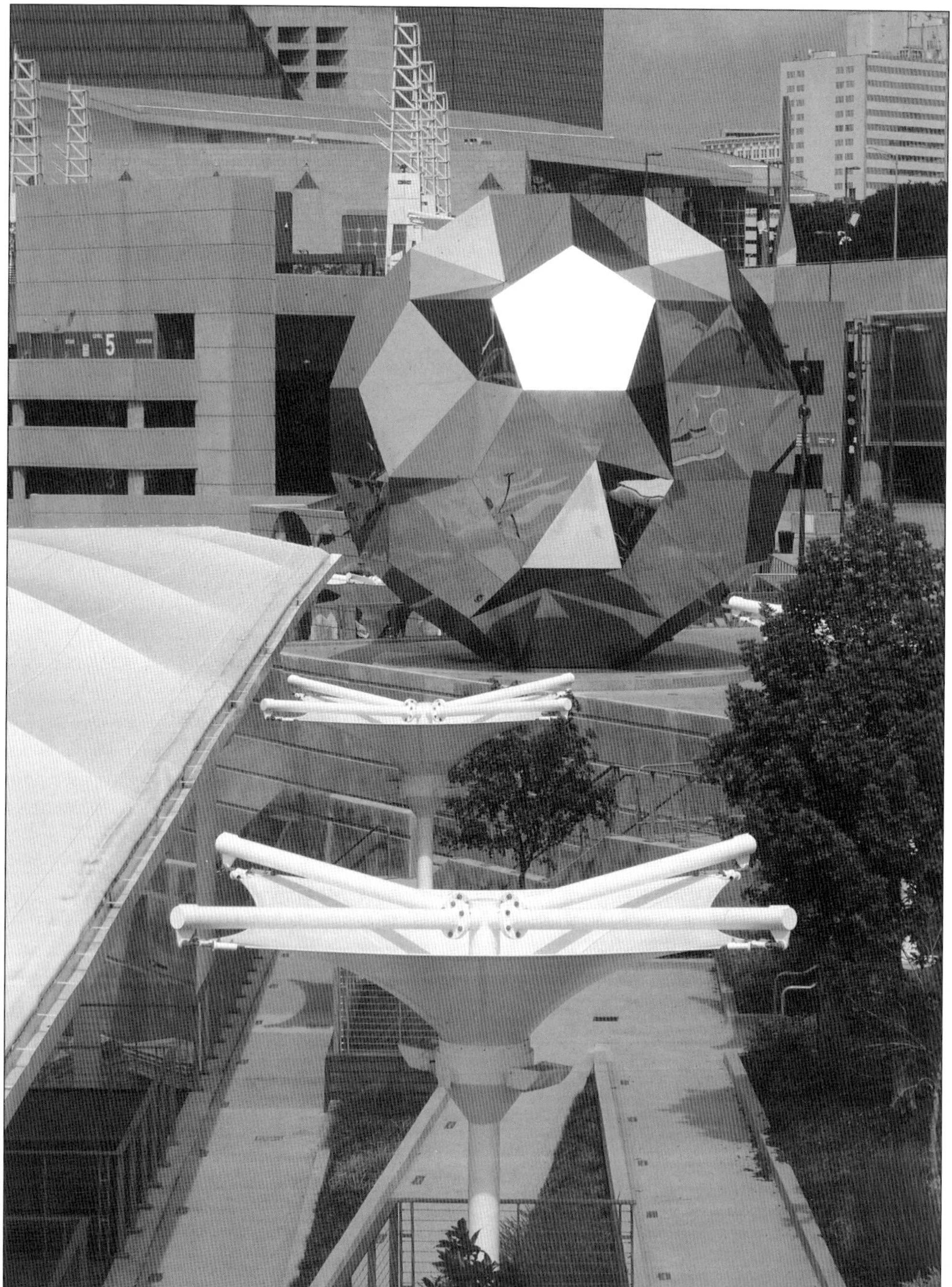

With Gábor Miklós Szőke's *Atlanta Falcon* sculpture (see page 127), this abstracted soccer ball inaugurated the art program at Mercedes Benz stadium, here honoring Atlanta United and the growth of soccer in the United States. *Telstar* by Studio Roso (2018) is a stainless steel spherical truncated icosahedron, containing pentagonal and hexagonal faces and referencing the standard Adidas Telstar-style soccer ball, transformed here to an Archimedean solid of flat surfaces, comparable to Buckminster Fuller's geodesic domes. (RMC.)

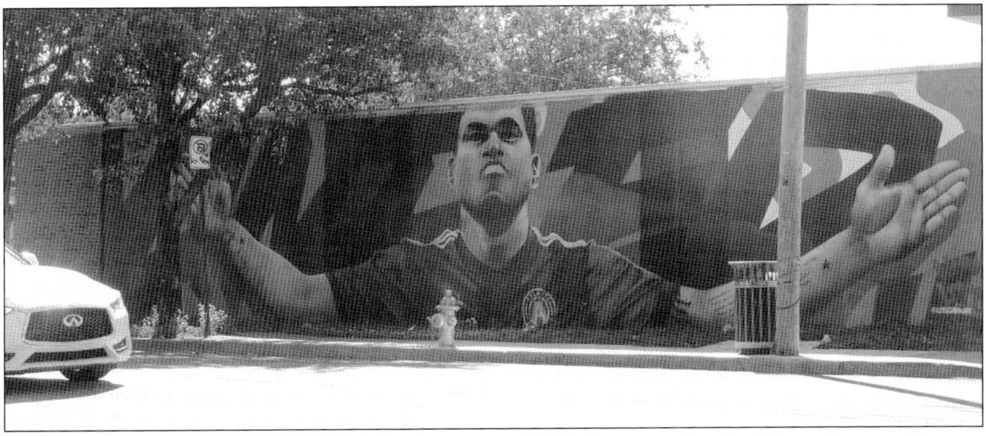

Venezuelan footballer Josef Alexander Martínez (1993–) is a striker for Major League Soccer (MLS) club Atlanta United FC. In 2018, he became the most decorated single-season player in MLS history by winning the League MVP, All-Star Game MVP, Golden Boot, and MLS Cup Final MVP awards. The Matt Letrs (1982–) mural in Castleberry Hill was voted Atlanta's most popular in a 2020 *Atlanta Journal-Constitution* poll. (RMC.)

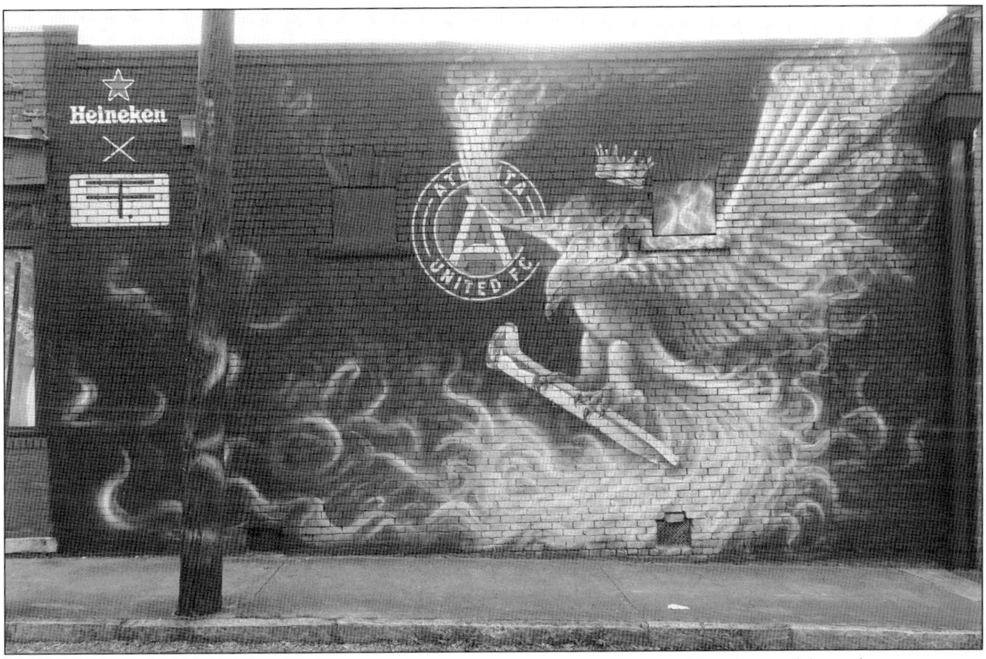

Muralist Thomas Turner (1987–) is skilled at painting animals and birds, and his phoenixes on local Atlanta United murals have taken on status as an unofficial symbol of the Atlanta footballers club. Examples are his *Time to Soar* mural at Sequoyah Middle School celebrating Atlanta United's victory in the 2019 Campeones Cup, his *Rooted in Royalty* in Summerhill, and *The Accolade*, seen here, at the Rocky Mountain Pizza Company. (RMC.)

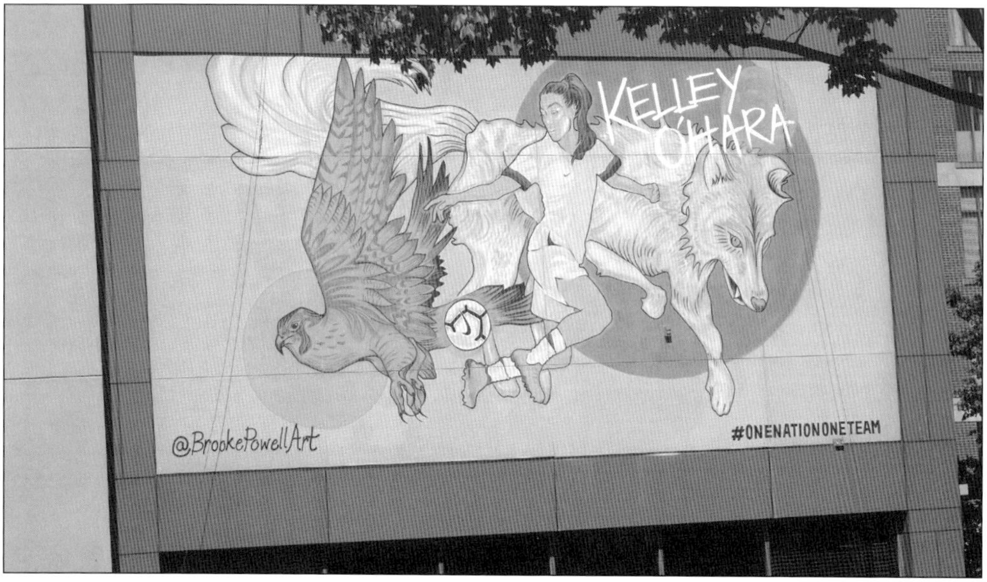

Women's soccer is represented in an Atlanta mural celebrating the achievements of Georgia-born Kelley O'Hara (1988–), Olympic gold medalist in 2012 (one of three players for the United States to play every minute in the tournament), and twice FIFA (Fédération Internationale de Football Association) Women's World Cup Champion (2015 and 2019). She has recently played for the Utah Royals in 2017 and, in late 2020, was traded to the Washington Spirits. (RMC.)

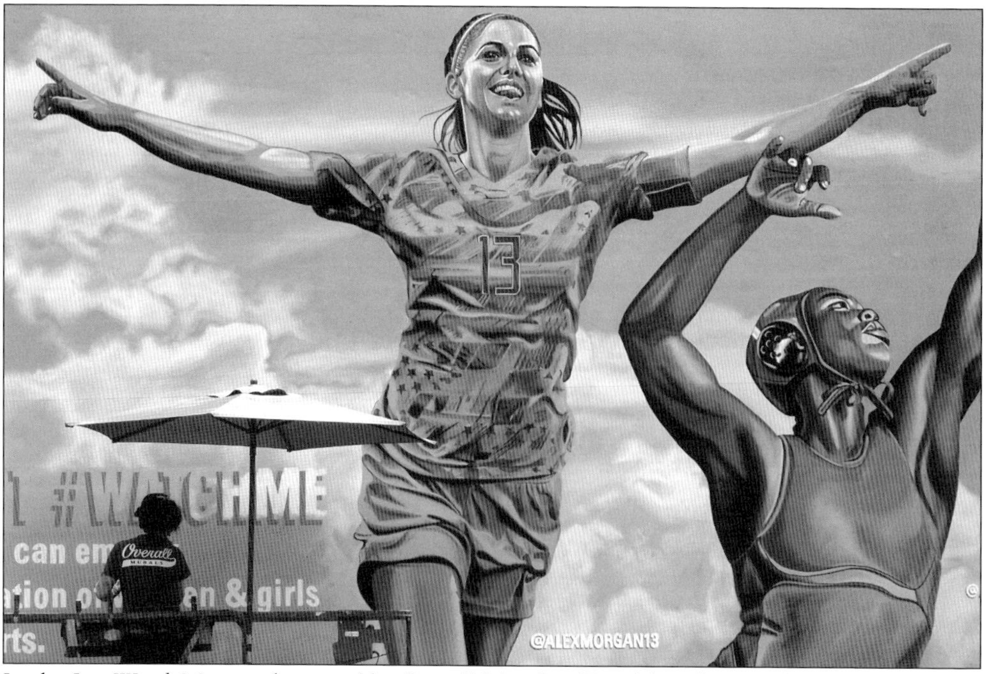

In the *Just Watch Me* mural painted by Overall Murals of Brooklyn, five notable woman athletes representing different sports are presented in a photorealistic style against a blue sky. The mural is part of a national campaign to encourage more spectators to "empower a generation of women and girls in sports." Soccer player Alexandra Morgan Carrasco (1989–) from the United States women's national soccer team is featured. (RMC.)

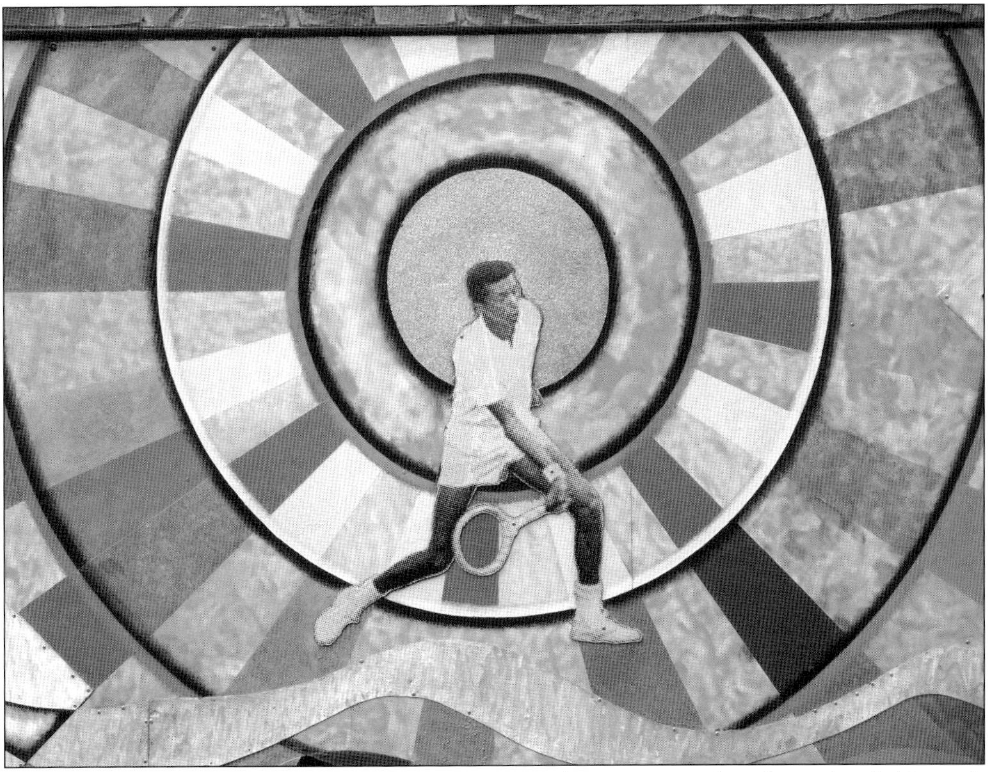

The historically black Washington Park Tennis Center features a mixed-media work titled *Legends* by Carl Joe Williams (1970–) of New Orleans. The 2003 mural features an abstract background of concentric circles and horizontal wave details along the lower half of the piece that employs a photograph and paint process on metal. Black and white images of famous African American tennis players such as Arthur Ashe are featured. (RMC.)

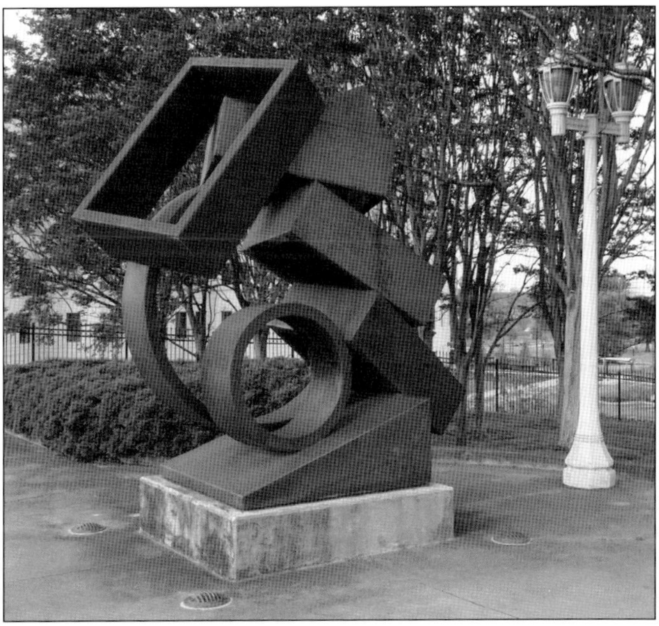

Games (1996) is an abstract Corten steel sculpture by Spanish sculptor Elisa Arimany (1933–) commemorating the 1996 Olympic Games. It features five open boxes and two open circles positioned asymmetrically on a concrete base. Sponsored by the Cultural Legacy Initiative, the sculpture is part of a cultural exchange program between the two host cities of the 1992 and 1996 Olympic Games. (RMC.)

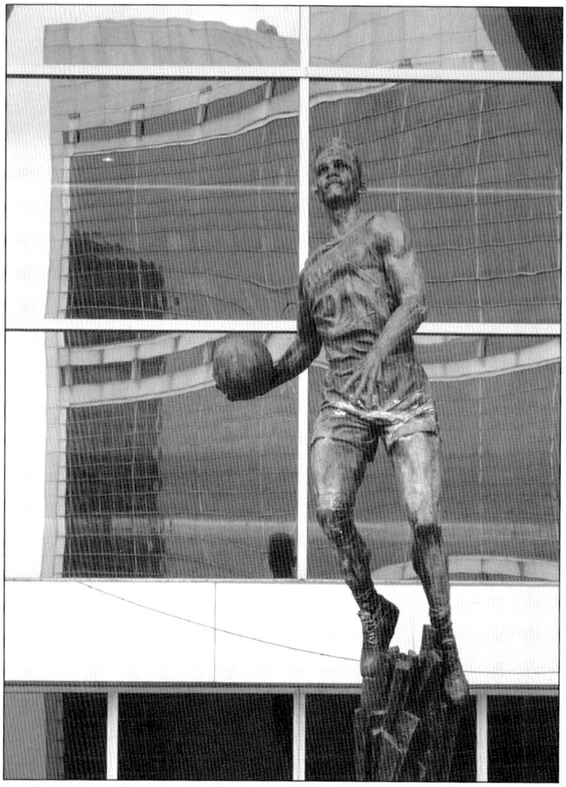

The 13.5-foot granite 2015 sculpture of Atlanta Hawks' Dominique Wilson (1960–) weighs 18,500 pounds but springs to life as sculptor Brian Hanlon (1961–), the official sculptor of the Naismith Memorial Basketball Hall of Fame, captures Wilson about to execute a right-handed dunk. The nine-time All-Star Wilkins is widely viewed as one of the best dunkers in NBA history. The franchise has retired his number, 21. (RMC.)

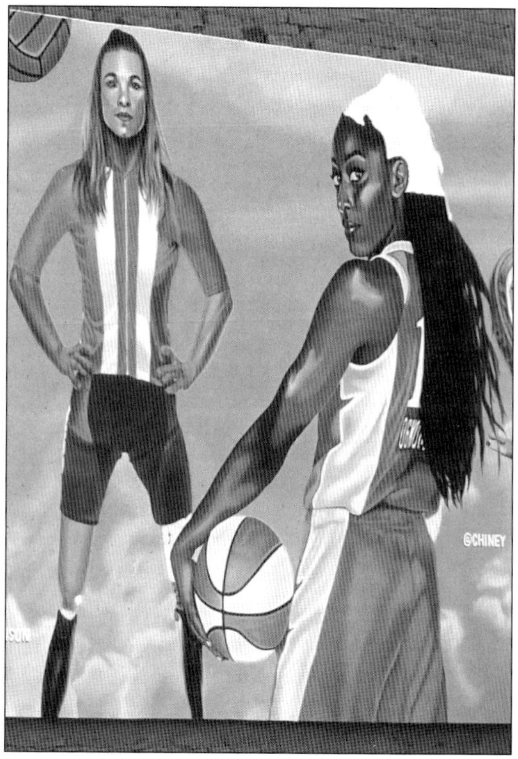

Women's basketball is represented on the 2021 *Just Watch Me* mural by Chinenye "Chiney" Ogwumike (1992–), a Nigerian American professional player for the Los Angeles Sparks of the Women's National Basketball Association. Behind her is Oksana Masters (1989–), a Ukrainian-American Paralympic rower and cross-country skier who won the first-ever US medal in trunk and arms mixed double sculls in 2012. (RMC.)

In 2015, after breaking records for all-time career saves at Princeton University, Ashleigh Johnson (1994–) was part of the American team that won gold at the 2015 World Aquatics Championships. The following year, she became the first African American woman to make a US Olympic Women's Water Polo Team; her Team USA won gold at the Olympics in Rio. She is considered one of the best goalkeepers in the world. (RMC.)

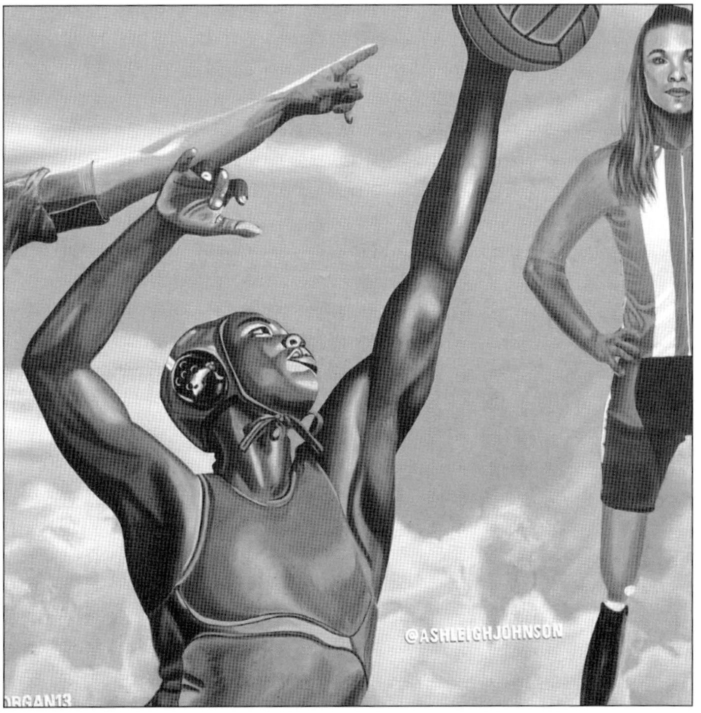

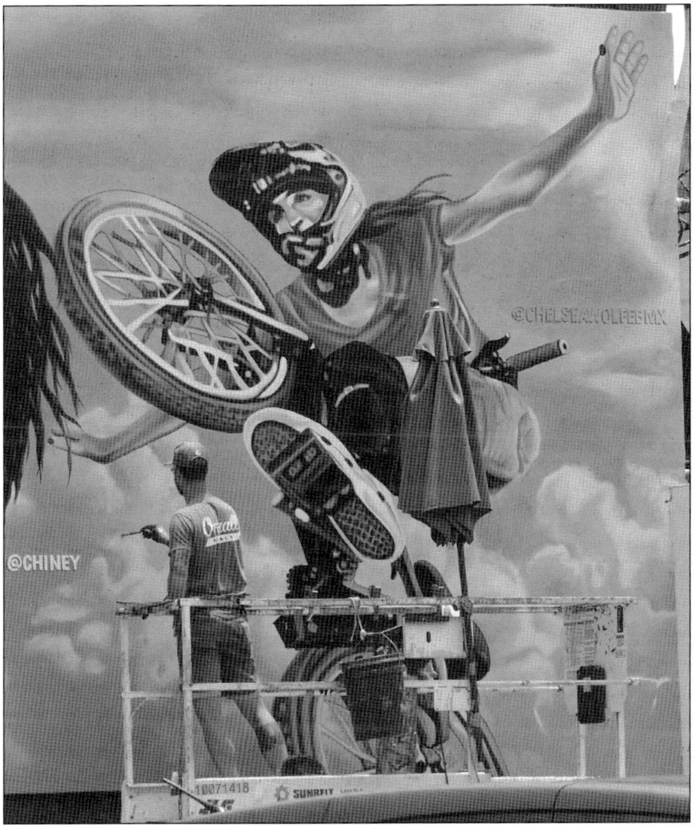

BMX (bicycle motocross) freestyle cyclist Chelsea Wolf (1993–) took fifth place in the recent World Championships—enough for Wolf to qualify for the Tokyo Olympics. It is notable because Wolf is a female trans athlete, the first transgender Olympian, although she will not race unless one of her teammates drops out. She is one of the female athletes featured in the 2021 *Just Watch Me* mural. (RMC.)

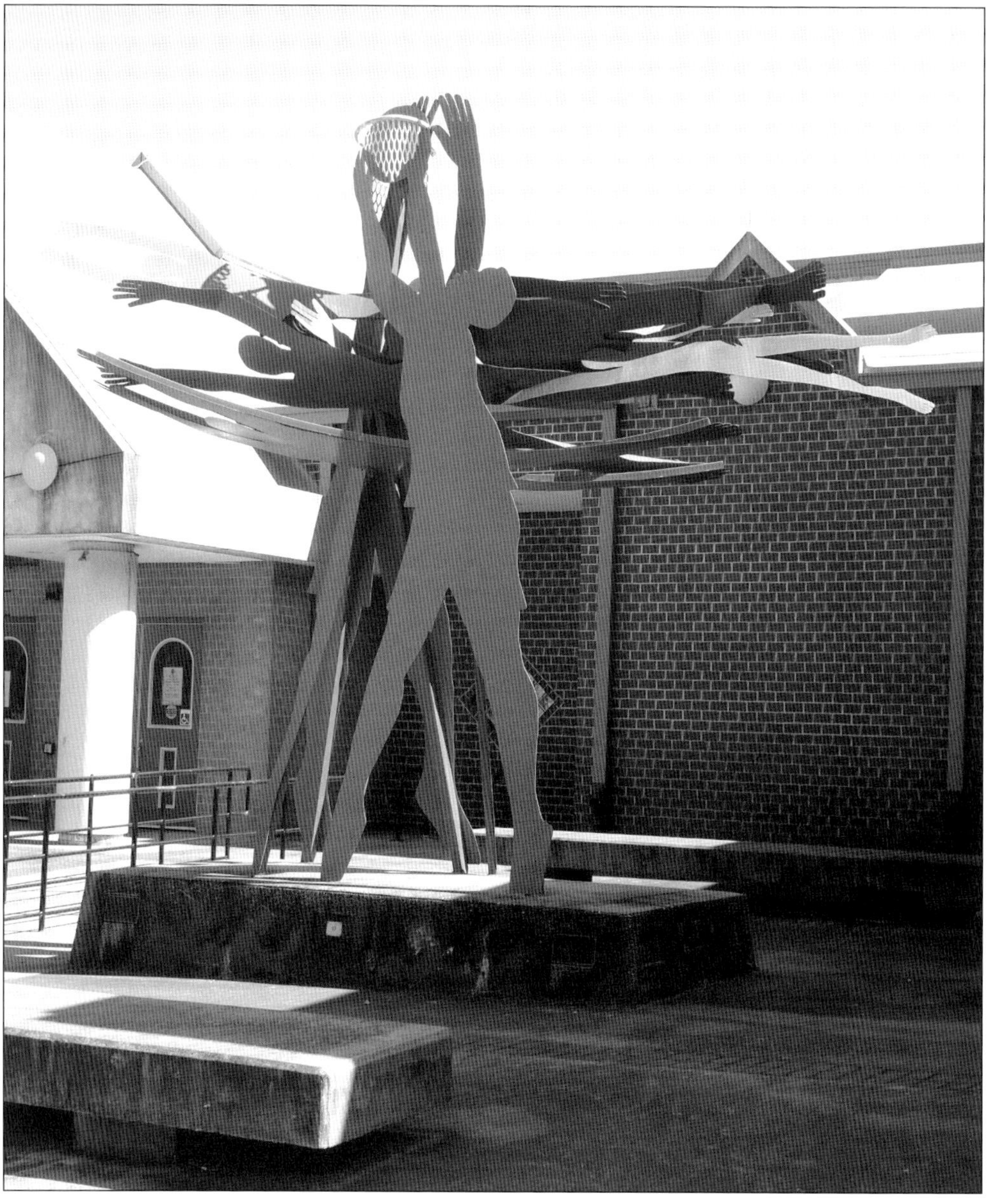

Robert Clements's sculpture displays flat cutouts in steel, brightly painted, and composed to encourage the observer to walk around the sculpture and look up to the silhouetted profiles against the sky in order to see the figures in sharp outline, gradually transformed from edge line to profile as one circumnavigates the sculpture. Clements's delightfully silhouetted individuals are engaged in such activities as reading, sports, or playing a musical instrument, and his work is intentionally aspirational and motivational: a title such as *Attaining Goals* (seen here), *Flying* (in Decatur), or *The Muse of Learning* at the Athens Public Library makes evident his purpose of encouragement of youth. Clements taught art at the University of Georgia for 25 years before his retirement in 1994, intent then on creating art full-time. His *Attaining Goals* of 1994 features a group of three vertical and three horizontal human figures made from his familiar painted steel cutouts, fabricated this time as profiles of basketball players. It is sited outside the Rosel Fann Recreation Center, where neighborhood youth may still find lessons from the professor emeritus. (RMC.)

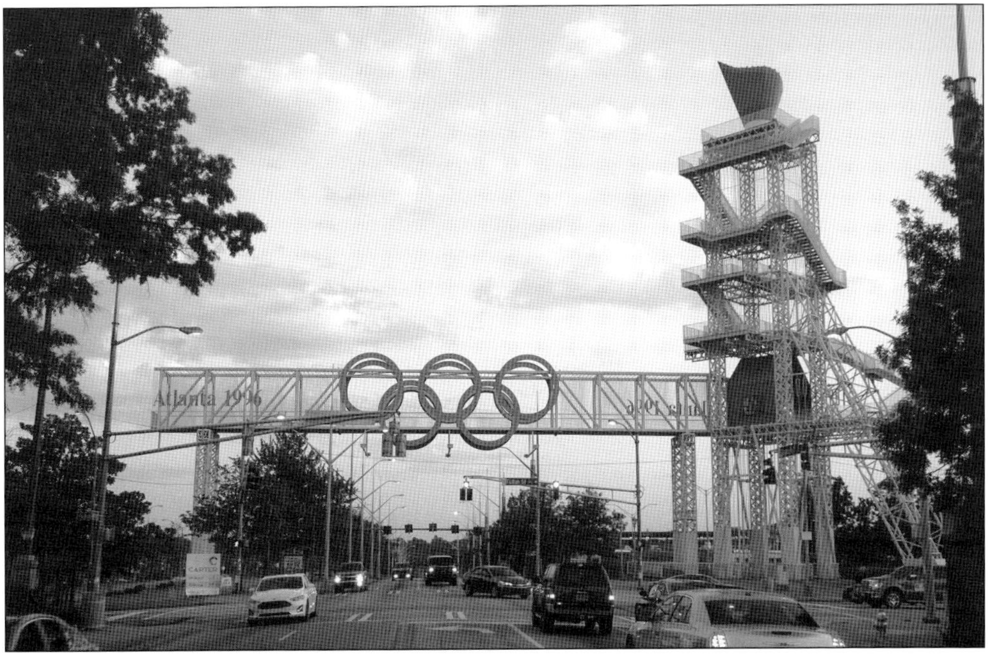

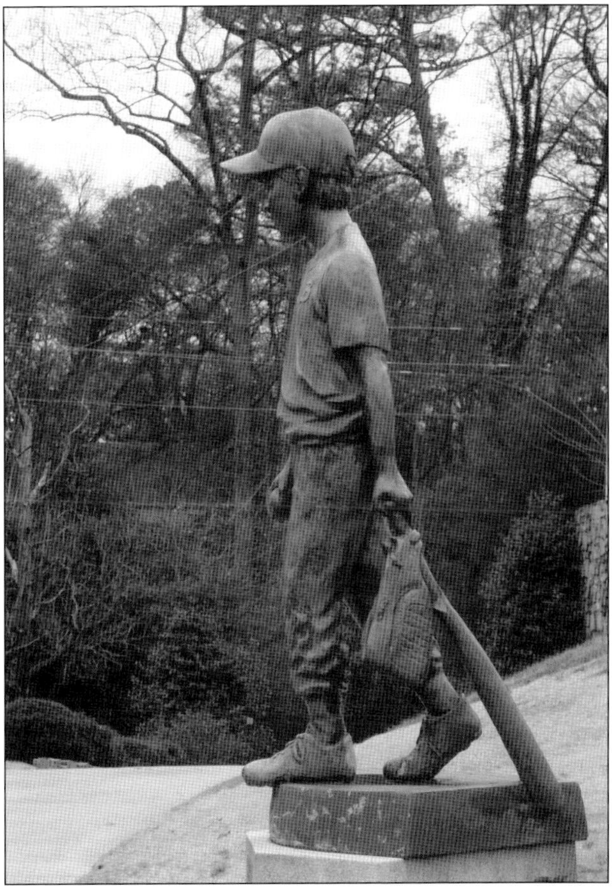

The five rings of the Olympics, a symbol first sketched by modern Olympic Games founder Pierre de Couperin in 1913, represent the five continents [Africa, Asia, Australia, the Americas, and Europe] from whose nations world-class athletes convene at a selected site to engage in "fertile rivalries." Atlanta's gate and flame tower survive from the 1996 Centennial Games, a reminder of sports history and the continuing aspirations of young athletes.

Just a Little Boy, inscribed on its base with a sentimental poem, is a tribute to youth sports programs and encapsulates the hopes and dreams of future athletes represented by this engaging young baseball player. As youth of all ages, with dreams of hopeful accomplishment, pass by this statue in Frankie Allen Park, they are viewing the alpha of the Olympiad omega. Perhaps this boy will grab the five rings. (RMC.)

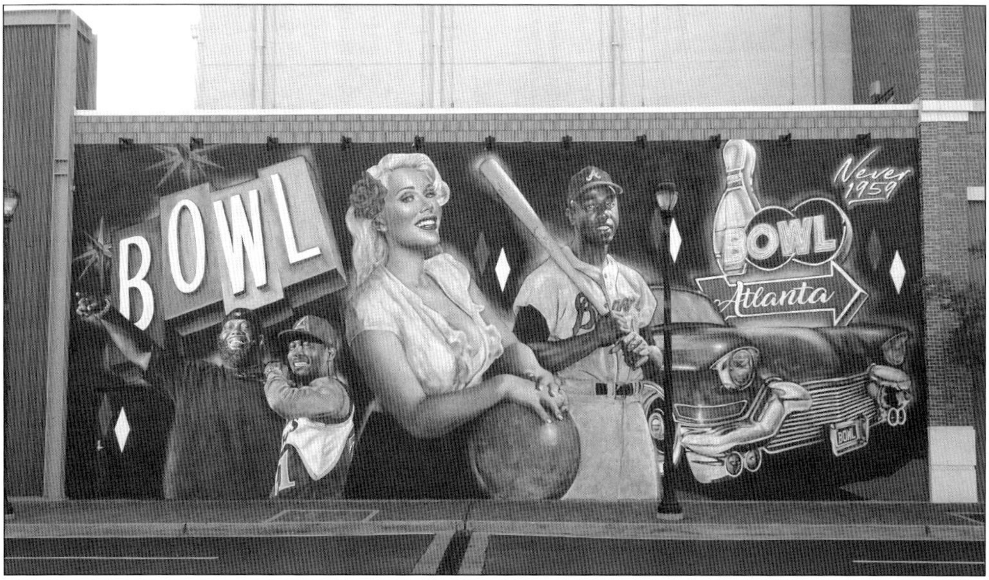

Jonas Never (1981–), also known as Never1959, painted these murals in 2019–2020 for Bowlero Atlantic Station (Market Street at Nineteenth Street NW). The mural above is typical of the artist's work in mixing sports, celebrities, and pop culture, here depicting Hank Aaron as an icon of pop culture, in a setting with a muscle car, neon sign, bowling alley advertisements, and Atlanta rappers Michael Santiago Render (1975–), also known as Killer Mike, and T.I., or Clifford Joseph Harris Jr. (1975–). Around the corner is Never's also nostalgic scene envisioning Bowlero in a setting with foregrounded "classic" 1950s cars while a steam locomotive passes nearby, an image based on an iconic 1956 photograph by O. Winston Link of a drive-in theater in West Virginia. (RMC.)

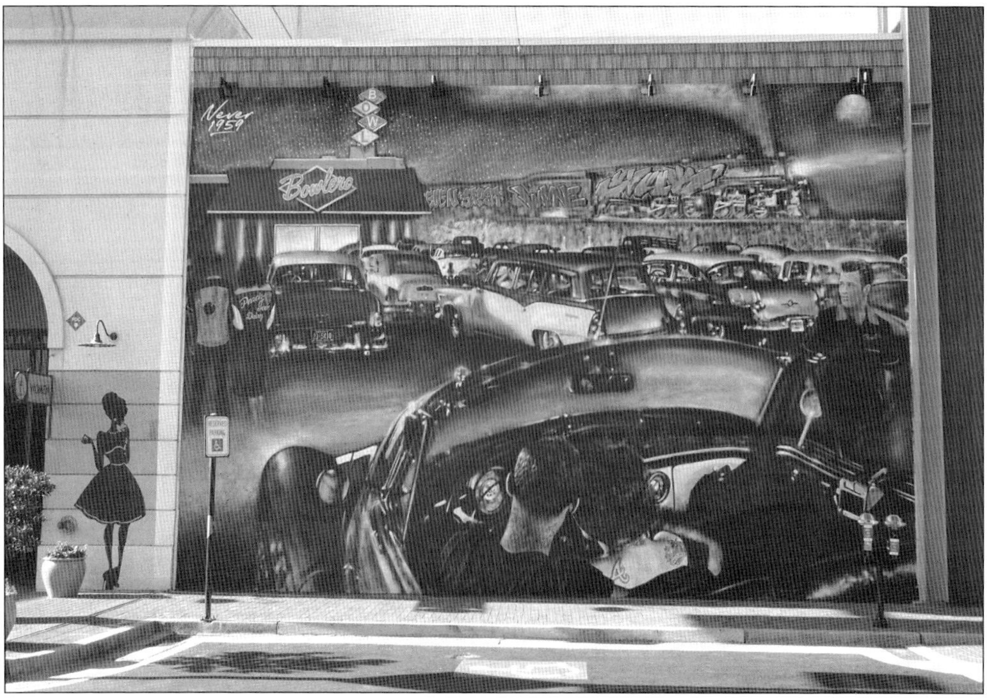

Eight

Popular Culture

The variety of influences on street artists and the individuality of their styles is so diversified that it is impossible in an introductory compendium such as this to be comprehensive. One cannot ignore, however, the theme of pop culture. Many muralists began as graffitists, graphic artists, or illustrators, and comic strip imagery, calligraphy, and popular pulp imagery influenced their forms and colors. Everyday objects were familiar subjects although, like Claus Oldenburg or Andy Warhol, the objects may appear at unexpected scale and with realistic detail to create an ironic art garnering an unexpected or startling reaction from viewers. Such is the sculpture *Autoeater* by German artists Venske and Spänle, depicting a fish swallowing a car, on public view at Tenth and Peachtree Streets. Or along the Chattahoochee River in Roswell's Riverside Park, one finds (fabricated in fiberglass, steel, and holographic film) Ask the *Fish 2.0* by Dr. Stephen Fairfield, a giant hand holding a fish. Pop art is immediate and engaging, requires no art history degree to appreciate or deride, and may walk that thin path between fantasy and deviant art, between nonacademic and naïve art, and between populist low art and kitsch. It may even satirize high art.

Subjects of pop art embrace popular icons of the day. In Atlanta, the hip-hop capital of the South, artists memorialize rappers, especially when they overdose or are perceived as victims of societal behavior, but also because contemporaries are buying millions of their recordings. Artistry in the visual arts encourages reference to artistry in the performing arts, and among the images of the Atlanta mural scene are Corey Barksdale's visual translations of New Orleans jazz, Dixieland, ragtime, and African American improvisational dance. "I am working out the essence of a situation like a jazz musician playing his instrument," the artist has written, "or people dancing in the streets that animate you to join in." Ashley Dopson's 2019 Atlanta Music Project Mural on Dill Avenue is packed with musicians, singers, and even a piano keyboard painted on the sidewalk as foreground. It is difficult to view such images without hearing music in one's mind's eye (or ear).

Moreover, the immediacy of pop art can result in a readily identified subject matter, whether it be quotations from high art, as when Van Gogh's self-portrait is projected at large scale on a building elevation, or the recognized influence from a past style such as Cubism, abstract expressionism, surrealism, or hard-edged minimalism. Muralists are not working in a vacuum, and their personal styles may merely be a reflection of those currents of influence most attractive to them. Portraits in spray-can art are translated from photographs into striking images of hyperrealism at a huge scale. What may be plagiarism in writing may only be degrees of influence in the visual and performing arts: Ralph Vaughn Williams's borrowings from folk music, or Puccini's expropriation of a musical line from the American national anthem in *Madama Butterfly*, are purposeful allusions, with visual parallels, for instance, in Chris Wright and Killimari's quotations from a *Dick Tracy* comic strip in a tribute mural on Wylie Street in Atlanta dedicated to rapper MF DOOM.

However illegal graffiti tagging may be, an artist like Mister Totem has taken graffiti script and its "robotic armored letters and characters" to a new level in his explosive graffiti mural compositions, only one aspect of his versatile styling. In 2019, the music app Pandora partnered with local street artists nationwide to create "Sound On" murals, each with a QR code that viewers can scan with their phone to pull up a playlist curated by each artist. Quite literally, "the audio allows the vibes of the graffiti to be heard." Moreover, testifies the muralist, "These [songs] are the basic DNA of my soul. You can get a very good understanding of where I'm coming from as an artist via the music I listen to." If that is true of the artist, it may also be true of the observer.

In his extensive study *The Creators: a History of Heroes of the Imagination*, published by Random House in 1992, historian Daniel J. Boorstin speaks of "creators of all the arts [who] have enlarged, embellished, fantasized, and filigreed our experience." There are some extraordinarily talented artists who have adorned Atlanta's urban infrastructure walls, commercial building sidewalls, abandoned warehouse walls, and back-alley elevations with surprisingly well-observed images, executed with skill, displaying talents that are indeed trained and continuing to develop, and enriching our urban scene. The regrettable dimension is the lack of longevity of the art, its susceptibility to the erosive ill effects of exposure to weather, pollution, and time, the disrespect of some graffitists who tag or paint over the art, and the reliance on building owners to allow and then preserve the work. The joy of this free and always open outdoor museum of art is ever one of discovery. There is always something new, just around the corner.

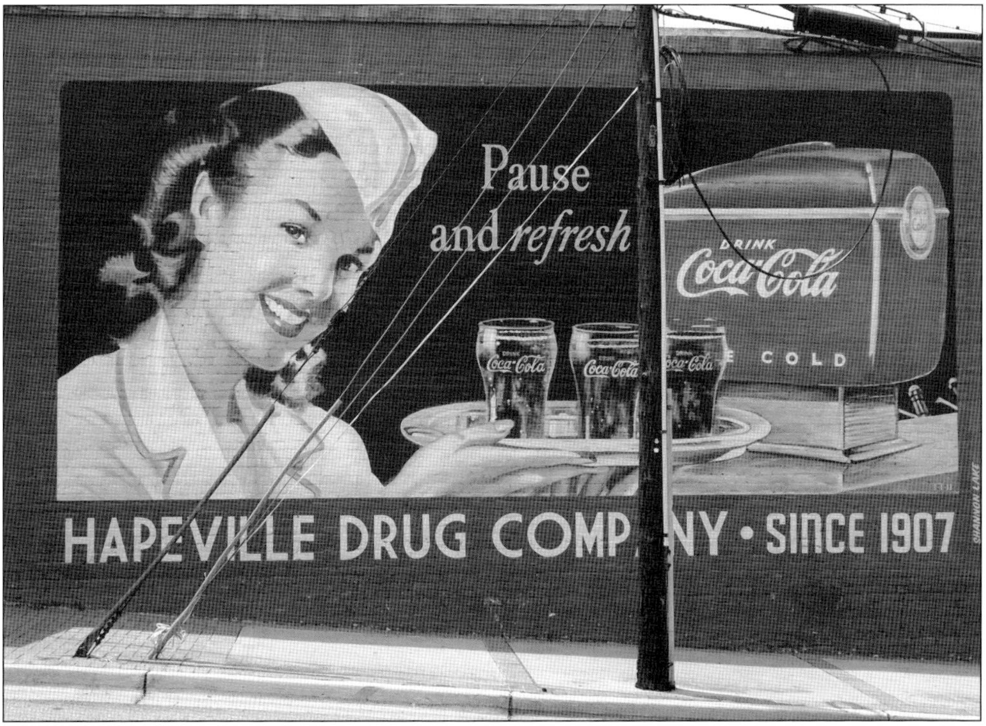

Popular culture historians have long valued and documented early outdoor advertisements on mercantile, industrial, and farm structures—from "See Rock City" painted on rural barns to iconic Coca Cola signs in neon or painted on city walls. Societal love of nostalgia has prompted a continuing admiration for Coca-Cola's universally recognized script, merchandise profiles, red and white colors, and models holding a trademark bottle or fountain glass of Coke. Taking advantage of the universally recognized designs, Coca-Cola signage is revived at Manual's Tavern in Atlanta (see page 32) and at the Hapeville Drug Company building, seen above, painted by Georgia artist Shannon Lake (1970–). Squirt is a caffeine-free, citrus-flavored, carbonated soft drink first manufactured in 1938 and a precursor of 7 Up, Mountain Dew, and other yellow-green bottled drinks. The nostalgic Squirt advertising sign seen below is on Little's Food Store in Cabbagetown. (RMC.)

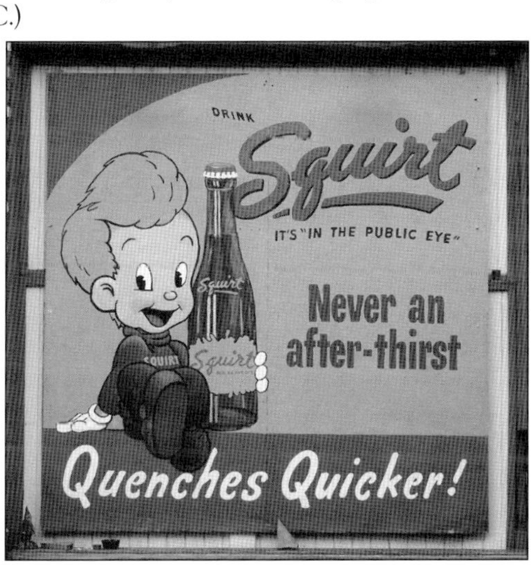

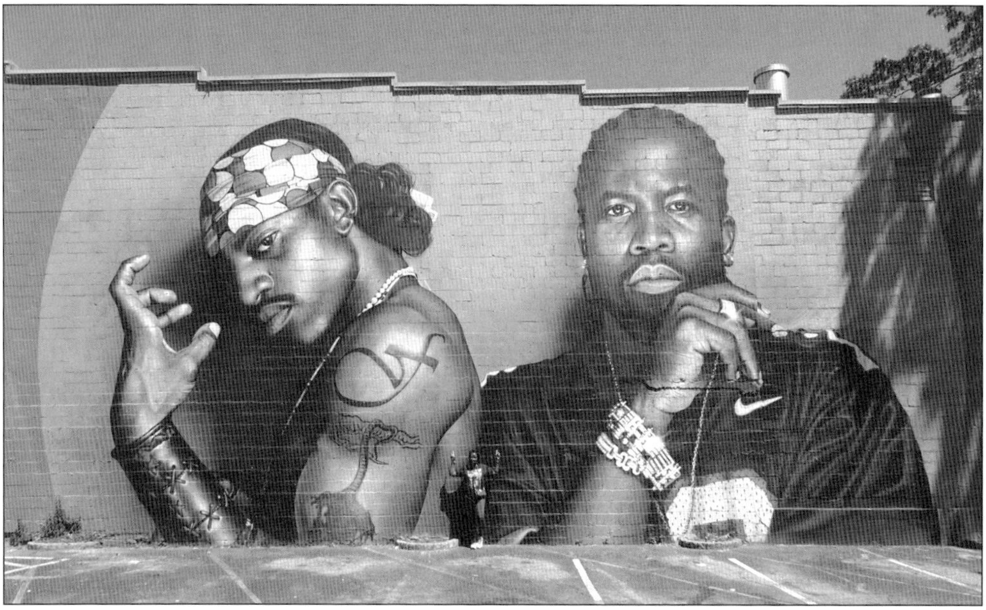

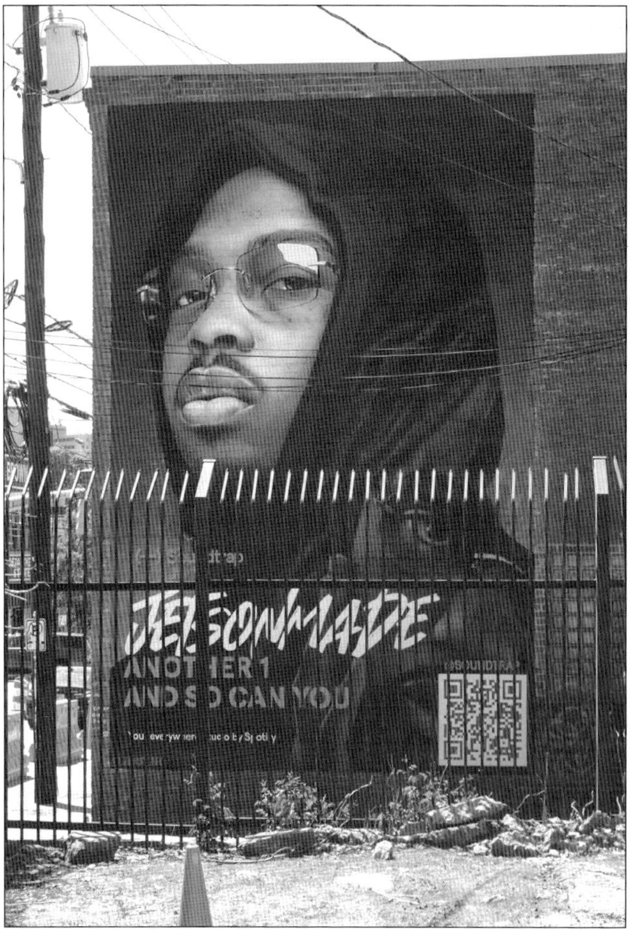

One of the most remarkable murals in Atlanta features hip-hop rappers Outkast (above) in a hyper-realistic image based on a photograph by Jonathan Mannion. Antwan André Patton (1975–), also known as Big Boi, and André Lauren Benjamin (1975–), also known as André 3000, dwarf the scale figure below, giving an indication of the 2019 mural's 30-by-65-foot dimensions. The Little Five Points mural is by Brian Lewis (1982–), also known as Jeks of Greensboro, North Carolina. Jeks also painted the Jetsonmade mural seen left. Tahj Morgan (1996–), also known as Jetsonmade, is a pioneer of the rap scene in the Carolinas, where muralist Jeks is based. A record producer, songwriter, and record executive, Jetsonmade produced such hit songs as "Suge" and "Bop" by rapper DaBaby; His producer tag is referenced in the mural: "Oh Lord, Jetson made another one!" (RMC.)

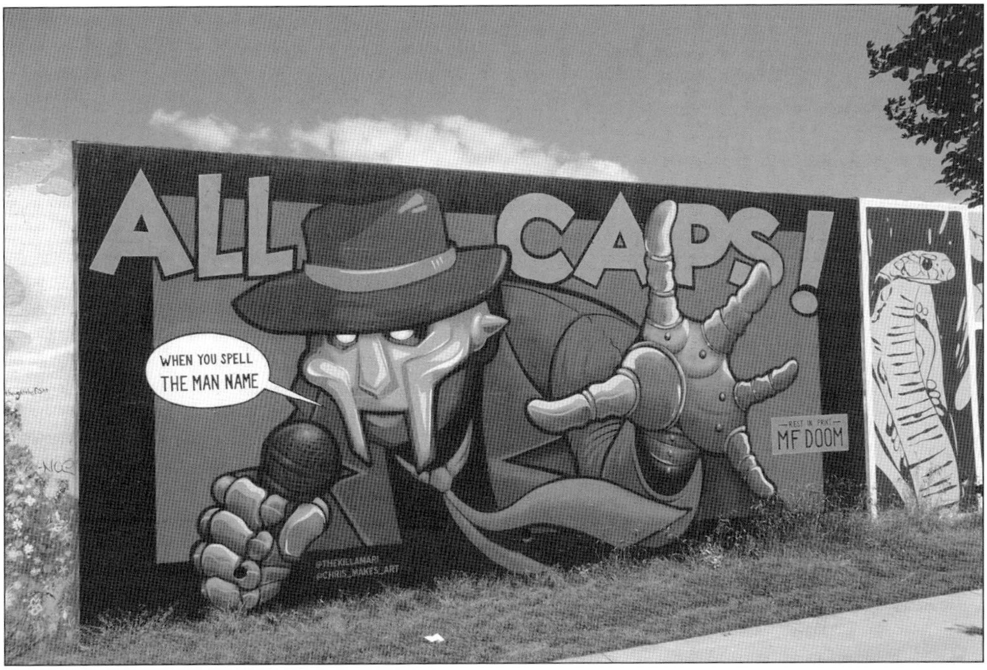

Daniel Dumile (1971–2020), also known as MF DOOM, sometimes simply DOOM, was a British rapper and record producer, living mostly in the United States until 2010. His signature metal mask and supervillain stage persona, combined with the intricate wordplay of his rap, made him a leader of the underground and alternative hip-hop scene of the 2000s. The comic-book style of the "ALL CAPS! When You Spell The Man Name" mural above is the work of Chris Wright (1987–) (@ChrisMakesArt) and Rod Ben, also known as Killimari, a full-time illustrator and designer in an animation studio, who not surprisingly has worked with Marvel Entertainment. Killimari is the founder and leader of a group of muralists, animators, illustrators, and designers known as The Lotus Eaters Club. The mural of DOOM below is by Wes Holland. (RMC.)

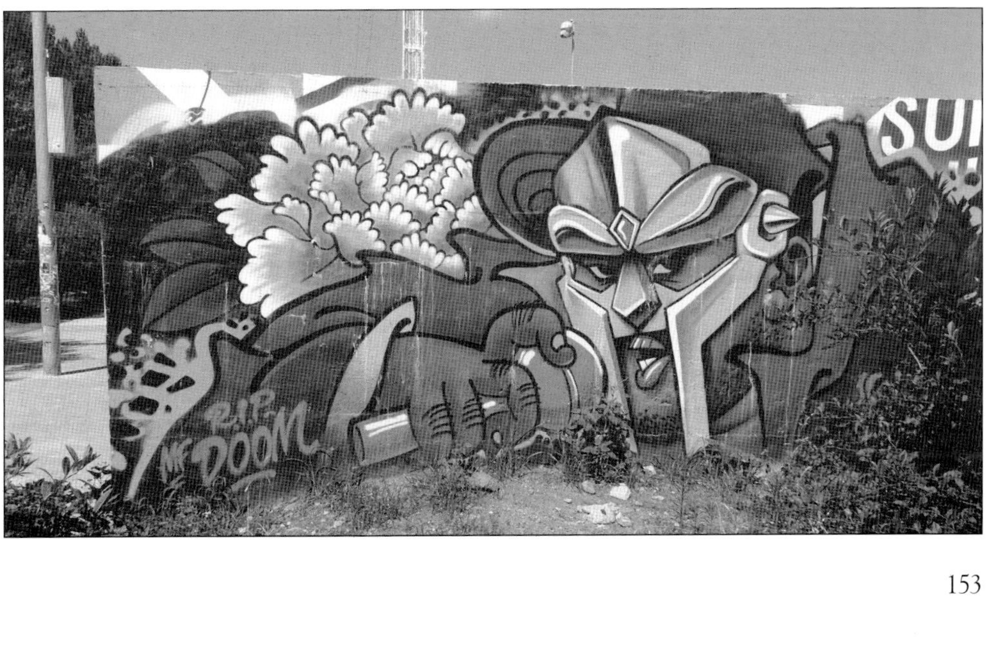

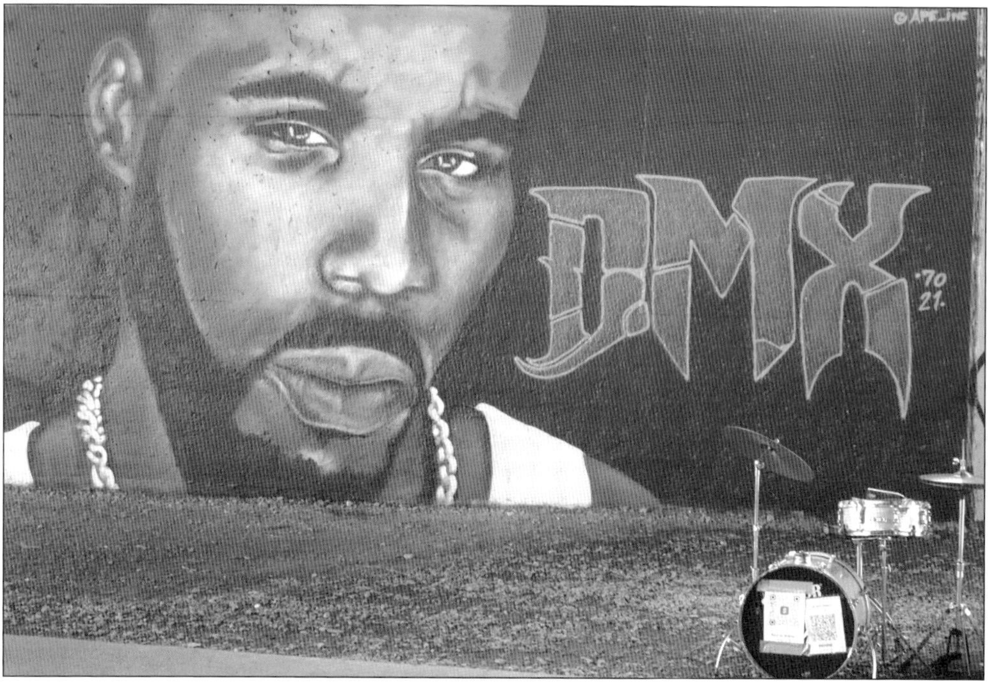

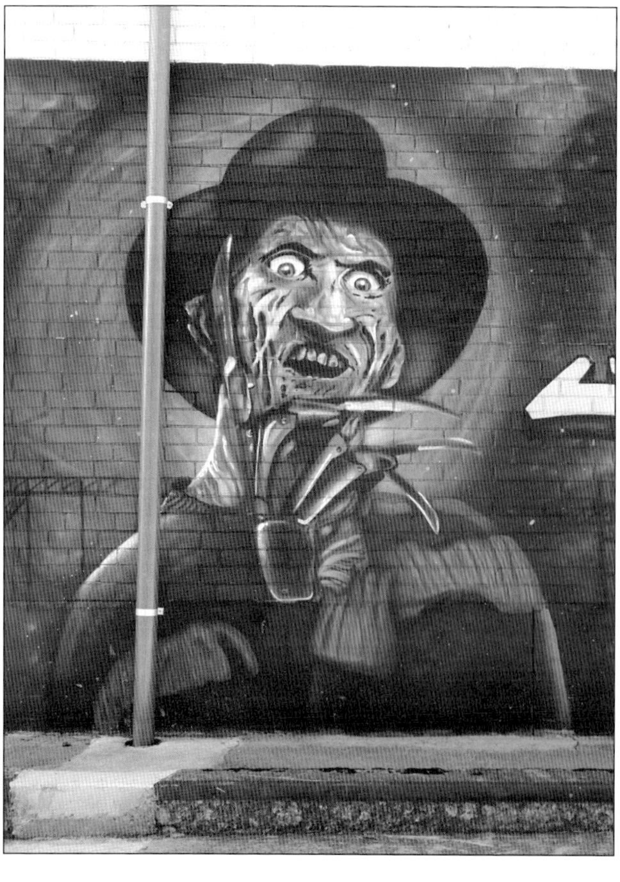

American songwriter and rapper Earl Simmons (1970–2021), known famously as DMX, died April 9, 2021, and the next day Armondo Monoletti began painting a tribute mural on the East Beltline at Old Fourth Ward Skate Park. Like the work of Jeks, the mural displays the skill of a photorealist. As pop culture figures, hip-hop rappers are well represented in the people's art. (RMC.)

The fictional character Freddie Krueger, painted on the "mural wall" of one of the long studio blocks at the Met (680 Murphy Drive SW), references the 1984 slasher film *A Nightmare on Elm Street*, now a cult film firmly planted in pop culture. Atlanta-based satiric muralist Chris Veal (1981–) is a popular street artist often painting comic-strip, teary-eyed females and handsome men, including speech balloons from comic book conventions. (RMC.)

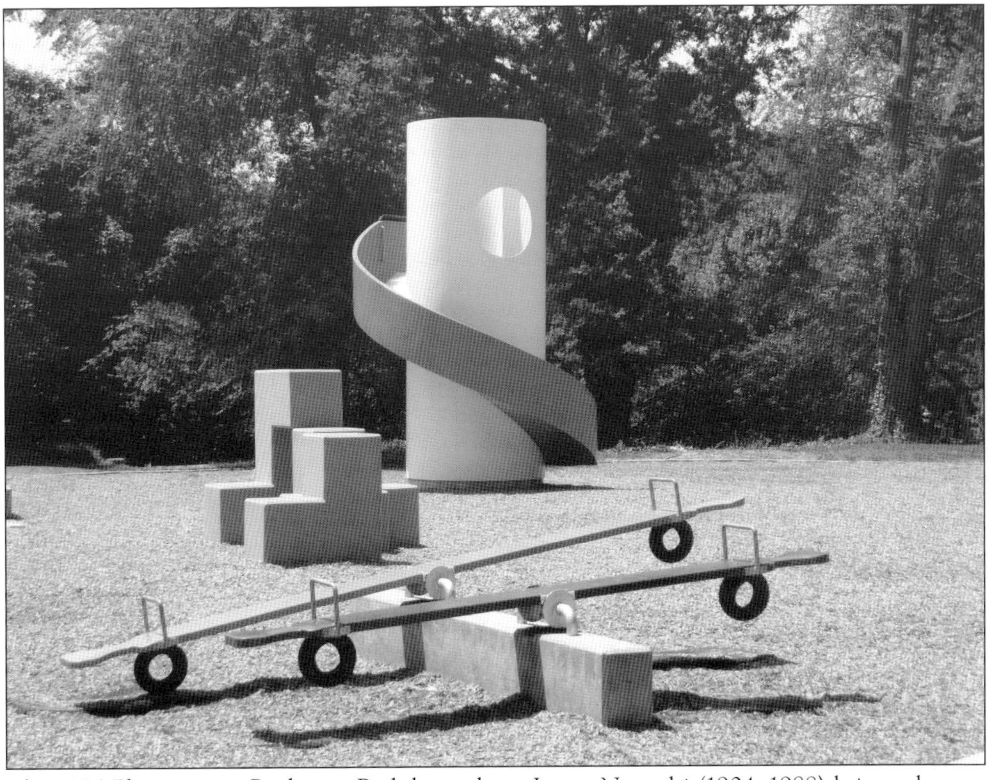

The 1976 *Playscapes* in Piedmont Park by sculptor Isamu Noguchi (1904–1988) brings abstract expressionist minimalism into the realm of functional playground design. Noguchi commented, "I think of playgrounds as a primer of shapes and functions; simple, mysterious, and evocative; thus educational." Art critic Tomas Hess observed that "instead of telling the child what to do (swing here, climb there)," Noguchi's Playscapes "becomes a place for endless exploration." Commissioned by the High Museum of Art and the National Endowment for the Arts, the project was touted at the time to be Noguchi's only executed playground in the United States after decades of thinking and unrealized playground designs by the sculptor and landscape artist. As a synthesis of architecture, outdoor functional sculpture, and landscape architecture, the Playscapes are a nationally significant work by one of America's most important Mid-Century Modern artists. (RMC.)

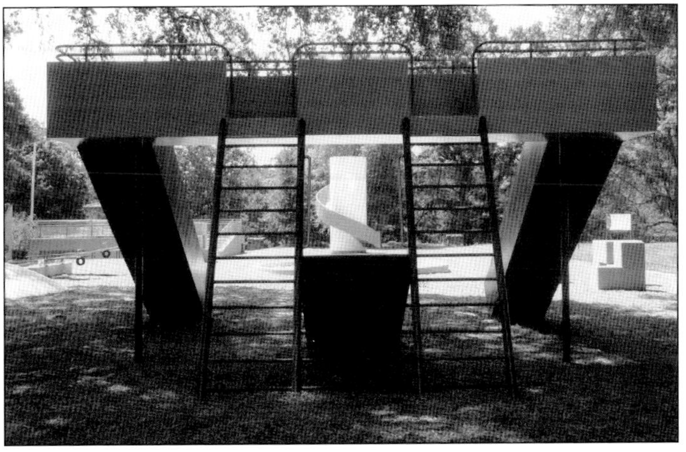

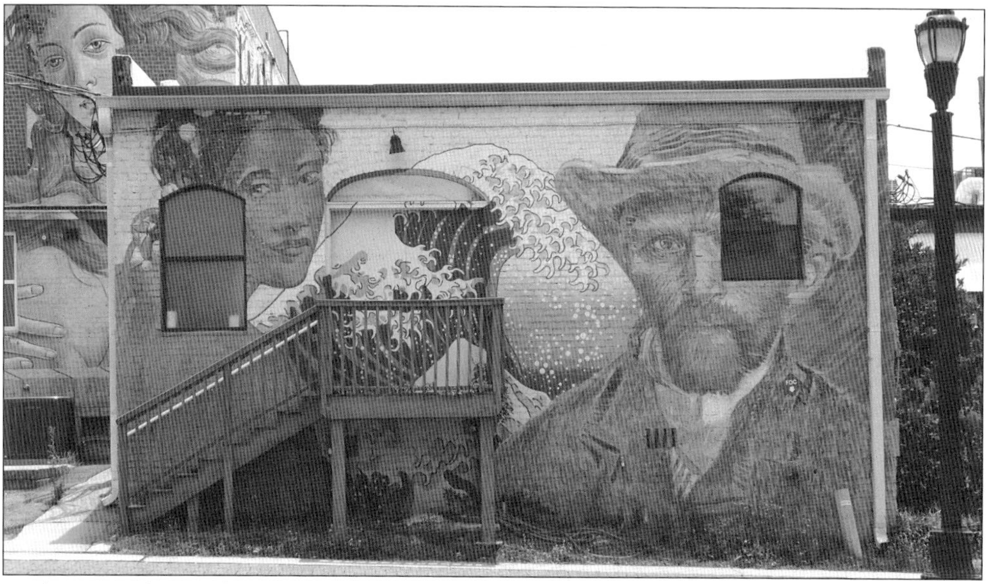

High art is referenced in murals behind the Academy Theatre at 599 N. Central Avenue (US Route 41) in Hapeville. Here, one finds Van Gogh's 1887 *Self Portrait* from the Rijksmuseum in Amsterdam (right) and *The Great Wave off Kanagawa*, a c. 1820–1831 Japanese woodcut print by Katsushika Hokusai in the Met in New York City (center); the left image is borrowed from Paul Gauguin's *Maternity (Three Women by the Seashore)*, 1899, at the Hermitage Museum. (RMC.)

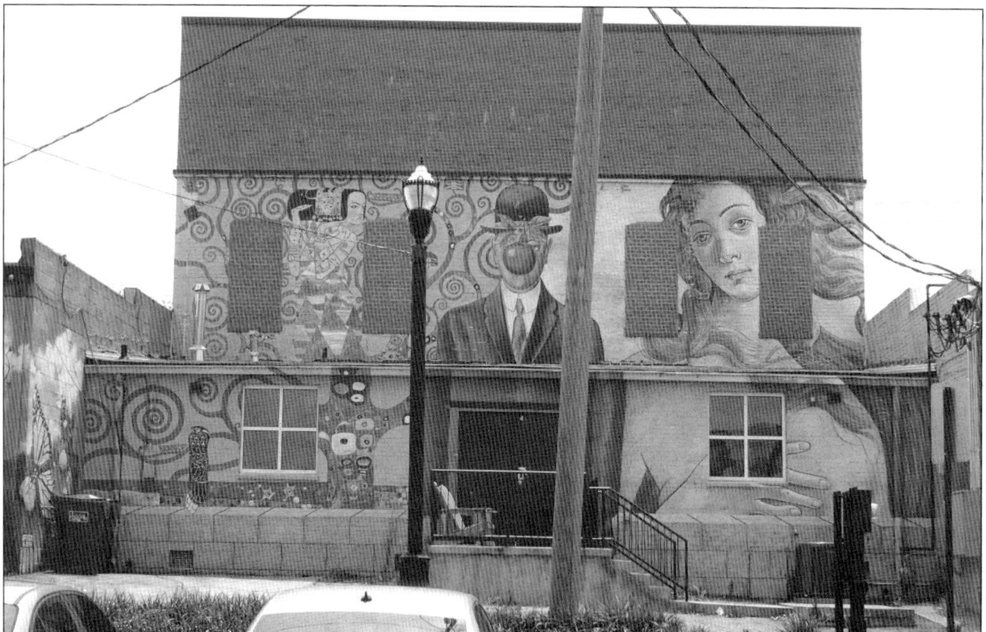

Artist Shannon Lake looked to other sources for the mural on the theater itself: Sandro Botticelli's c. 1484–1486 *Birth of Venus* from the Uffizi in Florence, Italy (right); René Magritte's self-portrait *Son of Man*, 1964, from a private collection (center); and Gustav Klimt's Viennese Secessionist painting *Tree of Life, Stoclet Frieze*, 1909, from the Museum of Applied Arts in Vienna (left). The art history murals overlook the civic plaza and city hall. (RMC.)

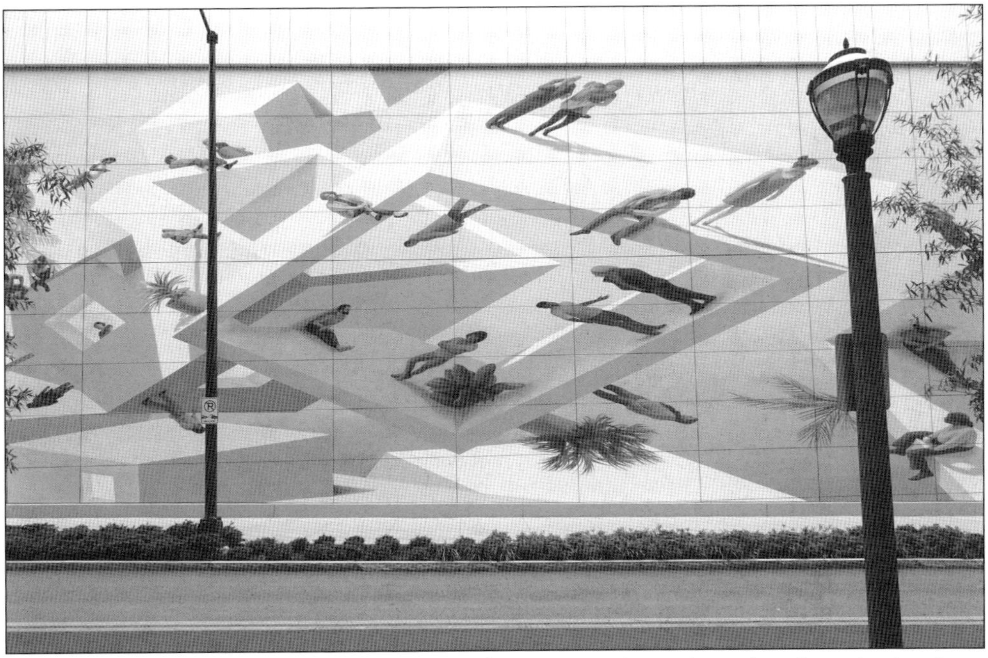

The muralist at John Portman's CODA complex appears also to have found inspiration from an earlier master artist. A long wall along Armstead Place features Cinta Vidal's M.C. Escher–inspired mural titled *Merge*. Escher's well-known 1953 *Relativity* drawing in which the observer's eye questions the logic and impossible play with perspective, is a not-so-distant cousin of Vidal's double anamorphosis, offering two vantage points from which to view the work. (RMC.)

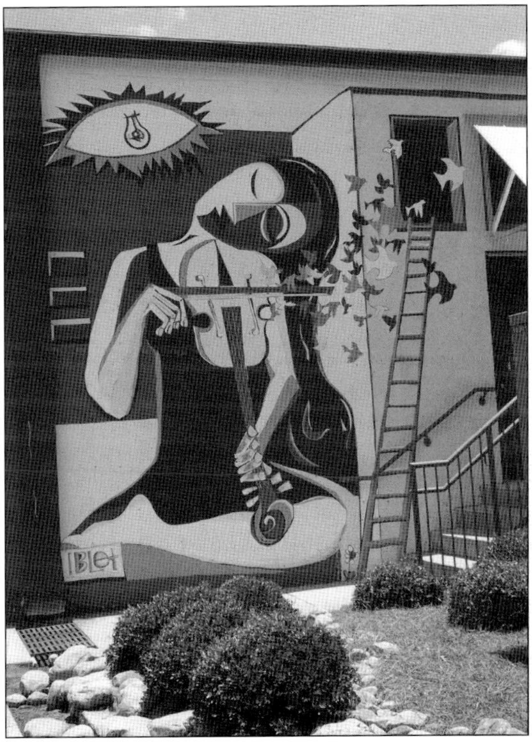

The work of Picasso, although here without the planarity, spatial simultaneities, and transparencies of Cubism, influences the work of Brandon Morrison (1979–), also known as Iblet, at the artist's studio at the Beacon in southeast Atlanta. The palette, more subdued than Iblet's usual, is mostly black, white, and pale ochre, except for the multiple colors used for the birds that flutter off as though symbolic of the violin's tones. Morrison is also a musician. (RMC.)

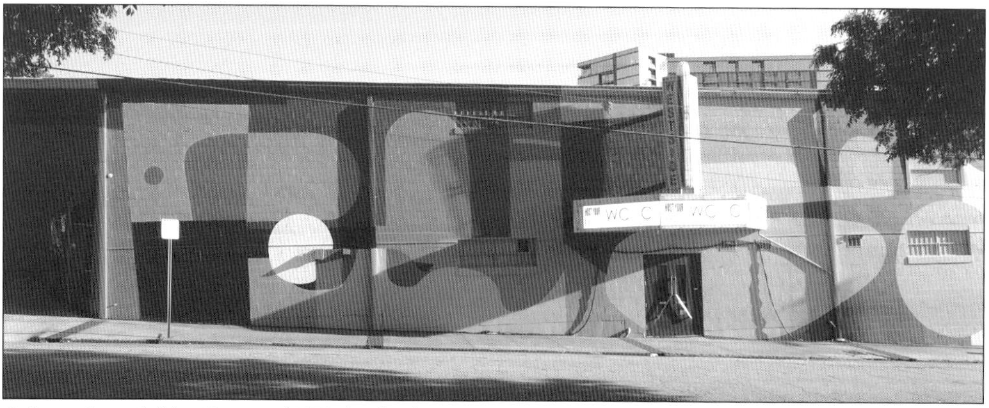

Atlanta-based Alex Brewer (1978–), also known as Hense, began as a graffitist and has developed a worldwide reputation for his hard-edged minimalist abstractions, unified by tonal harmonies, and full of color. He reupholsters whole buildings, as seen here at the Westside Cultural Arts Center. He has a huge mural on Midtown's Icon Tower, recently completed the Beltline underpass mural at Monroe and Tenth Streets, and has major work in Peru, Australia, and Washington, DC. (RMC.)

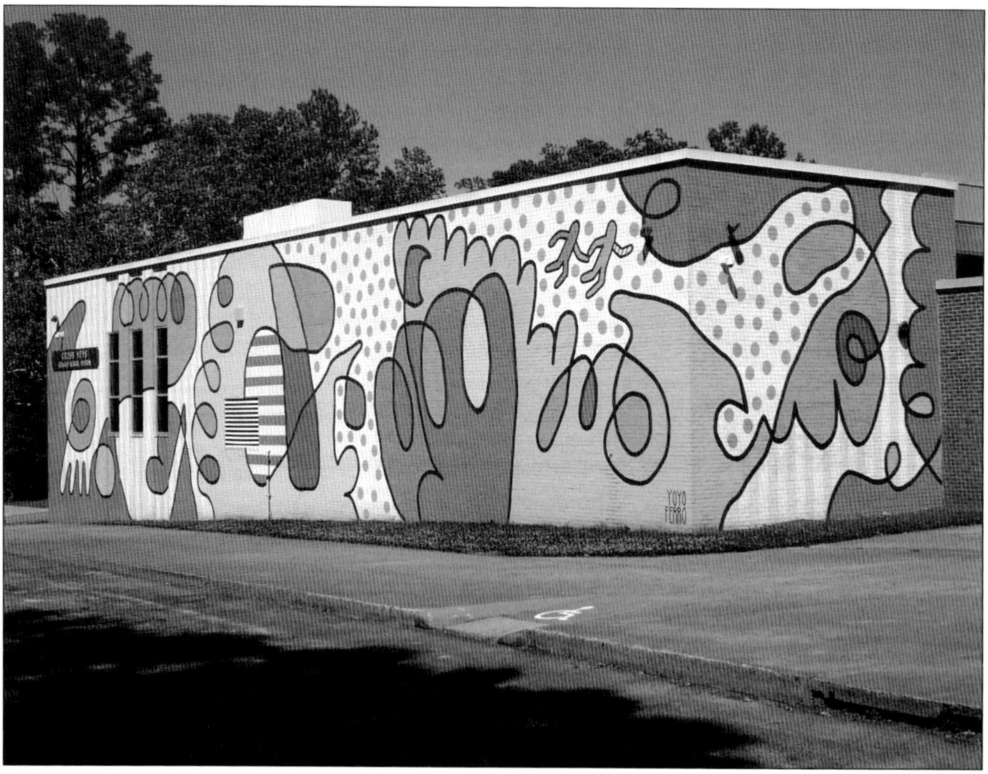

In musical terms, Yoyo Ferro (1986–) is the Mozart among Atlanta muralists: full of delight, embodying sheer happiness, and with a childlike charm in all his work. He too can upholster whole building facades in paint, as here at Cross Keys Elementary School, but smaller and always inviting murals adorn every Atlanta neighborhood. His work is always welcomed: who can resist the stylized figures that humanize his otherwise abstract patterned work? (RMC.)

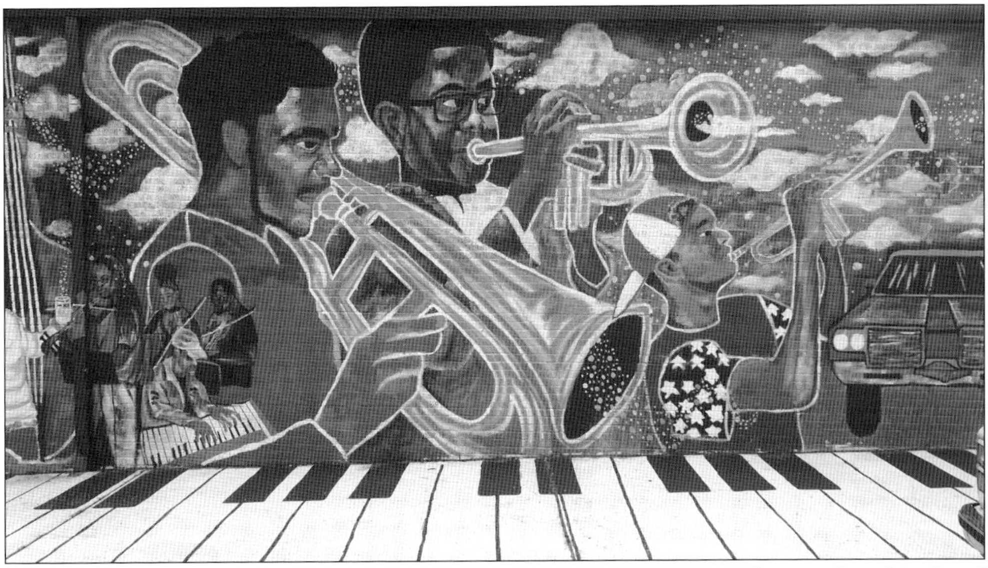

The Atlanta Music Project (AMP) was founded in 2010 to teach music to underserved neighborhood youth in order to empower positive social change. In 2019, at the southwest Atlanta facility, Ashley Danielle Thomas (now Ashley Dopson) painted a piano keyboard on the sidewalk and a mural that captures the spirit of this noble mission, a 150-foot-long composition depicting musicians, singers, choral groups, and dancers engaged in making music. (RMC.)

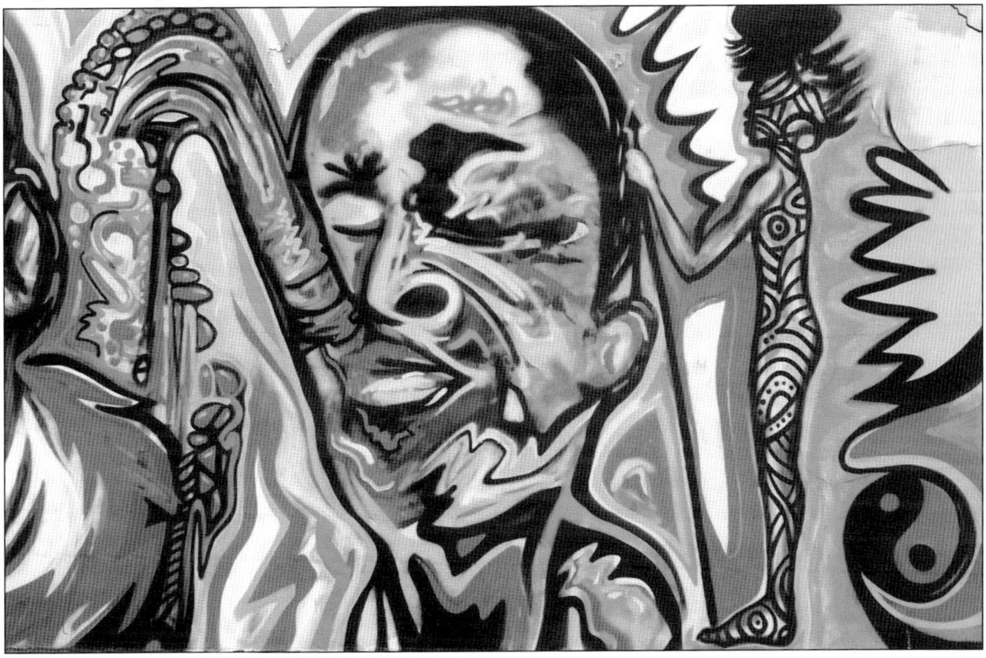

The vibrant colors in the work of Corey Barksdale (1972–) pulsate among strong black lines and waves of vibrato, transporting an atmosphere reminiscent of John Coltrane's primordial shrieks of improvised free jazz. Barksdale's abstract expressionist colors look to both the Fauves and Der Blaue Reiter art movements and African American masters, while his subjects illustrate and express the dynamic and energetic dimensions of African American life and music: ragtime, jazz, nightclubs, and jitterbug/free street dancing. (RMC.)

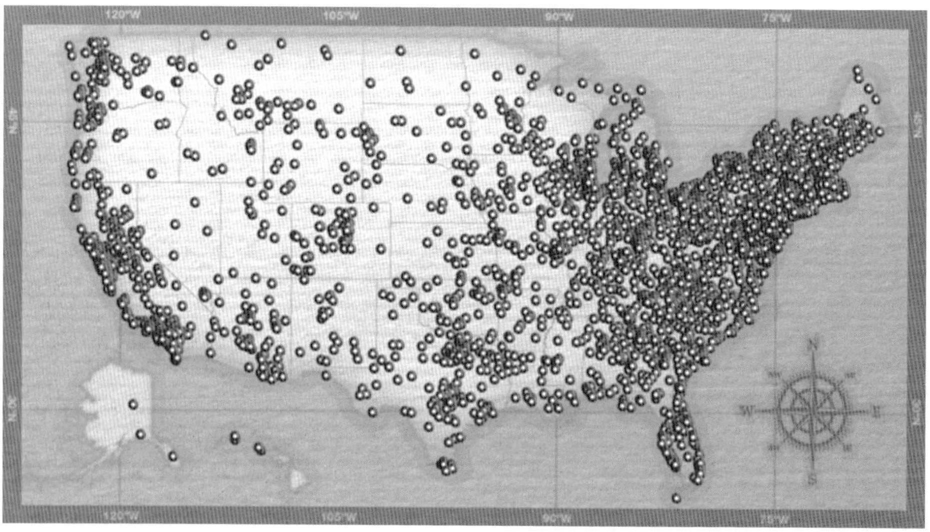

Consistent with our mission to preserve history on a local level, this book was printed in South Carolina on American-made paper and manufactured entirely in the United States. Products carrying the accredited Forest Stewardship Council (FSC) label are printed on 100 percent FSC-certified paper.

MADE IN THE USA